P9-CQJ-992

Other books by Vince Staten:

Unauthorized America Harper & Row
Real Barbecue Harper & Row

Acknowledgements for photographs and other credits are found on page 192.

Second Printing October, 1991
Third Printing 1992.
Fourth Printing, 1994

Library of Congress Cataloging-in-Publication Data

Staten, Vince
The Jack Daniel's Old Time Barbecue Cookbook
(includes index)
Title; No. 90-71739

THE SULGRAVE PRESS
2005 Longest Ave.
Louisville, Ky. 40204

ISBN 0-9624086-2-X

Jack Daniel's Old Time Barbecue Cookbook

By Vince Staten

TABLE OF CONTENTS

FOREWORD

It's a combination as natural as Waylon and Willie; barbecue and Jack Daniel's Whiskey.

Both barbecue and Jack Daniel's have been around as long as anyone can remember. Both take lots of patience and lots of time. And both are still made the old-fashioned way.

They're perfect partners. You can barbecue with a Jack Daniel's baste, add Jack Daniel's to your sauce or just sip it while tending a barbecue pit.

That's why this book was a natural: a pairing of two Tennessee traditions.

And that's why I was a natural to write it. I'm a Tennessee tradition, too. I was born in Tennessee, raised in the hollers, and even graduated from college there. It was when I was in college that I first visited the Jack Daniel's Distillery. Garland Dussenberry took me on a tour. He's still there at the Distillery, leading tours, showing folks how Jack Daniels' is made.

In this book I'm not going to tell you how to make Jack Daniel's.

Barbecue is another story. I've been a barbecue connoisseur since before I could spell the word; *connoisseur* that is. I've always known how to spell barbecue. And how to cook it.

One of my hobbies is checking out different barbecue joints. I've sampled more than 600 places. I've traveled as far north as Curtis' All-American 9th Wonder of the World Bar-B-Q in Putney, Vermont and as far south as Shorty's in South Miami, Florida. I've been coast-to-coast in search of great barbecue and I've eaten at places within sight of each ocean.

And any time I taste truly magnificent barbecue, I make it a point to seek out the pitman or pitwoman. To compliment them, of course, but also to talk barbecue. I'm not trying to steal their secrets, for in barbecue there are no secrets. There is only one constant: patience.

But I enjoy swapping barbecue tall tales and comparing notes.

Since I'm on a lifelong quest in search of the perfect barbecue, in this book I'm going to share some of the lessons I've learned in my quest.

I haven't found the perfect barbecue yet.

But, to tell the truth, I hope I never find it. I'm enjoying the quest too much to end it.

AN INTRODUCTION TO BARBECUE

The story of barbecue is the story of America: Settlers arrive on great unspoiled continent, discover wondrous riches, set them on fire and eat them.

Barbecue was there at the beginning. ("Went up to Alexandria to a barbicue," George Washington confessed to his diary, misspelling and all, in 1769.) And barbecue is there today, scattered along countless country roads, still served in the same slow-cooked, smoky way that transforms ordinary meat into a delicacy so meltingly tender and suffused with flavor that mere mortals ought to thank their lucky Wet-Naps that the gods didn't keep it to themselves.

As America's genuine grass-roots cuisine, barbecue is also the nation's most fussed-over and feuded-over food.

Go into a crowded room, a place where you don't know anyone, and, as casually as you can, mention the word "barbecue."

Suddenly someone will toss out a boast, "Where I come from has the best barbecue in the world."

Someone else will shoot back a retort, "Where you come from they call a Sloppy Joe barbecue."

All you have to do is mention barbecue and the arguing begins.

Lyndon Johnson always claimed the best barbecue came from Texas. Owensboro, Kentucky calls itself the barbecue capital of the world. So, too, does Memphis. And Kansas City. And Lexington, North Carolina. And... the list goes on.

"The best barbecue in the entire free world, bar none, is at Craig's Bar-B-Q in Devall's Bluff, Arkansas," says Baltimore radio executive Bob Moody, who just happens to hail from Arkansas.

"Paducah barbecue is the best anywhere in the world," claims retired newspaperman Bill Powell, who happens to live in Paducah, Kentucky.

And in barbecue arguments, it is not enough that your home state has the best, it is also that your friends' home state doesn't have a clue.

"They don't have barbecue in Texas," says Memphis native Lucious "The King" Newsom. "They might think they do, but they don't."

"That silly bunch up in Owensboro, they don't know what they're doing; they're kidding themselves," says Paducah's Powell.

The fact of the matter is: they're all right. They have great barbecue in Texas. And in Tennessee. In Paducah and in Owensboro.

There is no one great barbecue because there is no one barbecue style. In Texas it's beef. In Owensboro it's mutton. In Memphis it's pork.

I know about great barbecue. I've eaten it everywhere, from California to Cape Cod, from Minneapolis to Miami, and all points in between. I've eaten at more than 600 barbecue joints and cooked it myself scores more times. And the fact is: great barbecue is where you find it.

And one place you'll find it is in this book.

This book is a guide to cooking great barbecue the way they do it in Lexington, North Carolina, population: 16,000; barbecue joint population: 16. It's also a guide to cooking great barbecue the way they do in Lexington, Virginia and in Lexington, Kentucky. In Lexington, Texas and in Lexington, Tennessee.

By the time you get through trying out all the barbecue styles in this book, you'll be a certified pitmaster, with a double major in beef and pork.

But enough of this introduction. Let's get to cooking, so we can get to eating.

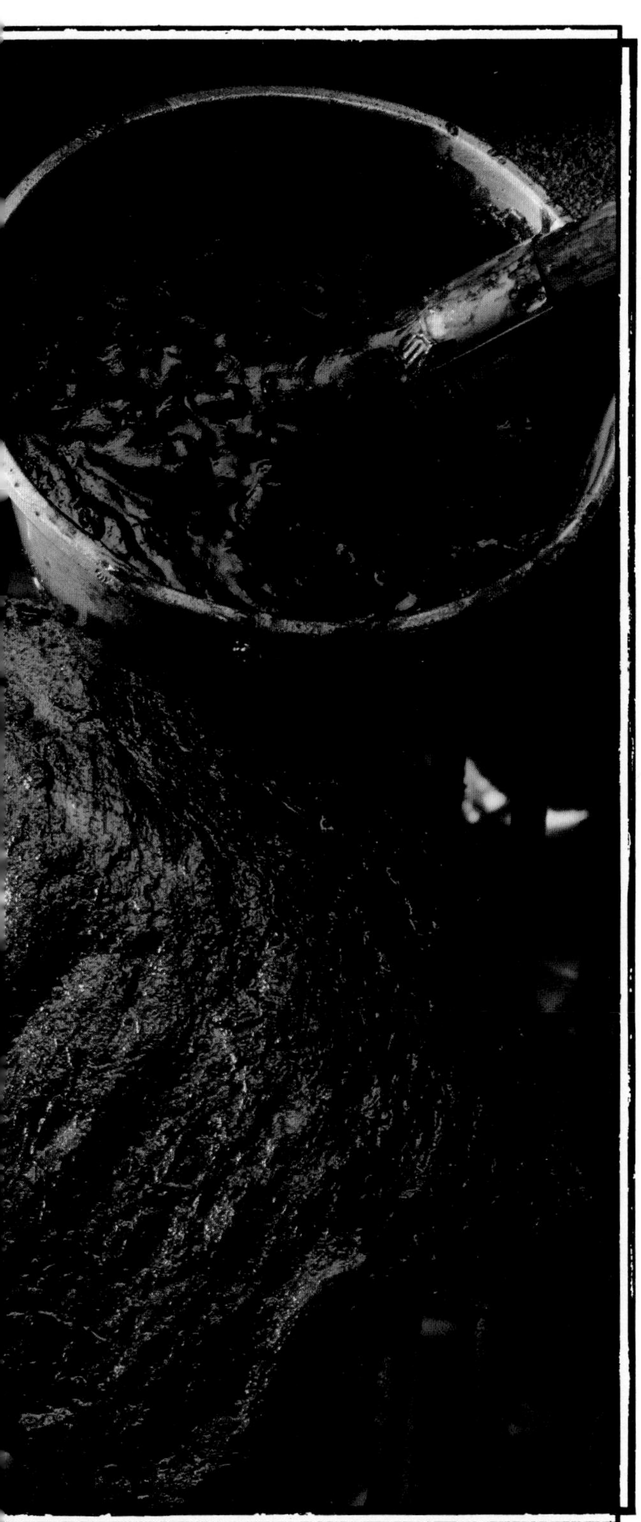

COOKING GREAT BARBECUE

Barbecue is 99 percent perspiration and 1 percent sauce.

It's that simple.

You don't have to spend days in the kitchen concocting experimental sauces to cook great barbecue. You don't need to study ancient Chinese manuscripts to discover the ultimate secret ingredient. You don't have to learn the intricacies of meat packing or thermal engineering.

Remember these three magic words as you begin your barbecue cooking career: tender loving care.

Take care with your fire. Take care with your sop. Take care with your sauce. Take care with your meat. And the barbecue will take care of itself.

This is not some recent scientific breakthrough. The great pitmen of America have always known this.

"Patience and slow cooking, that's it," says Bud Roach of Jeffersonville, Indiana, head of the Ole 97 barbecue cooking team, which took first place in the 1990 Missouri state championships.

Think of it this way: cooking barbecue is a lot like making Jack Daniel's Whiskey. It takes time to make good whiskey. It takes time to make good barbecue. You can't rush either one.

THE REAL THING

Before we can talk about the hows of barbecue, we have to determine the whats of barbecue. What is barbecue? It's different in different parts of the country. In eastern North Carolina it is a whole hog, sitting atop a hickory fire, waiting to be "picked" clean of its meat. In Texas, it's a beef brisket slowly sizzling away atop a mesquite fire. In south Georgia, it's a goat that's roasting. In Vermont, it's chicken. In Owensboro, Kentucky, it's mutton.

In Texas they use a closed pit. In South Carolina they like an open pit (although health regulations are making it more difficult to do commercially).

Who's right?

They all are. Barbecue can have many characteristics as long as it adheres to a fairly strict definition created by the U.S. Department of Agriculture in the early part of this century. The USDA defines "barbecue" as any meat "cooked by the direct action of heat resulting from the burning of hardwood or the hot coals therefrom for a sufficient period to assume the usual characteristics ... which include the formation of a brown crust. ... The weight of barbecued meat shall not exceed 70 percent of the fresh, uncooked meat."

Simple enough: any meat, whether pork, beef, mutton or chicken.

The heat can come from burning hickory, oak, mesquite or any hardwood or from the coals of those woods.

And the final product must be cooked long enough and slow enough that some 30 percent of the original weight, usually the fat, will have been cooked away.

The phrase "usual characteristics" doesn't mention it, but the usual characteristics include a meat that is tender and moist, smoky and flavorful.

One thing all barbecue cooks agree on: Real old-time barbecue is cooked not by the fire, but by the heat and the smoke of the fire.

Never put a barbecue meat directly in a flame.

Because there are so many methods and so many shortcuts, this book is intended as a starting point for your barbecue cooking. As you continue to cook barbecue, you will develop your own tricks, your own methods.

EQUIPMENT

You can't barbecue without a cooker. It can be a handsome $10,000 model, hand-crafted by Memphis barbecue man John Willingham, or it can be a Rube Goldberg-looking homemade model assembled from old parts you found in the garage. It can be a hole in the ground or a stack of cinder blocks.

It doesn't matter what it looks like. You don't build it to look at. It's like the Jack Daniel's aging house, surely the ugliest building in Lynchburg. They'd have to spruce it up to turn it into a prison.

It's not the outside that's important: it's what happens inside. With the Jack Daniel's aging house, it's where the mash turns to whiskey. With a barbecue cooker, it's where the raw meat turns to barbecue.

You can buy a starter cooker at the local hardware store or a deluxe model from a mail-order company. Just make sure your cooker has some sort of firebox, enough room to keep the meat away from the flame, a top to hold in smoke and a grate to put the meat on. You also need a way to control the draft so you can control the temperature and a way to add coals to the fire. Past that it's whatever you like.

Then you need to get to know your grill. Practice on it.

"Grills are like cars: each one has its own little accelerator," says Shane Best, winner of the Best Ribs in the World title at the 1990 World Invitational Rib Championship in Richmond, Virginia. "You have to get to know your own grill. ... What takes a half-hour on one may take 45 minutes on another."

Big Daddy

Take another look at the cooker on the cover of this book. That's my cooker (that's also me pretending to cook on it). It's called Big Daddy simply because that's what it looks like. It was a simple contraption to make: two 55-gallon barrels, some stovepipe, a few firebricks, a couple of hinges, a little ingenuity, some manual dexterity, and a lot of time.

Big Daddy is a double-barrel, dual-purpose cooker. I can slow-cook and smoke meats by making a fire in the bottom barrel. I can barbecue and grill using only the top barrel.

When I want to cook something for at least 12 hours, I use the bottom fire compartment. When I want to shorten my cooking time, I build the fire in one half of the top barrel. If I'm barbecuing, I put the meat on the other half. If I'm grilling, I put the meat directly over the fire.

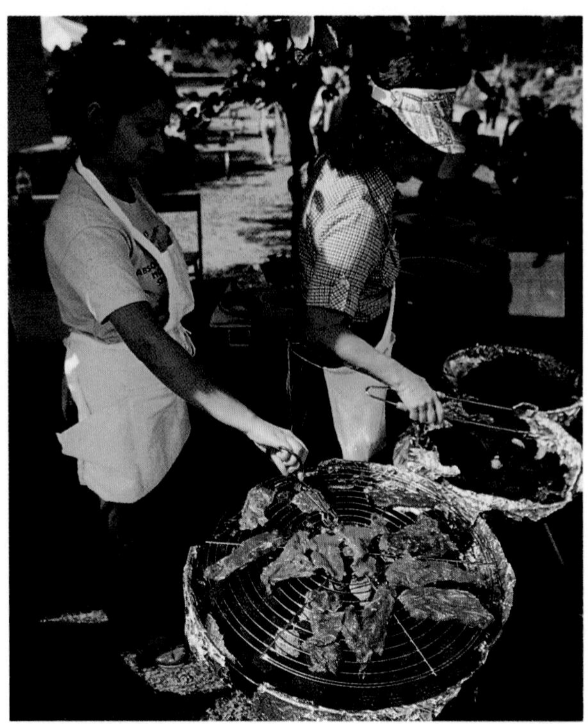

Weber Kettle

One of the most common barbecue cookers around is the Weber Kettle. Thousands have been sold over the years. You can cook real barbecue on a Weber almost as easily as you can cook it on a dedicated barbecue pit.

The shortcomings of a Weber Kettle are size – you can't cook much meat on it – and fire stoking: you have to jimmy up the cooking surface to add coals to the fire.

But you can cook great ribs and great shoulder on it because I've done it.

Here's how:

Build your fire as you usually do, piling the charcoal briquettes in a mound. When they are white-hot, shovel them to one side of the fire grate. On the other side place a tin plate filled with water. When you are cooking, the water will add moisture to the meat.

Soak wood chips overnight in a bucket of water. Add them to the fire as needed to keep a steady stream of smoke. You can drop them through the bars of the top grilling surface.

Now put the grate on. Place the meat over the plate. Replace the kettle lid, making sure that the smoke holes are open.

Those NewFangled Gas Grills

I know you've seen them. Every deck in America seems to have one. They're those boxy-looking gas grills that are rapidly taking over from the Weber Kettle as America's favorite backyard barbecue grill.

Barbecue purists – of which I am one – hate them because barbecue purists hate gas cooking. Evelyn Grogan of Reidsville, North Carolina, says the experience is not the same cooking with gas. And gas can add a subtle, and not particularly pleasant taste to meat.

But as much as I dislike a gas cooker, I have to admit they have their advantages. There's no hassling with a fire. It starts up quickly and gets up to speed just as quickly. And there's no sooty smoke.

So I own one.

And you can cook barbecue on one. Be sure to light only one half of your grill. Then put the meat on the other half of the grill. Keep your heat gauge as low as it will go.

Expensive But Worth It Dedicated Cooker

You will have to look around, ask friends, check out mail-order sources, check the Yellow Pages, but it will be worth the time and the money spent on a professionally built cooker. They almost all have an outside firebox, that you can easily stoke, and a covered grill large enough for a small pig. Bells and whistles vary but usually include sophisticated temperature gauges and intricate vent windows.

Cinder Block Pit

Did you love Legos as a kid? How about Lincoln Logs? The Cinder Block Pit is for the builder in us all.

You'll need some sort of hard surface for the base of your pit. Your driveway will suffice. Or a public road, if you can pull it off.

Now stack the blocks in a square or rectangle three to five high. Be sure to leave a gap of at least a block to enable you to add coals to the fire. Otherwise you'll be pulling blocks in and out of your pit all night. You may even want to leave an entire end open.

The size of your pit will be determined by the size of metal grid you can find. Check the local scrap yard. You'll need something with a mesh pattern sturdy enough to support your choice of meat.

The grid should be about three feet above the ground. You can cook either over burning hardwood or you can burn the wood down to coals in a firebox and add them to the fire. If you use coals, keep them about six inches thick. Either way, the meat is cooked directly above the fire, not to the side of it.

Barbecue men are of two minds when it comes to the smoking process on this pit. Some leave the meat in the open air. Others cover the top of the pit, including the meat, with pasteboard, to hold in the smoke. Try it both ways and see which you like best.

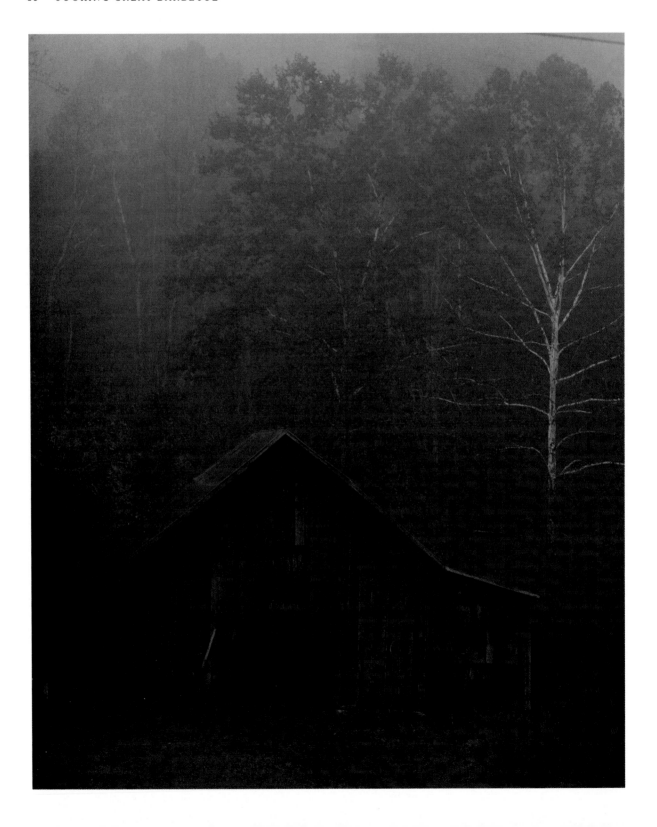

Real Pit

Sometime in your life you should cook barbecue over a real pit. After all, that's where the name barbecue pit came from: a hole in the ground.

Cooking in a real pit is sort of like the folks at the Jack Daniel's distillery using ironfree water from the Cave Spring; it's a tie to the past. The water from the Cave Spring keeps the folks at Jack Daniel's faithful to their old methods. It's the same with a real pit.

Find a suitable location, preferably in someone else's backyard, with no overhanging tree limbs. Dig a hole three feet wide by five feet long by one foot deep.

Build a hardwood fire in the pit about an hour before you plan to start cooking. This dries the inside walls of the pit and also heats them up.

Spread out your coals. How hot should the fire be? Just hot enough to allow you to hold your hand over the pit about 10 seconds. You don't want any flames. They will cook the meat too fast. A good idea is to build a separate fire next to the pit to supply coals as necessary.

You'll need some sort of rack to hold the meat above the fire. Chicken wire will work with a few iron pipes run crossways of the pit for support. You'll also need something to cover the meat, holding the heat and smoke in. Pasteboard will work. Sheet metal too (although it will get hot to the touch). You could even use three or four garbage can lids. Just make sure they're clean; preferably new.

Whatever type cooker you use, just be patient. Don't give up on it too quickly. The great pitmen of America don't believe a pit is broken in good for at least two years. It has to mature, they say. And these are guys who cook on their pits everyday!

And how do you know if your pit has matured? You'll know, the pitmasters say.

Jack Daniel's Whiskey has to mature, too. And at the Jack Daniel's distillery, maturity is also a matter of judgment, not days. The tasters decide when the Jack Daniel's is ready and it's not just a matter of counting days, months or even years.

Other Equipment for the Complete Barbecuist

A cotton mop for basting
Tongs for turning meat (cast-iron coal tongs are best)
Thermometer (for those who get nervous)
Garden hose with spray nozzle (for dousing flare-ups in the fire)
Sugar needle (optional: for injecting sauce into the meat)
Beverage cozy (to keep your drink cold)

Fire

Every barbecue begins with fire. If you weren't a Cub Scout or a Brownie, now is the time to question what you were thinking back then. And also to learn how to build a fire.

My Aunt Esther Shanks, who lives in Leesburg, Tennessee, is the best I ever saw at building a fire. Here's how she builds one:

"First take a big handful of Johnson City Press-Chronicles (newspapers). Wad 'em up and put kindling on top. Then strike your match. After it starts blazing good add you some hickory wood until it gets to cracking and a-popping. Add small sticks of hickory until it gets started good. Too large a sticks puts it out. It's no trouble keeping it going. Just add a little dry wood to it. And if you want more smoke, you can use wet wood."

You don't need a thermometer to gauge the heat. Your hand is a natural thermometer. Jack Dempsy of Ty Ty, Georgia, has been cooking barbecue for half a century using only the palm of his hand as a heat gauge. Just hold your hand about eight inches above the coals. If you can stand the heat for five seconds, you have a low or slow fire; four seconds, a medium fire; three seconds, a medium-hot fire; and two seconds, a hot fire.

If you use charcoal and wood chips, soak your wood chips overnight. That will make them smoke more. And if you use charcoal, try to find good lump charcoal. It doesn't have fillers in it and burns better.

Or try Jack Daniel's Charcoal. It's made of staves from the barrels used to age the whiskey.

Wood

Look for hardwood. Softwoods burn too fast and also emit resins that coat the meat. Hardwood burns slow and clean, or as clean as smoke ever is.

The most popular woods for barbecuing are hickory, oak and mesquite. What you use will depend, in large part, on what is available in your area.

Fruitwoods, such as cherry and apple, are a good addition to your fire. Shane Best says he adds cherry and apple wood to hickory. "Sometimes hickory bites a little too strong for people."

One word of warning from Arkansas native Steve "Buck" Greene: "You can't use pine. It has too much oil ... and makes it taste like gasoline."

You can cook with either direct flame or hot coals. At Owensboro's Moonlite Bar-B-Que, Ken Bosley says, "We keep the fire under the meat at all times." A hundred miles away at Starnes Bar-B-Q in Paducah, Kentucky, they burn the hickory down to red-hot coals and then shovel them under the meat.

Experiment with woods. Hickory may be too strong for your taste, oak too bland, mesquite too harsh, apple too sweet. Just remember the most important fact about wood selection: you don't eat the wood.

Meat

Start by buying the best cuts of meat. Many barbecue cooks think this is the real secret to great barbecue: top-grade meat. It's a secret that folks at the Jack Daniel's distillery already know: the highest quality ingredients yield the best product.

The particular cut of meat you use is a matter of personal preference.

The standard barbecue cuts are ham, loin, shoulder or Boston butt for pork, brisket for beef, ribs for pork or beef.

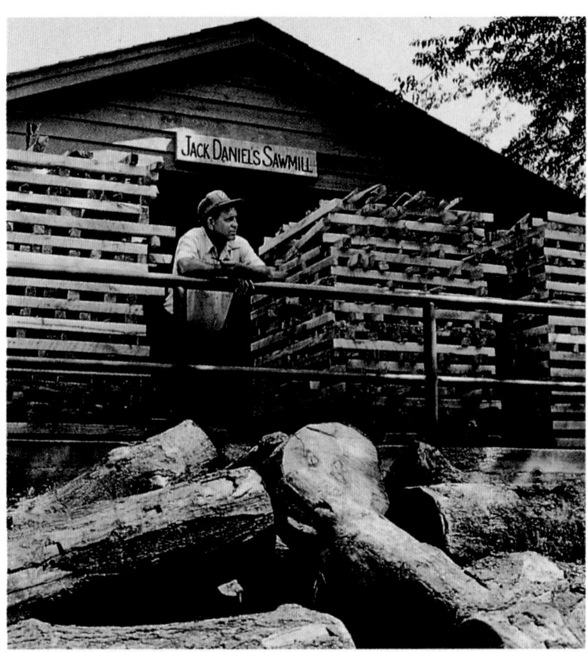

Steve "Buck" Greene favors green ham for his backyard barbecuing. "It's a fresh ham, one that hasn't been cured with sugar or salt. In Arkansas you can get them off the shelf. Other places you have to order one and wait three days."

Your meat should be room temperature before you cook it. Fish and poultry can be cool, but they should not be frozen.

Preparing the Meat

This can mean anything from rubbing it with salt and pepper or secret herbs and spices to marinating it, depending on what style barbecue you want. See next chapter.

Cooking

Now you're ready for the fire. Cook according to the recipe. Cooking specific cuts is discussed later in this chapter.

How to Tell When Your Meat is Done

How long do you cook?

"There's no magic number," says Shane Best. "Cooking barbecue is just like making mayonnaise. You just have to break enough eggs to make it right."

Some use the rule of thumb of an hour a pound. With larger cuts, such as a whole hog, this won't work, since no one wants to tend a pit for 90 straight hours.

Wayne Monk at Lexington No. 1 in Lexington, North Carolina, says pork shoulder is done when it pulls away from the bone. You can use a similar rule for beef.

With ribs when the outside meat begins to feather, the ribs are done.

With chicken the meat is done when you can easily pierce the flesh near a joint with a fork.

There are some who say you need to open up a bottle of Jack Daniel's as you put on the meat. When the bottle is empty, the meat will be done.

When you cut into the meat you should see three layers of color. The outside should be black. Just under the black should be a pink layer. This doesn't mean the meat isn't done. It's the smoke ring, created by the penetrating smoke. The innermost layer should be that of well-done meat.

Here are some tips for cooking various cuts of meat.

RIBS

One of America's barbecue kings once told me not to worry about the temperature when I cooked ribs. "Ribs don't burn," he said. So I was cooking for a large party at my house once, barbecuing a pork shoulder on my Big Daddy cooker and smoking two racks of ribs on my Weber Kettle. I was paying much more attention to the shoulder because my barbecue king friend had told me not to worry about the ribs, they wouldn't burn.

They burned, to a crisp, charred black; they fell apart to the touch.

The moral of this story is that ribs do burn. Pay as much attention to them as to any other barbecue meat.

There are three kinds of ribs – loin ribs (when cut from a young hog they are called baby back ribs), back ribs (also called country-style ribs) and spareribs (also called long ribs) – and all are perfect for barbecuing. The loin ribs are the meatiest, and also the most expensive.

Ribs are cooked fat side up for the entire time they are on the grill.

POPPY BROWN'S LOIN BACK RIBS

2 slabs baby back ribs
Warmed honey
Dry rub mix:
3 tablespoons paprika
1 tablespoon onion powder
1 tablespoon garlic powder
1 tablespoon ground basil
1½ tablespoons mustard powder
1 tablespoon red pepper
½ tablespoon black pepper

Combine dry rub ingredients and rub into ribs. Cook ribs over hickory coals at 190 to 200 degrees for 4 to 5 hours. 15 minutes before serving, coat ribs with heated honey.

Lucious (and Luscious) Ribs

Recipes on packages have a bit of a bad reputation. From undrinkable "summer coolers" reeking of cheap rum to "mock apple pie" stuffed with Ritz crackers, most such recipes seem designed mainly to force you to buy more of whatever package you found them printed on.

In one sense, the recipe you find printed on Lucious the King's Southern Seasoning is exactly the same: it'll make you want to buy more packages. But the difference is, it's great – a fast, simple method of cooking dry-rub ribs that leaves them meaty and juicy, with a rich mahogany surface that begs to be gnawed.

The basic technique that The King advocates (cooking ribs hotter for a shorter length of time) will work with any dry rub. Still, the spices in the package are as good as the recipe on it, and I suggest you seriously consider ordering some. It's available from Lucious the King's Southern Seasonings, 428 McCallie Avenue, Chattanooga, Tennessee 37402. It's $1.75 for a 2½-ounce pack or $16.68 for a dozen packs. In either case, add $2.50 for shipping and handling.

And here's what you do with it:

Lucious' Luscious Ribs

Spareribs, 3-pound rack or under, "skinned"
1½ tablespoons dry rub
1 750-ml bottle Jack Daniel's Whiskey

First, take your ribs out of the refrigerator and make sure they're "skinned" (have had the membrane removed from the bone side). If not, skin 'em yourself with a sharp knife. Then sprinkle the dry rub onto them, massaging it into the meat. Use 1 tablespoon on the meat side and ½ tablespoon on the bone side. Set them aside and allow them to come to room temperature while you build your fire.

Make yourself a good, self-sustaining bed of coals in one half of a closed grill, and make 'em hot: 325 degrees. Use charcoal with some hickory chips added, or else build a hickory fire and let it burn down to coals. Put the ribs on the grill side away from the coals, over a drip pan if possible. Place the ribs bone-side down and grill at 325 degrees for 1 hour and 45 minutes. Open the grill only to add wood or charcoal (if necessary) to maintain temperature. Pinch the meat between the ribs; when it's done, it will "give" under your fingertips. Cooking time may be as long as a couple of hours, not much longer. Oh, yeah. Pour the Jack Daniel's over ice and drink it.

David Coleman's Spareribs

Dave actually doesn't have any spareribs; this is just his recipe for cooking spareribs.

10 pounds spareribs
1 cup brown sugar
1 teaspoon salt
1 teaspoon pepper
1 teaspoon paprika
1/2 teaspoon garlic salt

Mix dry ingredients and rub into both sides of meat. Let stand 30 minutes.

Smoke for 4 to 5 hours at 200 to 225 degrees.

David Coleman's Rib Sauce

1 15-ounce can tomato sauce
1/3 cup brown sugar
1/3 cup apple-cider vinegar
1 teaspoon garlic salt
1 tablespoon paprika
1/3 teaspoon cloves
1/4 teaspoon cinnamon
2 tablespoons Worcestershire sauce
2 tablespoons onion, chopped
2 tablespoons Tiger sauce
1 teaspoon dry mustard

Mix well. Bring to a boil, then simmer 20 minutes.

PORK SHOULDER

This is a preferred cut across the South.

Buy the best, top-grade shoulder the butcher has. You may want to rub or marinate the meat before cooking.

Start it on the grill, fat side down. Cook it this way for the first hour. Then cook it the rest of the time fat side on top. This way the fat cooks down through the meat, giving it its distinctive sweet taste.

Cook the meat slowly. During the first couple of hours there should be virtually no change in the color of the shoulder.

Some say the meat is done when a meat thermometer inserted in the thickest part reads 170 degrees. I don't like that method. To begin with I don't like sticking my meat unless it's with a knife and the next act I perform is eating it. It lets some of the juices out. I judge by the appearance of the meat. When the meat has pulled away from the bone, it is usually done.

If you use the thermometer method, you can cook away all the fat by leaving the shoulder on the grill until the temperature in the thickest part is 200 degrees.

The hardest part of cooking shoulder is deciding whether to serve it pulled, pulled and chopped or sliced.

My personal favorite is pulled and chopped. I think it is more flavorful because there are more surfaces to make contact with your taste buds. But that's only my theory.

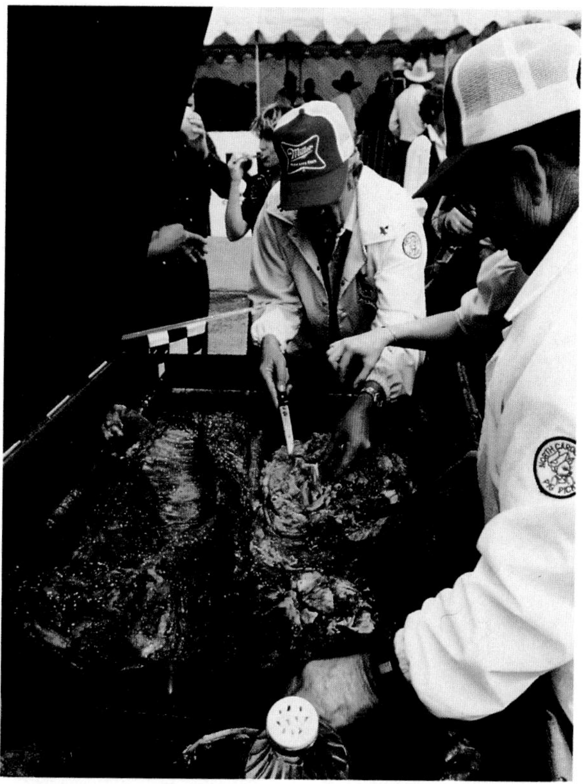

WHOLE HOG

A big pig is not for the beginner. It's cumbersome to work with, tricky to cook, near impossible for one person to turn and a whole lot more meat than a dinner party for four can handle. Only try a whole hog when you have help, lots of help, preferably experienced help.

When calculating how much pig to buy, figure a pound and a half per person. The meat will cook down quite a bit; in addition there are some parts on a whole hog, even one that's been dressed by the butcher, that civilized people won't eat.

Some people recommend buying a dressed pig, with its head and feet removed. I prefer leaving them on. Gives me somebody to talk to during those long hours.

Have the butcher saw the backbone through the center, leaving the skin intact. And don't pierce the skin.

When you put the hog on the pit, spread him apart. Start cooking him meat side down and skin side up. You will need to turn him several times as you cook.

Sop often enough to keep the pig moist, although you shouldn't need to start until the pig has been on the pit a good four hours. Use any of the sop recipes in the next chapter or make a solution of 1 quart water, 1 cup red cider vinegar and 1/4 cup salt. Brush it on with a small cotton mop.

Be sure and baste as quickly as possible so as not to lose the heat in the cooker.

A whole hog won't cook in a half-hour. Plan on barbecuing Mr. Pig only when you can stay up all night.

For a true pig pickin', serve the pig whole. Give each guest a pair of tongs and instruct them to pull their own meat. The experienced ones will head for the tenderloin first. Trail along behind the new-comers; they're liable to pick something they'll regret later, when they find out what it is.

BEEF BRISKET

The toughest cut of meat the aspiring barbecuer will come in contact with is the beef brisket. This is a piece of meat that definitely can use all the help it can get: marinating, basting, slow cooking. But when barbecued properly it is at the top of the taste list. If you don't believe me, just ask a Texan.

Some barbecue places in Texas cook their brisket 24 hours. Some places cook it even longer. At Hammonds in Glen Rose, Texas, they cook it 36 hours. That's not a typo, that's an incredible length of time: 36 hours! You just feel grateful that they'd consent to sell it to you.

CHICKEN

More chicken is cooked on barbecue cookers than any other meat. Not much of it is barbecued; most is grilled. But barbecued chicken, with its smoky, delicate flavor is one of Mother Nature's great delights.

Chicken is simple to barbecue. It cooks very easily using the method you use to cook pork shoulder. Put the chicken, skin side up, on the grill, away from the heat.

Turn the chicken every 10 to 15 minutes with tongs (a fork will puncture the skin and when barbecuing, you don't ever want to puncture the skin). Baste each time you turn the chicken. Chicken needs more mopping than pork or beef because it doesn't have as much fat.

The meat is done when you can easily pierce the flesh near a joint with a fork. Another method for testing for doneness is to grab the drumstick and shake it. If it feels like shaking hands with a contortionist, a loosey-goosey feel, it's done.

One trick you might try when barbecuing chicken is to remove it from the cooker after the first 10 minutes, to give it a rest. Let it stand about 10 minutes and then return it to the grill. It makes for a more tender chicken.

AUNT CINDY'S SINFUL LEMON CHICKEN

1 fryer chicken, cut in half
1/2 cup mayonnaise
1/4 cup lemon juice
1/2 tablespoon salt
1/2 teaspoon paprika
1 teaspoon onion powder
1 teaspoon dried sweet basil, crushed
1/4 teaspoon thyme, crushed
1/4 teaspoon garlic powder

Combine mayonnaise, lemon juice, salt, paprika, onion powder, basil, thyme and garlic powder. Mix well. Pour over chicken. Cover and refrigerate overnight, turning chicken occasionally.

Cook 30 minutes skin side up on the grill, brushing frequently with marinade. Turn and cook, continuing to baste with marinade until chicken is golden brown, usually another 20 minutes.

BEST RIBS

Shane Best has finally lived up to his last name. He can now tell people he cooks the Best Ribs in the World and show them the trophy to prove it.

Best and his Kentucky Cookout Company barbecue team won the Best Ribs in the World title at the 1990 World Invitational Rib Championship in Richmond, Virginia.

He also won $15,000 in cash: $5,000 for winning the Best Baby Back Ribs category and $10,000 for being named overall champion. And it was only the fourth barbecue cooking competition Best had ever entered.

His first contest was the 1989 World Series of Ribs, held in Minneapolis. "We finished 18th. Then we competed at Mansfield (Ohio) and finished 6th and at the North American Rib Championship in Detroit and finished 8th."

Best has only been cooking barbecue since 1983. He got into it by accident. Some folks called and wanted him to sell sandwiches at their fund-raising event. "I didn't want to because what was I going to do with a thousand cold sandwiches if they didn't sell? Then this misplaced Texan named Jim Yockey talked me into cooking barbecue for the event. He brought a unit up from southwest Texas and we cooked ribs on it. Then I started selling barbecue out of my store from there."

His store was the Prospect General Store in Prospect, Kentucky, a meat market renowned nationwide for its smoked country hams (the New York Times *regularly listed him in its annual "Christmas gourmet food" story.) He was forced to close in 1988 because the convenience store next door owned his property and needed it for a parking lot. That's when he got into the barbecue catering business.*

It was a natural progression for Best, a New Albany, Indiana native who says he has been fooling with meat for as long as he can remember. "One of my first jobs was at a market. I can remember the first night I got to slice the baloney. I was on top of the world."

He credits his victory in the Richmond contest to two things: "The whiskey sauce and taking the time. For four hours I babysat those ribs while they were cooking."

He cooked over apple-wood charcoal, with a chunk of mesquite and some persimmon wood.

He has one more secret to rib-cooking. "Only use the right-hand ribs. The hogs lay on their left side so those ribs are a lot tougher." He says this with a wink.

Here is a variation on his award-winning recipe:

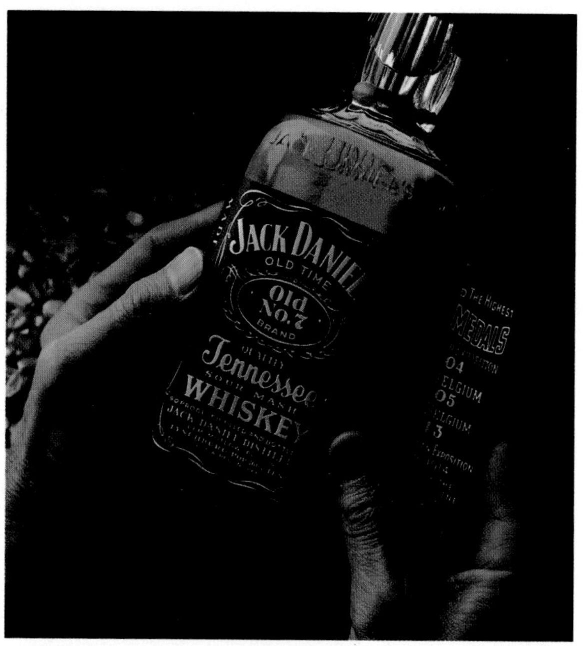

WhiskeyQue, Too Recipe

9 cups Worcestershire sauce
4 cups apple-cider vinegar
$1\frac{1}{2}$ cups tomato juice
$\frac{1}{2}$ cup Tabasco sauce
2 quarts ketchup
$\frac{1}{2}$ cup garlic, minced or put through a garlic press
2 cups brown sugar
2 cups sugar
$\frac{1}{2}$ cup paprika
$\frac{1}{2}$ cup black pepper
6 tablespoons onion powder
$\frac{1}{2}$ cup salt
Liquid smoke, to taste
1 cup Jack Daniel's Whiskey

Mix and simmer all ingredients except Jack Daniel's Whiskey for 1 hour. Add Jack Daniel's Whiskey after mixture has cooked and cooled.

Makes $1\frac{1}{2}$ gallons.

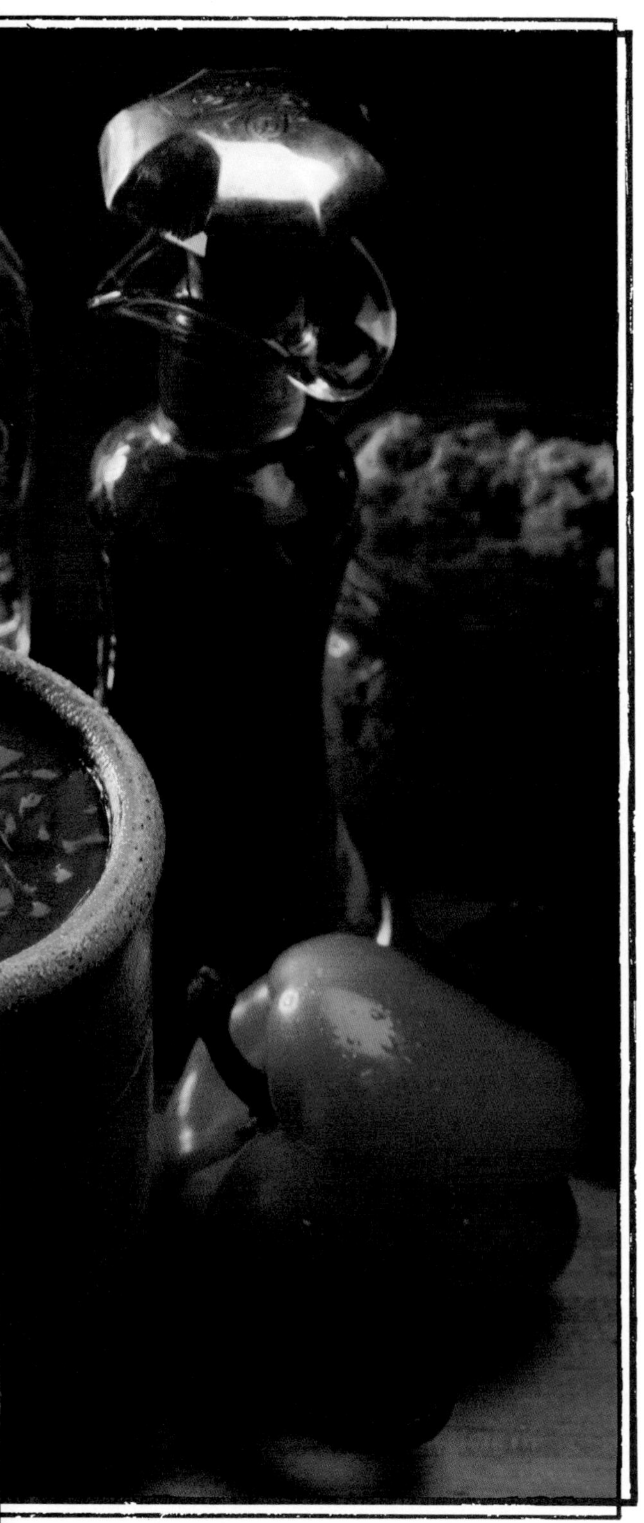

THE SEARCH FOR THE ONE TRUE SAUCE

Don't bother. There is no one true barbecue sauce. There are hundreds. And there are hundreds of variations on these.

Barbecue sauce was born in the Atlantic coastal region of America, specifically in Virginia and North Carolina, where the first American barbecues were held. They were barbecuing in these areas back when "pilgrim" was a word you heard in everyday conversation.

George Washington was an early barbecue fan. He frequently mentioned attending "barbicues" in his diary. Maybe he couldn't spell it, but he loved to eat it.

The first barbecue sauce, a variation on English ketchup, was almost pure vinegar, with only a dash of spice for kick. This was because the first barbecue cooks were at work in the days when the tomato was thought to be poisonous.

Then in 1830 a Col. Robert Johnson mounted the courthouse steps in Salem, New Jersey and chomped into a tomato. He didn't die and some barbecue pitman in the back of the crowd must have shouted, "Let's try it in the sauce." And thus was born the best known barbecue sauce, the tomato-based sauce.

As sugars were imported from the Caribbean, they, too, were thrown in the mix. Barbecue cooks in the various regions adapted their sauce to suit their available ingredients and the meat of choice. In Texas, where cattle was king, the sauce had to be hardy enough to overcome the strong taste of beef. In the deep South the more delicate taste of pork required a more delicate sauce. In the mid-section of South Carolina cooks found mustard a tasty addition to barbecue sauce.

Using only the primary barbecue sauce ingredients – vinegar, tomato, sugar, mustard, salt and pepper – you can create an almost limitless number of recipes for sauce.

TABLE SAUCES

The sauce recipes offered in this section should be considered a starting point. Dave Brandon of Brandon's Bar-B-Que in Louisville, Kentucky, says the fun of making barbecue sauce is creating your own. Start with a batch of sauce from one of these recipes and then make it your own. "Maybe marinate onions in a frying pan, throw in a couple of cloves of garlic, diced green peppers, maybe a cupful of vinegar to add extra spice, and mix. Experiment. Have fun. That's what outdoor cooking is all about."

DOWN EAST SAUCES

(vinegar-based)

If you are just beginning your quest for the perfect barbecue sauce, start with a vinegar-based sauce, the kind they favor in the eastern part of North Carolina. This is the kind of sauce George Washington used.

SOOOEY SAUCE

2 cups white vinegar
1 teaspoon cayenne pepper
1/2 teaspoon black pepper

Combine in a saucepan and bring to a boil. Reduce heat and simmer for 10 minutes.

EARL'S NO-COOK SAUCE

1 cup apple-cider vinegar
2 tablespoons salt
1/2 teaspoon red pepper
1 teaspoon red pepper flakes
1 tablespoon brown sugar

Combine ingredients. Let stand at least 4 hours; 4 weeks is even better.

FATHER OF OUR COUNTRY SAUCE

1 cup apple-cider vinegar
1 stick butter
1/2 teaspoon salt
1/2 tablespoon lemon juice
1/2 teaspoon cayenne pepper
1/2 teaspoon dried red pepper flakes

Combine vinegar, butter and salt in saucepan. Heat until butter is melted. Add lemon juice, pepper and pepper flakes. Allow to stand for 2 hours for flavors to meld. Serve warm.

These sauces can also be used as mopping sauces.

Lexington (North Carolina) Sauces

(tomato-based)

Travel west from New Bern and Goldsboro, North Carolina and you will observe a change in the barbecue sauce. As you cross U.S. 1, which runs through Raleigh, you'll find the sauce suddenly turning red. U.S. 1 is generally considered the line of demarcation between the vinegar barbecue sauces and the tomato barbecue sauces.

This thin tomato-based sauce is often referred to as Lexington Sauce, taking its name from the barbecue-crazy town of Lexington, North Carolina. This small community of 16,000 has 16 full-time commercial barbecue joints, one for each 1,000 residents!

Kernersville Sauce

1 cup white vinegar
1/2 cup water
1/4 cup ketchup
1 tablespoon sugar
1/2 teaspoon red pepper
1/2 teaspoon black pepper
1/2 teaspoon salt

Combine all ingredients in a saucepan and bring to a boil. Reduce heat and simmer for 10 minutes.

Piedmont Sauce

1 cup ketchup
1 cup water
1/4 cup apple-cider vinegar
1 small onion, minced
1 teaspoon garlic powder
2 tablespoons brown sugar
2 tablespoons molasses
2 teaspoons dry mustard
1 teaspoon chili powder

Combine all ingredients in a saucepan and simmer over low heat for 20 minutes.

Pork Butt Kicking Sauce

1 medium onion, minced
3 cups ketchup
2 tablespoons Worcestershire sauce
2 teaspoons chili powder
1 teaspoon cayenne pepper
3/4 cup sugar
1 teaspoon garlic salt
1/2 cup tarragon vinegar

Combine ingredients and cook over medium-low heat, stirring frequently, for 10 minutes.

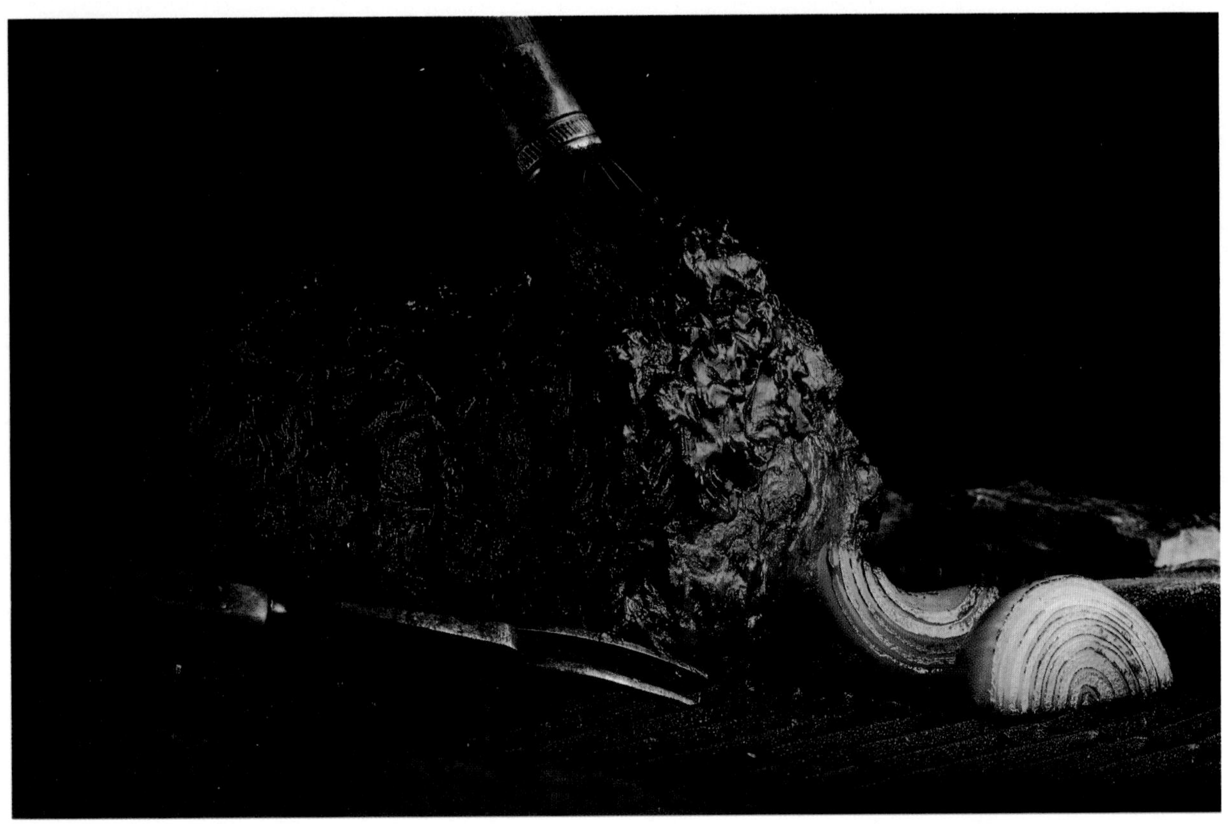

Little Bubba's Sauce

$1/3$ cup apple-cider vinegar
1 teaspoon salt
1 teaspoon celery salt
$1/2$ cup ketchup
$1/2$ teaspoon chili powder
$1/8$ teaspoon nutmeg
$1/2$ teaspoon brown sugar
1 cup water

Mix ingredients and bring to a boil.

South Carolina Sauces

(mustard-based)

Travel south from Lexington, North Carolina into South Carolina and you will observe another change in the barbecue sauce. As you near Columbia in the central part of South Carolina, you'll find the sauce suddenly turning yellow. That's right, yellow!

They pour a mustard-based sauce on their barbecue there. It's a different barbecue taste, but one every barbecue pilgrim should try.

Junior's Sauce

8 tablespoons mustard
$1/2$ cup heavy cream
1 tablespoon apple-cider vinegar
1 tablespoon dark corn syrup
$1/2$ teaspoon freshly ground black pepper
3 drops hot sauce

Combine all ingredients in a saucepan. Bring to a boil, then allow to simmer for 10 minutes.

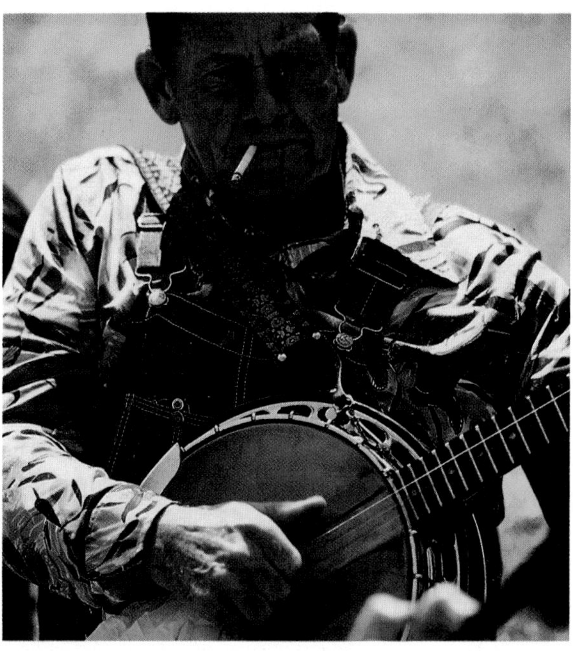

Pee Dee River Sauce

1 large (1-lb. 8-ounce) jar mustard
1 cup mayonnaise
$1/3$ cup ketchup
2 tablespoons Worcestershire sauce
1 tablespoon brown sugar
1 teaspoon Tabasco sauce
$1/4$ teaspoon cayenne pepper
$1/4$ teaspoon ground pepper
1 teaspoon seasoned salt
$1/4$ cup butter
$1/2$ cup water

Combine all ingredients in a saucepan. Bring to a boil. Reduce heat and cook uncovered for 8 minutes.

DEEP SOUTH SAUCES

(ketchup- and mustard-based)

Keep on heading south, from Columbia into Georgia, and you'll discover the sauce changing color again, back to an orangish-red. The folks here have discovered that tomato and mustard do mix, especially in barbecue sauce.

TY TY GOAT SAUCE

1 cup water
3/4 cup ketchup
1/4 cup vinegar
1/4 cup tomato juice
2 tablespoons light Karo syrup
2 tablespoons Worcestershire sauce
2 tablespoons mustard
1 tablespoon sugar
1 tablespoon hot sauce
1 tablespoon salt
1/2 tablespoon chili powder
1/2 teaspoon red pepper

Combine all ingredients and bring to a boil. Reduce heat and simmer for 10 minutes. Goat needs a strong sauce like this.

Mr. Jack Daniel

LEGENDARY BARBECUE

Legends are as thick as trees in the hills and hollows of Tennessee, but none are as famous as the legend of the distiller Jasper Newton Daniel, better known to the world as Jack Daniel. A little man, no more than five feet two inches tall, who hailed from the tiny town of Lynchburg, pop. 361, the county seat of Moore County, the smallest county in Tennessee, he made whiskey. Good whiskey. So good that Mr. Jack took samples to the Great Louisiana Purchase Exposition in St. Louis in 1904 to compete for the title of World's Finest Whiskey.

World Fairs and Expositions at that time judged spirits just as they judged other prod-

ucts: machinery, produce, livestock, textiles, art and a jillion other things. Inventors came from everywhere to compete and to introduce their wares to the world-at-large. Jack Daniel thought his whiskey was the best in the world and he wanted to see if the judges agreed with him. And he wasn't disappointed. When he returned to Lynchburg, he had in hand a medal for World's Finest Whiskey. And a new category, "Tennessee Whiskey," was born. This was not Kentucky Bourbon, nor Scotch, Irish or Canadian Whiskey. This was a new kind of whiskey, charcoal-mellowed through ten feet of charcoal. That process made a difference in taste and in category. This Tennessee Sour Mash was as mellow as the smile on Mr. Jack's face when he returned home.

Legends have been happening in the hollow ever since. Now that very whiskey is known all over the world. Lynchburg might not be on every map, even today, but it is known around the world as the home of Jack Daniel's Distillery. Legions of people have come to visit and tour his National Historic site, and while they are in the area they sample a little of the hometown product, sometimes in Southern dishes served in the local restaurants. It still has the reputation of the World's Finest Whiskey and some legendary recipes have been born using Mr. Jack's prize recipe as a key ingredient.

Dreamland Bar B-Q Drive Inn, Tuscaloosa, Alabama

Elberton Sauce

1 quart apple-cider vinegar
1 cup ketchup
1 cup water
1 cup chili sauce
1/2 cup Worcestershire sauce
1/4 cup mustard
1 stick butter
1 medium onion, chopped
1 green pepper, chopped
3 tablespoons lemon juice
1 tablespoon grated lemon zest (yellow part of rind only)
2 cloves garlic, crushed
1 teaspoon sugar

Mix all ingredients in a large pot and stir well. Bring to a boil, then reduce heat, cover and simmer for 30 minutes.

Enigma Sauce (from Enigma, Georgia)

1/3 cup minced onion
2 tablespoons butter
1 cup ketchup
1 cup mustard
1/2 cup water
1/3 cup lemon juice
2 tablespoons Worcestershire sauce
2 tablespoons brown sugar
1/4 teaspoon salt

Saute onion in butter. Add remaining ingredients. Combine and simmer for 10 minutes.

TEXAS SAUCES

(thick, tomato-based)

As you cross the Deep South, through Alabama, Mississippi and Louisiana, you'll discover the sauce getting sweeter. The color changes aren't as noticeable, but the sauces are definitely sweeter. That's because they started cooking barbecue in these parts about the time sugar cane was being imported from the Caribbean.

By the time you reach Texas, you have left pork barbecue country and entered beef barbecue country. The sauce is thicker and sweeter, to match the taste of beef and the aroma of the mesquite wood they cook it over.

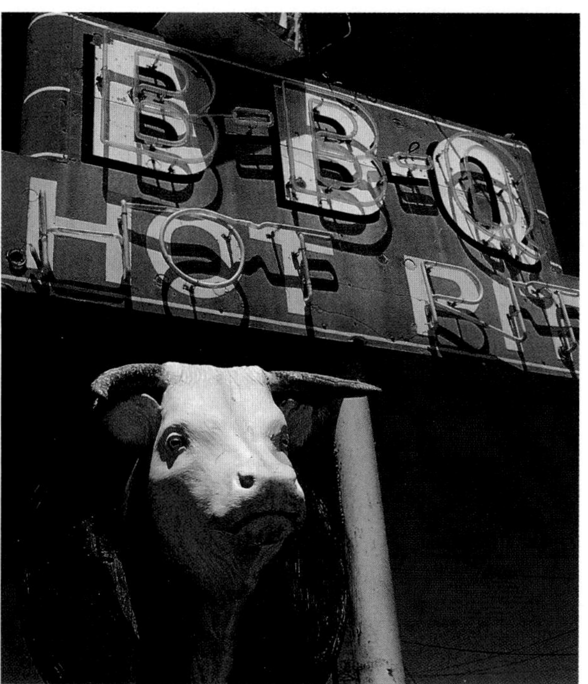

JOHNSON FAMILY SAUCE

President Lyndon B. Johnson often entertained his political friends with a barbecue. There are as many sauce recipes attributed to his barbecues as there are tall tales.

Here's another one.

3 cups ketchup
1 cup honey
1 medium onion, chopped fine
1 large green pepper, chopped fine
2 tablespoons Tabasco sauce
2 teaspoons garlic powder
2 tablespoons white vinegar
1/2 cup packed brown sugar
1/2 cup Worcestershire sauce
1/2 cup water

Combine all ingredients and bring mixture to a boil. Reduce heat and simmer until onion and peppers are tender.

LONE STAR SAUCE

1/2 cup butter
1/4 cup lemon juice
1/4 cup vinegar
1/4 cup ketchup
1/4 cup Worcestershire sauce
Dash salt
Dash pepper
2 teaspoons Tabasco sauce
Dash red pepper

Melt butter in saucepan. Add lemon juice, vinegar, ketchup and Worcestershire sauce. Bring to a boil, then add seasonings. Refrigerate 1 to 2 days. Serve warm as table sauce.

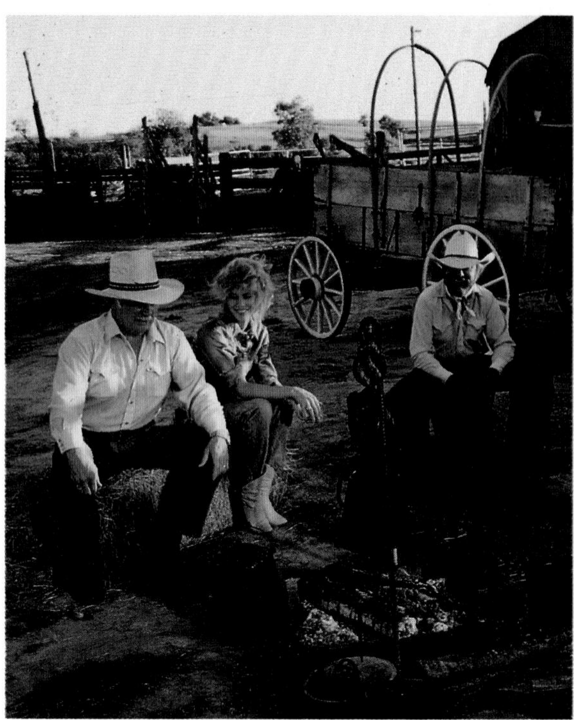

Long-Horn Brisket Sauce

Beef fat (cut from brisket)
2½ cups ketchup
1 cup Worcestershire sauce
1 cup lemon juice
½ cup brown sugar, firmly packed
½ cup onion, chopped
½ cup water
1 teaspoon cayenne pepper
1 teaspoon paprika

Cut fat into ½-inch pieces. Heat in a large skillet until melted. Pour 1 cup fat in a saucepan. Stir in remaining ingredients. Cover and cook over low heat until thick, about 1 hour.

Tall Sauce

½ cup butter
1 medium onion, chopped fine
1 rib celery, finely chopped
2 teaspoons minced garlic
1 cup tomato puree
1 cup beef stock
½ cup apple-cider vinegar
½ cup firmly packed dark brown sugar
¼ cup Worcestershire sauce
2 teaspoons freshly ground black pepper
2 teaspoons red pepper
2 teaspoons chili powder
1 teaspoon ground cumin

Melt the butter in a saucepan. Saute the onion, celery and garlic together until tender (about 10 minutes).

Add tomato puree, beef stock, vinegar, brown sugar, Worcestershire and spices. Simmer for 30 minutes, stirring frequently. Allow sauce to sit for 1 hour to allow flavors to meld.

Kansas City Sauces

By the time the migrating pitmasters reached this heartland town, they had perfected their craft and were willing to pass on the secrets. Kansas City is where the smoke meets the sauce, where all the barbecue traditions come together. But instead of becoming muddled in a big stew, each rises to another plain. Here you can find world class beef ribs, world class pork ribs, world class sliced pork and world class sliced beef.

You can't drive down a street here without passing a smokestack and pile of wood and hear the sighs of delight of satisfied barbecue eaters. The best seems once again to be at Arthur Bryant's, a joint made famous by writer Calvin Trillin, who proclaimed in a *New Yorker* article that it was the "single best restaurant in the world." Don't hold back there, Calvin.

Brooklyn Avenue Sauce

2 cups ketchup
1 cup brown sugar
1 tablespoon Tabasco sauce
1 medium onion, chopped
1 green pepper, chopped fine
1/4 cup lemon juice
1/2 teaspoon garlic powder
1 teaspoon paprika
1 tablespoon dry mustard
1 tablespoon white vinegar
1/2 cup brown sugar, packed
1/4 cup Worcestershire sauce

Combine in a saucepan. Bring to a boil. Reduce heat and simmer for 15 minutes.

Truman Family Sauce

This sauce is supposed to be as sweet as Bess Truman and as sharp as Harry's tongue.

1 cup tomato sauce
1 cup apple-cider vinegar
2/3 cup brown sugar
2 cloves garlic, crushed
1/3 cup Worcestershire sauce
1/3 cup water
1 medium onion, chopped
1/2 teaspoon paprika
1 teaspoon cayenne pepper

Combine in a saucepan and bring to a boil. Simmer on low for 10 minutes.

Owensboro Dip

(Worcestershire sauce-based)

In the central counties of Kentucky, they have developed an entirely different barbecue tradition. Because of the availability of mutton, that became the meat of choice. And because of mutton's stronger taste, they developed a new kind of sauce, a Worcestershire sauce-based dip. Because mutton has a fuller taste, you need to dip each bite into the sauce.

Daviess County Mutton Dip

1 gallon water
1 2/3 cups Worcestershire sauce
2 1/2 tablespoons black pepper
1/3 cup brown sugar
1 teaspoon allspice
1 teaspoon onion salt
1 teaspoon garlic powder
2 tablespoons salt
2 tablespoons lemon juice
2 cups vinegar

Combine ingredients and bring to a boil. Baste and use the rest as a dip for chopped or sliced mutton.

Tennessee Sweet Sauces

Because of its central location – it touches eight other barbecue-belt states – Tennessee has become the melting pot of barbecue. You can find almost any style sauce used somewhere in the state.

Uncle Luther's Pop Sauce

1 cup Coke or Pepsi
1 cup ketchup
1/3 cup brown sugar, packed

Combine ingredients in a saucepan and bring to a boil. Reduce heat to simmer and let the sauce cook down about 45 minutes.

Memphis Sauce

1 cup tomato sauce
1 cup apple-cider vinegar
1/3 cup Worcestershire sauce
1/3 cup water
1 tablespoon butter
1 small onion, chopped
1 1/2 teaspoons salt
Dash red pepper
Dash black pepper

Combine in a saucepan and bring to a boil. Simmer on low for 10 minutes.

JACK DANIEL'S SAUCE

1 medium onion, finely chopped
1 clove garlic, minced
2 tablespoons vegetable oil
1½ cups ketchup
¼ cup brown sugar
2 tablespoons Jack Daniel's Whiskey
1 teaspoon liquid smoke (optional)
2½ tablespoons apple-cider vinegar
½ teaspoon dry mustard
2 drops hot pepper sauce

Saute onion and garlic in vegetable oil until tender. Stir in remaining ingredients and bring to a boil over medium heat. Reduce heat and simmer for 10 minutes.

OTHER SAUCES

EVELYN'S SAUCE

2 cups apple-cider vinegar
1 cup water
¾ cup Worcestershire sauce
1 pound brown sugar (dark)
2 teaspoons dry mustard or 2 tablespoons prepared mustard
½ teaspoon Tabasco sauce
2 tablespoons black pepper
2 cloves garlic, chopped fine
½ cup dry onions or 2 medium onions, chopped
1 cup sweet pickle relish

Simmer the liquids and sugar about 10 minutes. Add the other ingredients and continue cooking 15 minutes or more. The onion and relish help thicken the sauce so it will stick to the meat in the oven or on the grill.

Spoon sauce over pork shoulder or loins as they cook. Keep meat damp with sauce at all times. When meat is tender, slice or chop and serve with warm sauce.

POSSUM SAUCE

(for use on barbecued possum, of course)

2 cups apple-cider vinegar
1 cup ketchup
1 cup oil
½ cup sugar
2 tablespoons cayenne pepper
2 tablespoons black pepper
½ teaspoon chili powder
4 drops Tabasco sauce

Combine all ingredients in a saucepan. Bring to a boil; reduce heat and simmer 10 minutes.

Rickyard Ribs

Some folks really believe you can't make charcoal outside in the open air. But that's not true. The rickyard at the Jack Daniel Distillery makes charcoal this old fashioned way every day. Just the way Mr. Jack made it when he started making whiskey. Ricks of cut sugar maple are stacked out in the open and burned to produce the charcoal which uniquely characterizes the whiskey from this little distillery. These men know how to handle fire. They know all about charcoal. It stands to reason they would also know about cooking over this charcoal when the opportunity arises. The combination of what these men do best, supervising the fire and watching the coals, make these ribs outstanding. The fact that they also use generous amounts of Jack Daniel's in the sauce makes eating them a rib-tickling experience.

1 cup ketchup
1/4 cup Jack Daniel's Whiskey
1/4 cup molasses
1/4 cup apple-cider vinegar
1 tablespoon lemon juice
1 tablespoon Worcestershire sauce
1 tablespoon soy sauce
1/2 teaspoon pepper
1/2 teaspoon dry mustard
1 clove garlic, crushed

Combine in a saucepan. Bring to a boil, then reduce heat and simmer for 10 minutes.

Jerry Roach's Arkansas Sauced Sauce

1 cup ketchup
1/3 cup Jack Daniel's Whiskey
1/4 cup vinegar
1/4 cup molasses
2 cloves garlic (crushed)
1 tablespoon Worcestershire sauce
1 tablespoon lemon juice
2 teaspoons soy sauce
1/2 teaspoon dry mustard
1/4 teaspoon pepper

Combine all ingredients, mixing well.

Colvin Lake Hunt Club Finishing Sauce (for duck)

1 cup orange juice
1 tablespoon brown sugar
1 1/2 teaspoons apple-cider vinegar
Grated zest of 1 orange (orange part of peel only)
1 1/2 tablespoons flour
1 1/2 tablespoons butter
1 tablespoon black currant jelly
1/4 cup port wine

Combine orange juice, brown sugar, vinegar and orange zest and use as a basting sauce. When duck is done, pour off all floating surface fat from the gravy. Melt flour in butter, work smooth and thicken gravy in the hot pan. Add jelly, and reduce this sauce in pan until thick and gummy, then add wine, stir once and pour over the bird.

Wide Awake At Midnight Sauce

1 cup strong black coffee
$1\frac{1}{2}$ cups Worcestershire sauce
1 cup ketchup
$\frac{1}{2}$ cup butter
$\frac{1}{4}$ cup lemon juice
2 tablespoons sugar
1 tablespoon salt
1 tablespoon cayenne pepper

Combine ingredients in saucepan. Simmer for 30 minutes, stirring frequently.

Don't Hold the Mayo Sauce

3 cups mayonnaise
1 cup lemon juice
$\frac{1}{2}$ cup sugar
$\frac{1}{2}$ cup apple-cider vinegar
$\frac{1}{2}$ cup Worcestershire sauce
2 teaspoons salt
1 tablespoon pepper

Mix all ingredients. Allow flavors to blend at room temperature for 15 minutes before use.

31 W. Sauce

1 cup ketchup
$^1/_2$ cup white vinegar
$^1/_4$ cup brown sugar
$^1/_4$ cup Worcestershire sauce
1 teaspoon chili powder
1 teaspoon seasoned salt

Combine ingredients in saucepan. Bring to boil, then simmer for 10 minutes.

Marinades, Rubs and Sopping Sauces

When people talk about barbecue sauce, they are usually talking about table sauce. But there are actually three kinds of barbecue sauce, each with its own distinct use.

Marinades are used to flavor and tenderize the meat before cooking. Sops are used to flavor and tenderize the meat during cooking, while also keeping it moist. Table sauces are used to flavor the cooked meat. (Sometimes table sauces are basted on the meat in the last half-hour of cooking and called a finishing sauce.)

Dry rubs cross the line between marinades and sops. They flavor and tenderize the meat before cooking and continue their work during the barbecue process.

Marinades

The process of barbecuing is quite enough to tenderize any cut of meat, so the traditional reason for a marinade – to soften the meat – is unnecessary in the barbecue world.

But that doesn't mean you should necessarily skip this type of sauce.

You can also marinade for flavor. Besides, marinades are fun and a good opportunity to impress your friends. "You put what in the marinade?" they'll ask with astonishment, when you mention your secret ingredient. One good secret ingredient for a

marinade is a cup of whiskey or wine. Almost any marinade can benefit from a healthy dose of either. Enough to bring it to life but not enough to get it drunk.

Brother Marvin's Marinade

$1^1/_2$ cups olive oil
$^3/_4$ cup soy sauce
$^1/_4$ cup Worcestershire sauce
2 tablespoons dry mustard
2 teaspoons salt
1 tablespoon freshly ground black pepper
$^1/_2$ cup wine vinegar
$^1/_3$ cup lemon juice
$1^1/_2$ teaspoons dried parsley flakes
2 cloves garlic, mashed

Combine all ingredients in a pan. Can be used to marinate beef, pork or chicken. Marinate for 2 to 4 hours before cooking. (Can also be used as a baste.)

MOO MARINADE (for beef brisket)

3 cups red-wine vinegar
1 medium onion, minced
Juice of 1 lemon
1 teaspoon red pepper
1 teaspoon black pepper
1 teaspoon chili powder

Combine and pour over meat. Marinate for 12 hours, turning meat at 2 hour intervals.

PIGGY'S PORK LOIN MARINADE

1/2 cup sherry
1/2 cup soy sauce
1 clove garlic, minced
Dry mustard
Thyme

Combine sherry, soy sauce and garlic. Rub pork loin with dry mustard and thyme. Then marinate for 2 days in sherry marinade.

MONKEY'S EYEBROW MARINADE FOR BARBECUED VENISON AND OTHER LARGE GAME

1 large mild onion, chopped
2 tablespoons spring onion, chopped
2 large carrots, chopped
1 cup tarragon vinegar
5 tablespoons olive oil or butter
3 or 4 whole cloves
1/2 teaspoon each of usual sweet herbs
Lots of salt and pepper

Fry vegetables in oil, add vinegar, herbs and seasonings, dust with lots of pepper and enough salt, and pour this marinade over the meat. Soak for 8 hours, turning every 2.

SOPPING SAUCES

Sopping sauce is another name for basting sauce. You brush the sauce on the meat at regular intervals with a cotton mop (available at restaurant supply houses) or some other soft brush. (Some hard-core Texas types tie a bandanna on the end of a broom stick and mop with that.) Virtually any barbecue sauce can be used as a sopping sauce, provided it doesn't contain tomato or sugar. Those two ingredients will burn and coat the crust of the meat with a tarlike finish.

When should you begin mopping the meat? Anytime after it is warmed up to pit temperature. Don't mop cold meat. It will merely roll off.

Barbecue cooks have different theories about how often to mop. A good rule of thumb is not to mop more than once an hour if you are using a closed cooker. Every time you open the cooker lid, you allow heat to escape and it will take time for the cooker to build that heat back up. Another rule of thumb is to mop every hour, so you can check on the meat, smell the aroma, feel the sizzle of the fire.

Joyce Rogers of Pa & Ma's Barbecue in Indianapolis believes there is one time and one time only to sop the meat: as it begins to swell and "opens up." She says that's when it is most receptive to a sopping sauce.

Red Doug's Pig-Sopping Sauce

1 gallon apple-cider vinegar
1/4 cup crushed red pepper
1 tablespoon black pepper
2 tablespoons salt
4 ounces pure honey

Combine and let stand for 12 hours. Heat before basting on pig. Start basting the pig after he's been turned (the first time). If the pig is on a spit, begin when the skin starts to pull away from the meat.

Razorback Sopping Sauce

1 cup water
1/2 cup vinegar
1/2 cup butter
4 tablespoons sugar
1 teaspoon pepper
2 teaspoons salt
1/2 teaspoon cayenne pepper
2 tablespoons prepared mustard
2 thick slices lemon
2 medium onions, sliced and peeled
4 tablespoons Worcestershire sauce

Combine water, vinegar, butter, sugar, pepper, salt, cayenne, mustard, lemon and onions in a saucepan. Bring to a boil and simmer for 20 minutes. Add Worcestershire sauce and baste is ready.

LBJ's Barbecue Sop

2 2/3 cups beef stock
2/3 cup Worcestershire sauce
1/3 cup apple-cider vinegar
1/3 cup vegetable oil
1 1/2 teaspoons dry mustard
1 1/2 teaspoons paprika
1 teaspoon garlic powder
1 teaspoon chili powder
1 teaspoon Tabasco sauce

Combine all ingredients. Let stand for 24 hours.

Rubs

Bridging the gap between marinades and sops is the rub, a dry mixture gently rubbed into the meat before cooking. It slowly seeps in and flavors the meat. Then during cooking it seals in the natural juices and flavors.

In Memphis, many barbecue cooks prefer to rub their ribs with a dry spice concoction instead of basting.

Moore County, Tennessee adds a whole new meaning to the name dry rub. You see, Moore County is "dry," meaning what it sounds like it means: you can't buy alcoholic beverages in Moore County. Which is kind of funny since the Jack Daniel Distillery is located in Moore County. The law says you can make whiskey here but you can't sell it or buy it.

Of course, you can drink it here or Moore County would be dry and empty.

Moore County, with a population of fewer than 4,500, is the smallest county in Tennessee. There'll probably never be enough people to vote the county "wet." The irony of the Jack Daniel Distillery in a dry

county rubs people funny. That's why I named this spicy mixture after the county. And like Moore County's most famous product, this dry rub will add a little spirit to any barbecue.

MOORE COUNTY DRY RUB

1 tablespoon paprika
1 tablespoon seasoned salt
1 teaspoon black pepper
1 teaspoon crushed red pepper
1 teaspoon garlic powder
1 teaspoon red pepper
1/2 teaspoon onion powder
1/2 teaspoon dry mustard
1/4 teaspoon celery salt
1/4 teaspoon chili powder
1/4 teaspoon cumin

Combine ingredients. Makes enough to rub 2 racks of ribs.

TEXAS RUB

3 tablespoons salt
3 tablespoons black pepper
3 tablespoons paprika
3 tablespoons sugar
1/2 tablespoon lemon pepper

Mix everything and rub into meat.

DOCTORING UP THESE RECIPES

You should treat the sauce, marinade, sop and rub recipes in this chapter as a starting point. There are countless ways to subtly alter each sauce.

Fruit adds a distinct taste to a sauce. Try your favorite fruit or even fruit juice in these recipes. Almost anything will work, from diced apple to minced pineapple, from orange zest to raisins. The Nightlife Bar-Crew in Owensboro, Kentucky make a tasty dip even better with the addition of orange juice.

That's the exciting thing about barbecuing. It isn't a science, it's an art. And it lends itself to experimentation.

You might even want to add your own "secret" ingredient. I've judged barbecue contests from Kansas City to Knoxville and I've heard about some amazing secret ingredients, from expensive wines to exotic beers; I've heard of buttermilk, chocolate, even peanut butter. See if you can top that.

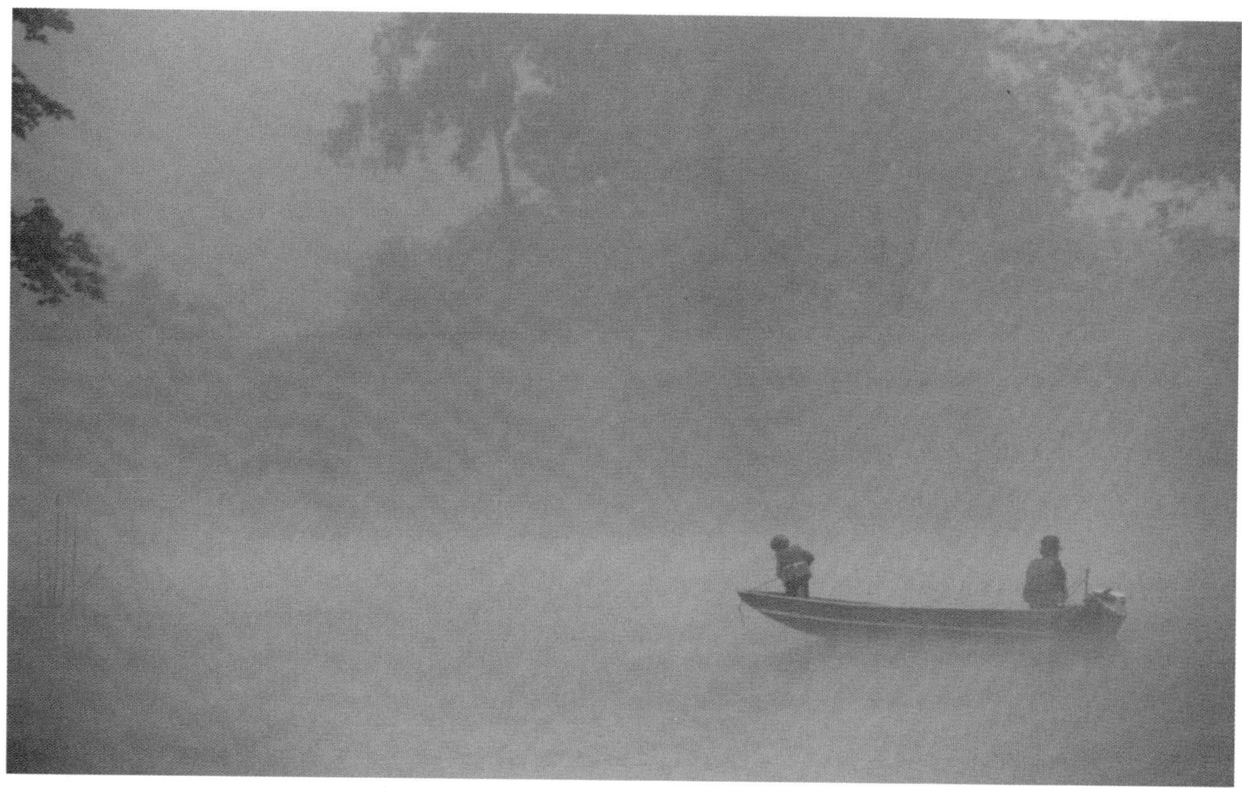

FISH SAUCES

Fish, because of its delicate texture, requires an entirely different kind of sauce from other meats.

10 BARBECUE SAUCES FOR FISH

1. Mrs. Buck's Best, a tested classic: 1 cup strained clam broth, 1/2 teaspoon hand-ground black pepper, 1/4 teaspoon salt (no more!). Then 1/2 teaspoon hot mustard, 3 tablespoons butter, 1 tablespoon flour. Do not use white pepper, or finely ground black. If no hand pepper mill is available, crush up whole peppercorns in a bowl, as visible pepper is part of the tradition. Melt butter and make roux with flour and mustard. Season, stir in clam juice slowly, heating very gradually. When it boils, note time. Draw off in precisely 2 minutes, no more!

2. Four Savory Butter Sauces: Very finely chopped mixed pickle, a little fine-chopped watercress, butter to suit. Anchovy paste, dash Tabasco, butter to suit. Finely chopped parsley, little lemon or lime juice strained, butter to suit. Anchovy paste, finely minced capers, butter to suit. Mix all of these well until butter is creamed and light. If sweet butter is used, add salt to taste.

3. A Fish Sauce from Dijon, which is in France: This is very tasty with barbecued fish, because it is derived from bastings. Put fish bastings through coarse sieve, add a trifle of fine-chopped chives, shallot or spring onion top, a pinch of basil. Add a little water and reduce slowly until very thick. Then add 2 teaspoons mild French mustard, 2 cups white sauce, 1 dozen finely chopped capers. Simmer up once more and it is ready.

4. Old Key West Lime Sour: This is a native classic from the Florida Keys. It is good in fish sauces, on fish itself in small quantities; also good for salad dressings for fish and green salads. To 2 cups strained lime juice add 1 level teaspoon salt. Stand in warm kitchen 2 weeks; cork then and keep in cool place; it's now ready to use.

5. A Sauce for Barbecue Fish: Rub 6 sardines through a sieve, cream with 4 teaspoons butter, juice of 3 limes or 2 lemons, 1 teaspoon fine-chopped parsley, 1/2 teaspoon scraped onion pulp. Brush over fish when it comes out sizzling.

6. A Shrimp Sauce Suitable for Barbecued Fish: Take enough white sauce to fill cream boat; stir in 1 1/2 teaspoons anchovy paste; juice of 1/2 lemon or 1 lime, strained; 6 shrimp tails broken small; cayenne to taste. Small cubes of lobster will also do, small chopped oysters, sliced hard eggs. Let sauce simmer up once, then serve. White sauce for fish should be made on base of 1/2 milk and 1/2 fish stock or court bouillon.

7. A Barbecue Sauce for Boiled or Grilled Fish of Size: Make roux of 1 1/2 tablespoons each butter and flour; don't brown. Add 2/3 cup warm sour cream. When worked smooth, add 1 1/2 teaspoons tarragon vinegar, salt to taste. Now add 2 tablespoons or slightly more freshly grated horseradish. Now 1/2 tablespoon chopped capers. Simmer all together once, and serve very hot.

8. Pepper Sauce for Barbecued Fish, Mainly: Here's one we found at a fine joint in Memphis. Pound 1 teaspoon whole peppercorns fine, simmer in 1/2 cup tart white wine. Reduce until nearly dry, then turn in 2 cups cream sauce based on half cream and half court bouillon. Boil up once; strain.

9. Buck Barr's Barbecue Sauce for Fish, and All Other Flesh: Pound yolks of 2 hard-boiled eggs with 1 teaspoon French mustard; pepper and salt, and 2 tablespoons olive oil. Mix well and add 3 tablespoons tarragon vinegar. Now add your preference of these: 1 tablespoon mushroom ketchup, walnut ketchup, or walnut pickle, or a few fine-chopped capers. Rub through a fine sieve.

10. A South Texas Green Sauce from a Favorite Haunt of Ours and Utterly Delicious on All Sorts of Delicate Fish, Lobsters and the Like: To 1/2 cup of thick sour cream add 1 cup good mayonnaise. Now add 1 tablespoon watercress or spinach, fine-chopped, for color. Next a speck of garlic pulp, enough green lime to suit tartness of taste; a dash of Tabasco. Whip thoroughly and rub through fine sieve, or toss in blender. Should be very cold for cold fish.

White Sauce

2 cups milk
4 tablespoons flour
1/2 stick butter
1 1/2 teaspoons salt
1/8 teaspoon pepper

In a medium saucepan melt butter. Add flour and stir well until mixture becomes a smooth paste. Slowly add the milk while stirring constantly. Add salt and pepper. Cook over medium heat, stirring constantly until mixture thickens and starts to boil. Remove from heat.

HOT ENOUGH FOR YOU?

Jake and Earl's Dixie Barbecue, in Cambridge, Massachusetts, is the only barbecue joint in America named for a dog and a doctor. The dog, of course, gets top billing.

Jake is co-owner Chris Schlesinger's Labrador retriever; Earl is Earl Wheaton, physician-father of partner Cary Wheaton.

Jake and Earl's, a carryout stand in the heart of Harvard country, is one of the few barbecue places in the Northeast, or at least one of the few with a regular address and hours you can count on. It's the result of Schlesinger's love of barbecue. He grew up eating pulled pork sandwiches in Williamsburg, Virginia, and went on to compete at the annual Memphis in May International Barbecue Cooking Contest.

He's even written his own barbecue book, "The Thrill of the Grill," published in 1990.

Schlesinger is a cooking wizard, a master chef who can dazzle you with his command of the kitchen. But his chief contribution to the barbecue world is his sauce, Inner Beauty Sauce, a menacing, yellow-colored concoction so dangerous it ought to be covered by the Geneva Convention. The label isn't lying when it says "Hottest sauce in North America." It is a scorcher. Schlesinger attributes the ferocity of the sauce to the Scotch bonnet peppers in it.

Before you sprinkle it on your barbecue – whatever you do, don't pour it on! – read the label carefully:

"Use Inner Beauty Sauce to enhance dull and boring food. Keep away from pets, open flames, unsupervised children and bad advice. This is not a toy. This is serious. Stand up straight, sit right and stop mumbling."

It means it, too.

Inner Beauty Hot Sauce is available at Jake and Earl's, Cambridge, Massachusetts.

McKinney's Meatballs

1 pound ground beef
1/2 cup dry bread crumbs
1/3 cup minced onion
1/4 cup milk
1 egg
1 teaspoon minced parsley
1 teaspoon salt
1/8 teaspoon pepper
1/2 teaspoon Worcestershire sauce
1/4 cup shortening
1 12-ounce bottle chili sauce
1 10-ounce jar grape jelly

Mix ground beef, crumbs, onion, milk, egg, parsley, salt, pepper and Worcestershire sauce. Gently shape into 1-inch balls. Melt shortening in large skillet. Brown meatballs. Remove meatballs from skillet. Drain fat. Heat chili sauce and jelly in skillet until jelly is melted, stirring constantly. Add meatballs and stir until coated. Simmer 30 minutes. Serve hot.

Some Dip

1 cup pecans, chopped
2 tablespoons butter
2 8-ounce packages cream cheese, softened
1 pint sour cream, room temperature
2 green peppers, chopped
3 tablespoons onion flakes
1/4 teaspoon Worcestershire sauce
1/2 teaspoon salt
1/2 teaspoon pepper
2 3 1/2-ounce jars dried beef

Saute pecans in butter. Pour off butter. Mix remaining ingredients. Put in 1 1/2-quart casserole. Top with pecans. Bake at 350 degrees for 20 minutes.

Itty Bitty Sausage Balls

4 1/2 cups Bisquick
10 ounces extra-sharp Cheddar cheese, grated
1 pound hot sausage, uncooked
1/2 teaspoon salt
1/2 teaspoon sage
7 tablespoons milk

Combine all ingredients and mix well with hands, making sure sausage is mixed in well. Pinch off bite-sized pieces and form into balls. Bake on cookie sheet at 350 degrees for 15 minutes.

Beth's Artichoke Dip

1 cup artichokes
1/2 cup sour cream
1/2 cup mayonnaise
1 cup grated Parmesan cheese

Combine ingredients and pour into 4-inch souffle dish. Bake at 350 degrees for 30 minutes. Serve with crackers.

Andrewe's Benedictine

1 8-ounce package cream cheese, softened
$^{2}/_{3}$ cup cucumber, peeled, seeded and grated
1 teaspoon Worcestershire sauce
2 tablespoons mayonnaise
Green food coloring

Blend ingredients until smooth. Serve with chips or crackers.

Popeye Dip

1 10-ounce package frozen spinach, thawed and drained
1 cup mayonnaise
1 8-ounce container sour cream
1 $1^{5}/_{8}$-ounce package dry vegetable soup mix
1 $8^{1}/_{2}$-ounce can water chestnuts, chopped
1 medium onion, chopped
1 round loaf dark rye bread

Combine all ingredients except bread and chill for 3 hours. Scoop out center of rye loaf and reserve pieces. Fill cavity with dip. Break pieces of rye and arrange around loaf.

Barbecue Red Dogs

2 cups ketchup
1 cup brown sugar, firmly packed
1 cup Jack Daniel's Whiskey
2 16-ounce packages hot dogs cut into 1-inch chunks

Combine ketchup, brown sugar and Jack Daniel's in a saucepan. Bring to a boil. Cover and reduce heat. Simmer 2 hours, stirring occasionally. Add hot dog chunks and simmer 5 more minutes. Serve in chafing dish with toothpicks.

Suzie's Macaroni Salad

2 cups uncooked macaroni
$1^{1}/_{2}$ cups celery, sliced
$^{1}/_{2}$ cup onion, diced
2 teaspoons parsley
1 cup mayonnaise
2 teaspoons vinegar
2 teaspoons mustard
$^{1}/_{2}$ teaspoon celery seed
$1^{1}/_{2}$ teaspoons salt
Shredded Cheddar cheese to taste

Cook macaroni as directed on package. Combine all ingredients and refrigerate.

Sooner State Caviar

2 16-ounce cans black-eyed peas, drained
$^{1}/_{3}$ cup peanut oil
$^{1}/_{3}$ cup wine vinegar
1 clove garlic
$^{1}/_{4}$ cup onion, finely chopped
$^{1}/_{2}$ teaspoon salt
$^{1}/_{4}$ teaspoon pepper

Combine all ingredients in a bowl and mix well. Cover and refrigerate for at least 24 hours. Remove garlic and serve.

The Great Tennessee Barbecue Safari

Bruce Haney never met a barbecue sandwich he didn't like.

Pork, beef, chicken, goat, he's had it all. And liked it all.

And still wants more.

He loves barbecue; it's that simple.

His job as a coal buyer with Tennessee Eastman in Kingsport takes him to cities across the state. So who better to take us on a guided tour of some of the Volunteer state's best barbecue joints than one who has been there?

There are 319 barbecue restaurants in Tennessee according to AT&T, which searched phone books for business listings with the word "barbecue" in the name. And Bruce says that number is too low because several great Tennessee barbecue places don't have phones (B.E. Scott's in Lexington, Tennessee, for instance).

Bruce says you can get a good taste of Tennessee barbecue by trying a couple dozen places.

East Tennessee

He suggests beginning a Tennessee barbecue safari in his native east Tennessee. "We have our own barbecue style around here. It's distinct from our neighbors across the mountains in western North Carolina and different from the folks out in the flatlands of the state. I call it Hillbilly Barbecue. It's sliced pork, flooded with a thick, sweet tomato sauce. This is the barbecue I cut my teeth on."

He picks the **Ridgewood** *in Bluff City as the best representative of the style. "It was the Ridgewood's Grace Proffitt who introduced this style when she opened her doors back in '48. Before you try any other places, you have to taste the original."*

He recommends the pork sandwich with Mrs. Proffitt's barbecue beans on the side. You won't be disappointed. The sandwiches are enormous.

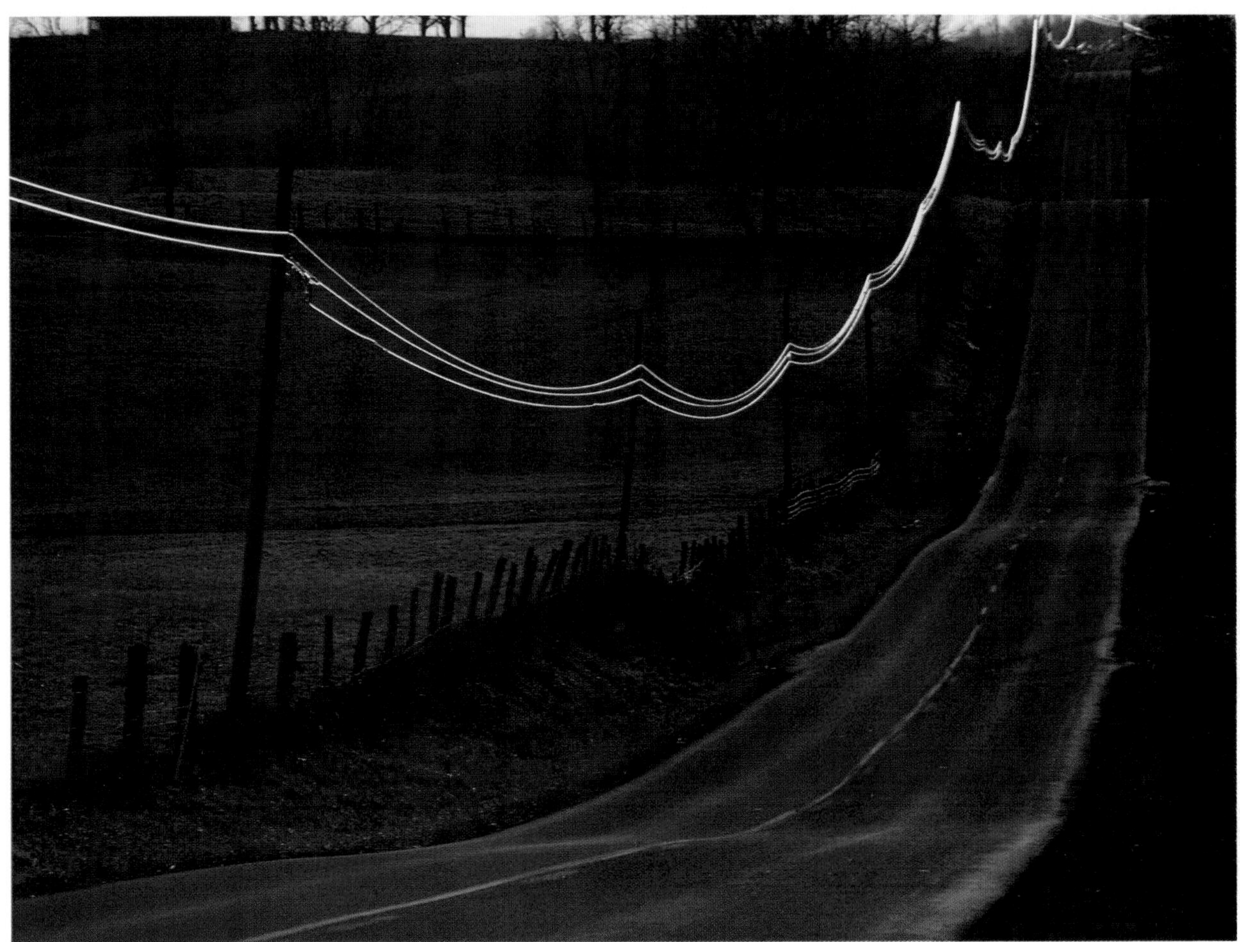

To get to the Ridgewood: from the airport take State Route 126 to Blountville. Head south on 19E to Bluff City. The Ridgewood is on the other side of town right on 19E.

Next, he recommends you head up 19E toward Elizabethton. A half a mile up you'll find Mrs. Proffitt's chief competition, ***Pardner's.*** *"If you detect a similarity, that's no coincidence. You see, J. Paul Bare, who owns Pardner's, was once associated with Mrs. Proffitt before heading out on his own." (There's a real story there; a lawsuit and... well, let someone at Pardner's tell you.) There are people in east Tennessee who will tell you Pardner's barbecue is better, that The Ridgewood is resting on its laurels, while Pardner's is trying to build its reputation. Bruce disagrees but respects the rights of those who think that.*

Next head to Johnson City. Bruce says the best ribs in east Tennessee are at the ***House of Ribs*** *on US 23 on the north side of town.*

Now jump on I-181 and head west to Kingsport. The road intersects with US 11W. Go east on 11W about 5 miles until you see the Big Indian and **Pratt's Barn.** *The giant concrete Indian used to guard the front door of a tourist shop. "He may be inappropriate at Pratt's, but he sure makes giving directions a lot easier," says Bruce. Pratt's barbecue is good – same east Tennessee style as the others – but the real reason Bruce directed you here is for the ice cream. A few years ago Tom Pratt bought a Marine surplus ice cream freezer. He set out to make the best ice cream in the world and he may have succeeded. "His ice cream is so rich that the Vanderbilts would be envious," says Bruce. Pratt uses the finest ingredients and it shows. His ice cream is 18 percent butterfat. Most premium ice creams are only 14 percent.*

There's only one more stop in upper east Tennessee: **Skoby's Barbecue** *on Center Street in downtown Kingsport. "Skoby's was cooking barbecue when I was growing up in the '50s, then they switched to fine dining." In recent years the restaurant has gone back to its roots, opening this diner-style place to cater to its barbecue-loving customers.*

KNOXVILLE

Knoxville is trying to gain a reputation in the barbecue world with its annual River Fest, a barbecue-cooking contest held each September at the site of the 1982 World's Fair. "If you're lucky enough to be in Knoxville during the River Fest, be sure and go by the booth of former mayor Randy Tyree. During one 5-year stretch his group won three times."

Bruce says, "The best barbecue in Knoxville used to be at **Brother Jack's,** *but he closed in 1989. A good choice now is* **Buddy's Barbeque.** *Buddy's has been around for 20 years so he must know something." There are four locations. Bruce favors the one on Kingston Pike, which is US 11-70.*

If you've never been to the National Rib Cook-Off in Cleveland, then you should stop by **Calhoun's.** *It won Best Ribs in America in 1985 and its baby back pork ribs are typical of what does well at the Cleveland contest: they're tender and well-sauced.*

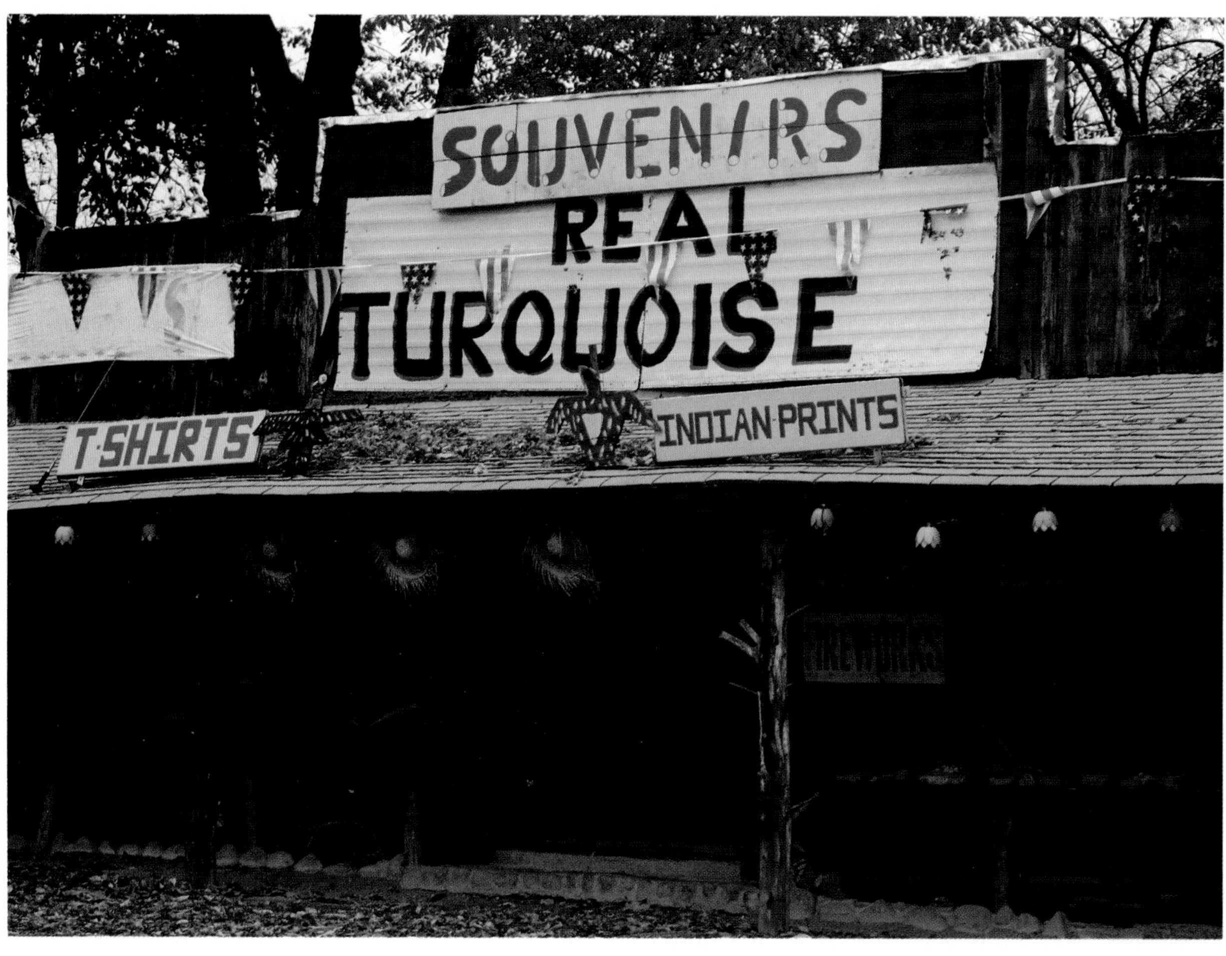

NASHVILLE

*"Go immediately to **Old Fashion Bar-B-Q,** northwest of town," says Bruce. Take I-24 to exit 35 (US 431). It's 5 miles up on the left. "This is one of the best pulled-pork sandwiches in the world. But it's only open Friday and Saturday."*

*Now head back I-24 to I-65, then south to the Hendersonville exit, number 96. Go east to US 31E and then turn north to **Center Point Barbecue.** "This is the place favored by a lot of country music stars." Ask for Dolly Loyd's chopped pork on corn bread. The address is 1212 West Main Street, across from the Colonial Drive-In Theater. Dolly is open daily from 8:30 a.m. to 9 p.m.*

WEST TENNESSEE

*"The absolute don't-miss place in west Tennessee is **B.E. Scott's** in Lexington," says Bruce. "Early Scott is the barbecue man who sleeps next to his pit when he is cooking."*

From Nashville head down I-40 to the Lexington exit, number 101, SR 22. He's on Highway 20, west of town. It's a stop you won't regret.

Now head on west on SR 20. It's only 18 miles to Jackson.

*Bruce's top recommendation is **Bill Case's BBQ Pit.** There are two locations. He prefers the trailer out on old 45 south. (The addresses are 36 Bond Bemis and 1427 Highland Avenue South.)*

*Another don't-miss in Jackson is **OD's,** aka Jolly Cholly's. It has been around since 1951 and calls itself the "Home of Holifield Real Pit BBQ."*

Only one more stop before Memphis: **Bozo's** *in Mason. (Get off at exit 35 and go north to US 70-79. Go east on it to Mason.) "Bozo's is right on the main drag, just east of what you might call downtown, if you're charitable." This is another long-time pit, opened in 1923 by Thomas "Bozo" Williams and now run by his daughter Helen. She is in a court battle with the Chicago TV clown over the name. "Bozo's looks like a highway patrol station from the '40s. But the barbecue is 10-4, which is Broderick Crawford talk for 'mighty fine.'"*

Memphis

You could write a book about Memphis barbecue. In fact, Carolyn Wells did. It's called "Barbecue Greats Memphis Style" (Pig Out Publications, $12.95).

"This is one barbecue-crazy town," says Bruce.

The Memphis Yellow Pages has a separate listing for "Barbecue" and there are 32 restaurants listed. And several barbecue places don't even list themselves in that specialty category. Altogether the Memphis Yellow Pages list 86 barbecue joints.

"There's no such thing as a bad barbecue place in Memphis. Some are just more equal than others." The must-visits, according to Bruce, are the **Rendezvous** *and* **Leonard's.** *"They've been around forever and for good reason."*

For barbecue pizza Bruce recommends **Coletta's.** *Another concoction unique to Memphis is barbecue spaghetti. Bruce's choices for this dish are* **Brady and Lil's** *(5353 Knight Arnold) or* **Raineshaven** *(630 Raines Avenue East).*

"There's a bunch of other places you shouldn't miss: **Payne's, Gridley's, Barbecue Shoppe, Smoky Ridge, Cozy Corner Fish & Ribs, Germantown Commissary, John Wills, Willingham's, Public Eye,** *and* **Interstate.** *Although it hasn't been around as long as* **Leonard's** *or the* **Rendezvous,** *for my money, the best barbecue in Memphis is at* **Corky's,"** *says Bruce.*

Bruce says his barbecue safari route is only a beginning. "I know I promised to keep it down to a couple dozen places but, when it comes to good barbecue, that's hard to do. There's other places I could have mentioned. Like **Goat City** *in Milan. And* **Lewis'** *in Moscow. And* **Baldwin's** *in Springfield. And* **R&R** *in Nashville. And..."*

ENTREES ON THE GRILL

While I believe that eating barbecue hot off the pit is the ultimate culinary experience, I also recognize that not everyone wants to slave over a scorching pit all day. There are occasions when you don't have the time to tend a fire and slow-cook barbecue for hours on end.

That's where these other outdoor cooking recipes come in.

You get the smoky flavor and the tender taste, but you don't have to spend all day over a fire.

Just about anything is good cooked on the grill.

BEEF

YODLER'S GRILLED BARBECUE STEAK

2 ½-inch thick steaks
4 oranges
1 clove garlic
Salt
Olive oil

Have the butcher pound the steaks thin or do it in domestic privacy with one of those small, square wooden mauls with the waffle-iron patterned face found in any household supply store. Next, cut oranges in half and rub and squeeze well all over steaks to get maximum oil from the rind onto every part of the meat. Crush garlic clove very fine and spread a trifle on each steak. Salt lightly and place in bowl, squeezing juice on each layer. Let marinate 2 hours, brush lightly with olive oil and grill over fierce heat, or live coals; searing briefly first on one side, then the other.

STONEWALL'S STEAK-IN-SALT-BARBECUED

Take a decent steak, and a bag of salt. Either semi-coarse Kosher salt or the ordinary non-pouring table variety.

Mix a bowl of salt and water until it is the identical mixture of a five-year-old's sand pies, then spread it evenly on one side of the steak until about ½-inch thick. Just to make it sound complicated, pat it with the hand to make firmly smooth on top. Put on grill, salt side up, about 1 inch from heat.

Broil as long as you usually do, no longer. A guide will be when the salt is a bit browned. Turn over, repeating the salt paste on the other side. Broil again. Take out and break the tile with any handy hard object. Butter and pepper the steak to taste. There will be no gravy yet, it's all in the steak. Nor will there be cooking bouquet. That is in the steak too. There are no burned, dried-out areas whatsoever, and you can cut it with an axe handle. Serve on fresh French bread as a sopper.

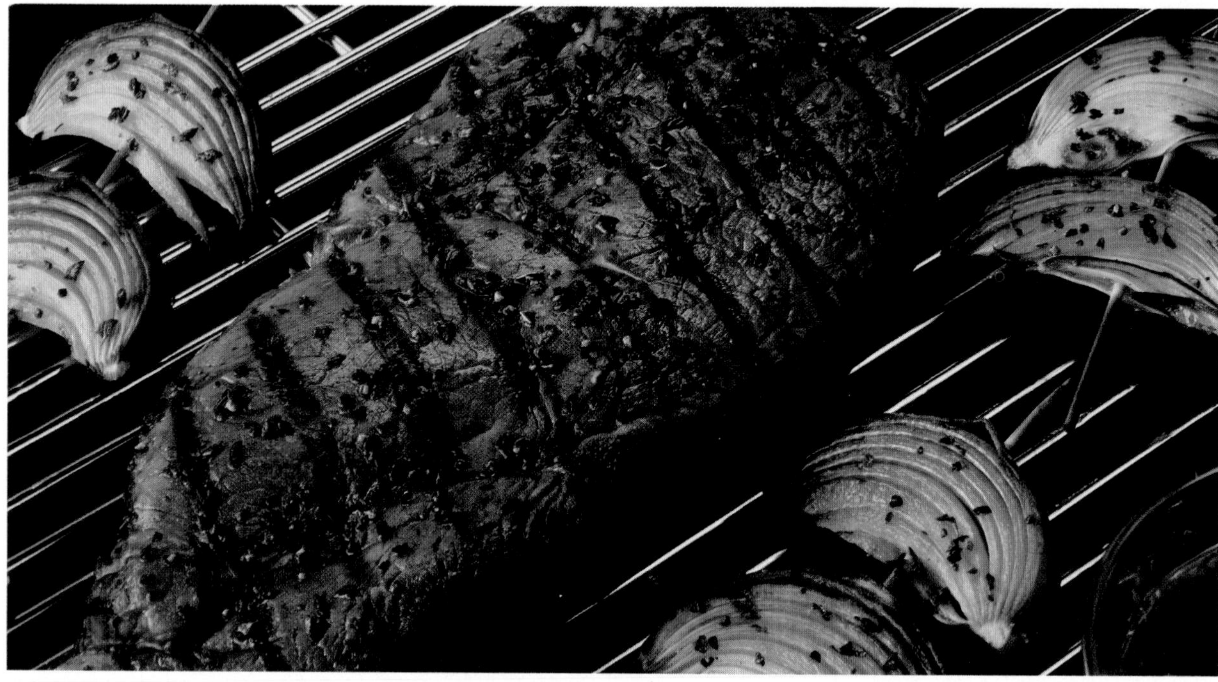

CHICKEN

MOONBEAM'S MONTEREY CHICKEN

2 whole chicken breasts, boned and skinned
$^1/_2$ cup Catalina salad dressing
1 medium onion, sliced
1 tablespoon butter
Salt and pepper
1 slice Monterey Jack cheese

Marinate chicken breasts in Catalina salad dressing overnight. Grill chicken breasts until tender. Saute onion in butter. Season to taste with salt and pepper. Top chicken breast with Monterey Jack cheese. Place under broiler until cheese is melted. Top with sauteed onions.

BAJA CHICKEN WINGS

2 pounds chicken wings
$^1/_4$ cup tequila
$^1/_4$ cup lime juice
2 tablespoons chili powder
$^1/_2$ teaspoon salt
$^1/_2$ cup olive oil

Cut wings in half at joint; remove wing tip and discard. Combine tequila, lime juice, chili powder, salt and oil until slightly thickened. Pour tequila mixture over chicken wings and refrigerate overnight.

Cook on grill for 15 minutes, turning frequently and basting with marinade. Serve with salsa.

BERT'S RIVER FARM BARBECUE CHICKEN

2 whole chicken fryers, cut in half
2 tablespoons garlic salt
1 tablespoon paprika
1 tablespoon black pepper
Baste:
1 cup water
1 cup ketchup
$^1/_4$ cup apple-cider vinegar
2 tablespoons instant onions
3 tablespoons Worcestershire sauce
1 teaspoon dry mustard

Mix garlic salt, paprika and pepper. Sprinkle over chicken, covering entirely.

Place chicken on grill, skin-side up, over medium-hot fire. Cover and grill 30 minutes. Turn and cook another 15 minutes.

While chicken is grilling, mix all baste ingredients in small saucepan. Bring mixture to a boil, then turn down heat and simmer 10 minutes.

When chicken is tender, baste entire surface and cook another 5 minutes. Turn and baste again. Chicken is done when it has a good glaze on it.

PORK

BETTY K'S PORK TENDERLOIN

1 4-pound pork tenderloin
1 clove garlic, crushed
1/2 cup olive oil

Rub meat with crushed garlic and olive oil. Cook at 325 degrees for 35 minutes. Let sit on top of stove. Slice very thin and serve on French bread with horseradish sauce.

PIEDMONT PORK TENDERLOIN

4 pork tenderloins, 3/4-inch thick
Flour
2 tablespoons white vinegar
2/3 cup heavy cream
1/4 cup mustard
1 tablespoon butter
1 teaspoon pepper

Pound meat until flattened to 1/2-inch thick. Dust with flour. Grill the pork on both sides until just done. In a saucepan mix vinegar, cream, mustard, butter and pepper. Bring to a boil. Reduce heat and simmer until sauce thickens. Pour over tenderloins and serve.

LAMB

MY LAMB PIE'S BARBECUED LAMB

This recipe is not just the usual grilled lamb, but with things besides, such as spiced vinegar for barbecuing. Order 5 pounds of lamb with a little fat. Cut into $1\frac{1}{2}$-inch squares about $\frac{1}{2}$-inch thick, first pounding lightly to flatten well. Marinate 2 hours in the Spiced Vinegar (recipe follows). Dry on a cloth, run onto skewers, alternating with squares of smoked bacon. First, brush with the spiced vinegar. Broil over coals or under broiler for about 10 minutes, turning now and then. Heat a little brandy or Jack Daniel's, put on with spoon, serve flaming.

Spiced Barbecue Vinegar for Grilling

Take $\frac{1}{2}$ cup red-wine vinegar (tarragon-flavored is best) and put in mixing bowl previously rubbed with a trifle of garlic and 1 teaspoon salt. To this add $\frac{1}{4}$ teaspoon black pepper, $\frac{1}{4}$ teaspoon cloves, $\frac{1}{4}$ teaspoon nutmeg, $\frac{1}{2}$ cup tart white wine and $\frac{1}{4}$ cup olive oil. Whip up well and pour over squares of lamb.

JEAN WOODLIEF'S LEG OF LAMB

1 5- to 6- pound leg of lamb, boned and butterflied
$\frac{3}{4}$ cup olive oil
$\frac{1}{2}$ cup white wine
1 onion, sliced
2 tablespoons fresh lemon juice
2 tablespoons crushed dried rosemary
2 cloves garlic, minced
1 teaspoon salt
1 teaspoon freshly ground black pepper
$\frac{3}{4}$ stick butter, melted
Additional salt and pepper to taste

Place lamb in a large glass or ceramic dish. Combine oil, wine, onion, lemon juice, 1 tablespoon rosemary, garlic, salt and pepper and add to lamb. Marinate for 2 hours or overnight, turning once or twice. Combine remaining ingredients for basting sauce. Drain meat and dry with paper towels. Grill lamb, turning and basting often, for about 35 minutes, or until done to taste.

VEAL

LOIS SHWAB'S VEAL CHOPS GRILLED OVER AN OAK FIRE

3 tablespoons virgin olive oil
1 shallot, finely minced
2 tablespoons fresh rosemary leaves
4 cloves garlic, peeled and coarsely chopped
1/2 teaspoon black pepper
3 bay leaves
1 tablespoon balsamic vinegar
1/2 cup dry white wine
4 veal rib chops
4 herb sprigs, for garnish

Warm olive oil in a small saucepan. Add shallot, rosemary and garlic. Sizzle gently for 2 minutes. Remove from heat. Add pepper, bay leaves, vinegar and wine. Stir well. Pour marinade over chops in a large baking dish, placing rosemary leaves and garlic on top of and under meat. Cover dish. Let stand at cool room temperature for 6-8 hours, basting often with marinade.

To grill: Prepare a wood fire and when it has burned down, break it up to form a thick bed of embers. Position a grill about 4 inches from the bed and let flames subside (when you hold your hand over the grill you should feel a deep, penetrating heat). Grill chops about 8 minutes per side. Rotate chops on each side to brown evenly, brushing occasionally with the marinade. Serve quickly.

GAME

BOBO FAMILY BARBECUED RABBIT

2 rabbits, quartered
1 cup vegetable oil
1/4 cup vinegar
1/4 cup red wine
1 small onion, minced
1 clove garlic, minced
Juice from 1/2 lemon
4 tablespoons A-1 sauce
5 tablespoons ketchup
1/8 teaspoon cayenne pepper
4 drops Tabasco sauce
1 teaspoon celery salt
1/4 teaspoon black pepper

Combine all sauce ingredients and simmer 20 minutes, stirring frequently. Baste quartered rabbits generously with sauce and grill over charcoal. Turn every 5 minutes and baste heavily each time. Meat should be ready in 30 to 40 minutes.

CAMP MANITUCKY'S CHICKEN-FRIED BEAVER

Cut a young beaver into serving-sized portions. Parboil in salted water with a sweet onion until the beaver is nearly tender. This parboiling helps to remove any excess fat. Drain the beaver pieces and roll in crumbs or flour seasoned with salt, pepper, thyme or celery salt, and then brown slowly in a heavy skillet in butter or drippings over a hot grill or a hardwood fire. Make gravy by blending the pan drippings into a dehydrated soup mix and water.

Coon hound
PUPS FOR
SALE

Fanning Family Roast Possum

Down around Lynchburg we have lots of tasty fruit trees. Possum get fat on these ripe delights. These recipes are designed to get rid of the fat.

1. Parboil possum in salted water to cover for about 1 hour. Then place in roaster in a 350 degree oven, draining off fat as it accumulates. After the roast has browned a bit, season with salt and pepper and a sprinkle of sage, poultry seasoning or garlic salt. After an hour of roasting, add sweet potatoes which have been parboiled 20 minutes in their jackets and then skinned and cut in thick slices. Sprinkle the sweet potato slices with brown sugar and add a dot of butter to each slice. Continue roasting until possum and potatoes are tender, about 30 minutes.

2. Preheat oven to 450 degrees. Place possum on a rack in the roaster and roast at high heat for 15 to 20 minutes. Reduce the oven heat to 350 degrees, season with salt and pepper and roast uncovered for about 1 hour, draining off fat as it accumulates. Place clean sweet potatoes in their jackets in the roaster and continue baking till both are tender.

3. Cut a tender possum into serving-size pieces and broil over the coals of a campfire, turning frequently so the pieces are nicely browned. Serve with barbecued onions which have been roasting in the embers of the fire.

DANDY DAN'S VENISON

1 hindquarter venison
Jack Daniel's Whiskey Marinade:
1 cup Jack Daniel's Whiskey
1 teaspoon celery seed
7 whole peppercorns
Crushed garlic to taste
1 12-ounce can frozen orange juice concentrate, thawed
4 tablespoons concentrated liquid smoke

Combine marinade ingredients in a large pan. Put the venison in a pan, spoon marinade on top. Cover and refrigerate for 22 to 34 hours, occasionally turning the meat in the marinade.

Lightly oil the barbecue grill and place the meat on top of the grill. Baste the venison with marinade at 15 minute intervals. Turn the meat after a half hour. Cook for another 30 minutes.

JOE CARROLL'S BALLARD COUNTY FOWL

First you have to get your bird – any game bird will do.

Marinade
1 quart water
1 cup apple-cider vinegar
2 ounces pickling spice
1/8 cup non-iodized salt
3/4 pound brown sugar

Mix ingredients. Pour over bird in a non-metallic pan. Refrigerate overnight. Smoke over a hardwood fire.

SEAFOOD

NUTT BROTHERS GRILLED SWORDFISH

6 swordfish steaks, about 2 1/2 to 3 pounds total
3/4 cup olive oil
2 cloves garlic, minced
2 plum tomatoes, peeled, seeded and mashed
2 tablespoons balsamic vinegar
4 sprigs fresh rosemary, or 1 1/2 teaspoons dried rosemary
Salt and pepper to taste

Place swordfish in a shallow pan. Combine oil, garlic, tomatoes, vinegar, rosemary, salt and pepper and pour over swordfish. Marinate 2 hours. Grill swordfish over medium-hot coals topped with mesquite chunks or chips, covered. Do not overcook. It should take about 4 to 5 minutes per side. Pour some marinade over the swordfish while it is cooking and when serving.

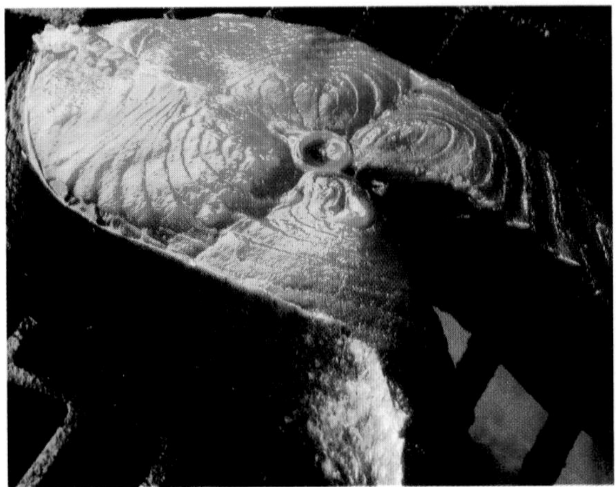

Buck Barr's Barbecue Salmon on the Grill

If you're lucky enough to catch or come on a whole salmon, here's a treat. Many grocers carry salmon, fresh or frozen, year-round. This same recipe will work with salmon steaks.

Take a 4- or 5-pound beheaded salmon and delicately cut lengthwise from the gills to the tail to open fish flat. The tail can be cut off. Use a sharp knife down the spine, being careful not to cut through the skin. Lay salmon skin-side up. Coat skin with olive oil or vegetable oil. Flip salmon over and season with plenty of lemon juice, salt and pepper to taste. Dot with butter.

Place salmon on the grill skin-side down. Cover top of fish with a loose covering of heavy aluminum foil. Continue to coat with lemon juice, butter, then add white wine to taste. Keep foil on during cooking. Salmon is ready when flesh turns from pink to white. If center bone loosens easily with a fork, the salmon is done. You never turn the salmon because the foil cooks the fish.

Remove fish to a platter. With a fork, remove bones easily. Garnish with parsley and serve. Allow about a half pound of salmon per person.

Uncle Buck's Grilled Salmon in Egg Sauce

1 3-pound fresh salmon fillet
1 tablespoon butter
Small bunch of fresh herbs
2 lemons, sliced

Egg Sauce (makes about 2 cups)
2 eggs, hard-boiled
4 tablespoons butter
4 tablespoons flour
1/2 cup cream (or milk)
2 cups chicken stock
2 tablespoons capers

Butter a large piece of heavy aluminum foil and place salmon fillet in the middle. Dot with any remaining butter. Sprinkle fish liberally with chopped fresh herbs and top with lemon slices. Seal the fish well inside the foil. Cook on an outdoor grill over high, direct heat – about 5 to 10 minutes per side, depending on flame. Do not overcook! Open the foil and check doneness from time to time. (You can use a frozen fillet without thawing it – it just takes longer to cook.)

Egg Sauce

Make egg sauce before or during cooking. Chop hard-boiled eggs into small dice and set aside. Melt butter in saucepan over medium heat. Add flour, stirring constantly, until mixture starts to bubble without browning. Add cream or milk and stock and stir with wooden spoon until thickened. Add chopped eggs and capers. Serve fish on a platter. Add sauce.

Commodore Joe's Barbecue Shrimp on a Stick

This recipe came from Commodore Joe Woodlief of the River Valley Club in Louisville, Kentucky. It's simple and colorful.

Buy some large shrimp in the shell and skewer them on metal or bamboo barbecue sticks. Put the shrimp on the cooker when everything else is about ready. The shrimp take only a few minutes to cook and the smoke adds to the flavor. Be careful not to overcook.

Ash Rapid's Barbecued Turtle Steaks

Steaks may be from green, hawkbill, loggerhead, pond or stream turtle, but not too thick or too aged – 1/2-inch to 3/4-inch thickness is correct. Rub with cut lime vigorously so as to get oil from peel into steak, rub with a cut clove of garlic, sprinkle with salt and let stand in squeezed juice of lime for 1 hour. Brush with lots of olive oil and broil like any steak over coals or under broiler, seasoning to taste.

Porky Heroes

$1^1/_2$ pounds ground pork
1 loaf Vienna bread
1 medium onion, chopped
1 rib celery, chopped
1 clove garlic, minced
$^1/_2$ cup your favorite barbecue sauce
$1^1/_2$ teaspoons chili powder
$^1/_2$ teaspoon salt
1 cup Cheddar cheese, shredded

Cut a small piece off top of bread and save. Hollow out inside to $^1/_2$ inch thickness.

Brown ground pork, onion, celery and garlic in large frying pan. Pour off drippings. Add barbecue sauce, chili powder and salt and stir. Line bottom of inside of bread loaf with $^1/_2$ cup shredded cheese. Add meat mixture. Sprinkle remaining cheese on meat. Replace top of loaf and wrap in foil, sealing top and ends. Place on jelly roll pan and bake at 450 degrees for 20 minutes. Let stand 10 minutes and slice.

Indoor Pork Loin

Here is a quick and easy method for cooking pork loin indoors. It comes from Evelyn C. Grogan of Reidsville, North Carolina.

"I often barbecue a pork loin, my favorite pork for barbecuing, in my pressure cooker. Place a rack in the bottom of a 6-quart cooker and place loin on the rack. A boneless 6- to 8-pound roast pork loin really is delicious. Salt lightly. Add 2 or 3 cups of water and pressure cook at 10 pounds for 10-12 minutes.

"Remove pot from stove. Release pressure and drain roast. Discard water.

"Add 2 or 3 cups prepared sauce to roast (pour over roast). Cook at 10 pounds pressure about 10 minutes longer. Remove from heat. Let pressure fall. Remove roast and slice. Serve with warm sauce from pot."

Virginia Oyster Barbecued Roast

First open oysters and save liquor; unless you're adept, better leave this to the oysterman. Wash deep halves of shells, rub each with a touch of cut garlic clove, and center up with 1/4 teaspoon scraped onion pulp. Strain liquor and put in saucepan. To each cup add juice of 2 limes, double dash Tabasco and reduce by 1/3. Stir in 1 tablespoon white wine, adding a little salt to taste. Thicken with a little flour and butter. Sauce should be thick, piquant.

Put oysters in half shells; mask with sauce, center with 2 1/4-inch cubes of rosy Tennessee ham. Pop under broiler until edges of oysters barely curl.

L.P. Malone's Barbecue Shrimp

2 pounds large (not jumbo) shrimp, uncooked and unpeeled
1 pound butter
1/3 cup Worcestershire sauce
2 tablespoons black pepper, finely ground
1/2 teaspoon rosemary, ground
2 lemons, sliced thin
1/2 teaspoon Tabasco sauce
2 teaspoons salt
3 cloves crushed fresh garlic

In a saucepan melt butter, add Worcestershire, pepper, rosemary, lemon slices, Tabasco, salt, garlic and mix thoroughly. Divide shrimp into 2 shallow glass baking dishes and pour heated sauce over them. Stir well. Cook at 400 degrees for 15 minutes, turning once. Shells should be pink and the meat white, not translucent. Serve with French bread for dipping and salad.

Land O' Sky Blue Waters Barbecued Snapper

5 pounds fish, red snapper is best*
Juice of 3 limes or 1 1/2 lemons
Salt
3 cups cashew nuts, chopped
1 cup grated mild cheese
1 small garlic clove, crushed
1 small onion, minced
1 cup milk
Cayenne pepper
1/2 teaspoon grated nutmeg
2 bay leaves, rubbed fine
1 cup bread crumbs, dry, fine
6 tablespoons butter

The secret to this recipe is that the fish is painted inside and out with lime juice, salted lightly, and iced that way for at least 4 hours before cooking. Take well-greased baking dish, place fish on bottom. Mix chopped nuts with cheese, garlic and onion, moistening with milk to make stiff paste. Add salt, cayenne, nutmeg and bay leaves. Then spread fish with this toothsome blanket and cover with dry fine bread crumbs. On this put generous walnuts of butter and brown in medium oven at 350 degrees, basting well.

*Also suitable for pike, bluefish, a big rainbow or black bass.

"Gramps" Malone's Alabama Unshelled Barbecued Shrimp – Browned

Buy as many shrimp as you estimate your guests can eat, then add 1/3 more. Have enough olive oil to fill your biggest frying pan, or deep-fat kettle. Don't use any other fat except olive oil. Heat oil to 370 degrees; chop 3 or 4 cloves of garlic and throw in with the first batch of shrimp. Discard when dark brown, and renew with fresh garlic as needed to disburse flavor. When shrimp are done, drain on paper towels, dust with salt and pepper.

Lacy's Smothered Turtle in the Mississippi Cajun Style

Trim 2 pounds turtle steak into 1½-inch squares, season well with salt and hand ground black pepper, squeeze on some lemon or sour orange juice and let stand awhile. Add plenty of chopped onion, a sweet pepper chopped well, 3 or 4 tomatoes cut into eighths, 3 bay leaves, a crushed garlic clove and mushrooms. Moisten well with stock made by boiling salted turtle trimmings and smother very slowly in tightly covered skillet until turtle is tender. Serve with big mounds of rice. This will nourish 4 farm boys.

Mr. Ed's Fish Sandwich

There's a tradition of independence in Kentucky, of stubbornly refusing to follow a trend just because it's a trend. It's a tradition that traces all the way back to the state's original restaurateur, D. Boone. (D. Boone Tavern, established 1767).

So it was no surprise to Louisvillians in 1985 when the city's premier chef, Ed Garber, opened a – what? – barbecue joint.

Garber, famous throughout the area for the gourmet meals served at his fine dining establishment, 610 Magnolia, opened Mr. Ed's Bar-B-Q Shop in May of that year.

Garber, a Kentucky native who learned his craft observing in the kitchens of France, New York and Montreal, stuck to his independent Kentucky ways and was determined to produce a better barbecue sandwich, profit be damned. He cooked pork shoulders over a slow hickory fire, gently basting and turning at half-hour intervals. The cooked meat was so tender you could slice it with a butter knife. He did produce a better barbecue, but he ran into a problem: the profit was damned. And Mr. Ed's Bar-B-Q Shop closed.

But in its short life, the joint spawned a new menu item for Garber's fancy restaurant, Mr. Ed's Fish Sandwich. It was so popular that Garber was forced to add it. That's right, a fish sandwich in a five-star restaurant.

Garber says there's no secret to his fish sandwich. "Just use fresh ingredients. And the

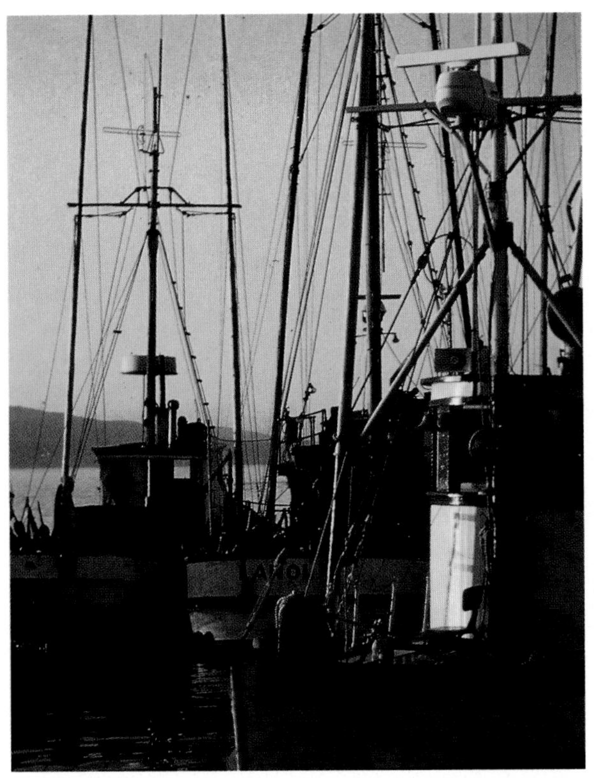

highest quality you can get." To insure the quality of his fish he buys from a retailer. "If I buy from a wholesaler, I'm just another small customer. But with a retailer I'm a significant customer. The guy will hand-pick my fish."

Garber collects rare bourbons and whiskies at his restaurant the way French restaurants collect rare cognacs. Among his finds are a 1917 bottle of Jack Daniel's. "Because of Prohibition, they couldn't bottle it until 1934." The spirits are not just for looks. For $20 you can have a shot of 1917 Jack Daniel's with your meal.

It's a perfect combination: a fish sandwich with Jack Daniel's Whiskey on the side.

Mr. Ed's Fish Sandwich Recipe

Fresh fillet of fish
Bread crumbs
Homemade tartar sauce (recipe follows)
Red onion slice
Leaf of lettuce
Tomato slice

Lightly turn fish in bread crumbs and deep-fry till done.

Serve on bun with tartar sauce, slice of onion, leaf of lettuce and slice of tomato.

Homemade tartar sauce

Combine homemade mayonnaise (recipe follows), capers, shallots, fresh lemon juice, white pepper and fresh parsley. (Ed insists he doesn't know the exact measurement of each. "I just cook. I don't read recipes.")

Homemade mayonnaise
Egg yolks
Vegetable oil

Beat egg yolks. Add oil slowly. Don't let mixture break down.

VEGETABLES & BARBECUE SIDE DISHES

Man cannot live by barbecue alone – although a few have tried. No, barbecue requires, even demands, a healthy sideboard of complementary dishes.

The good news is there are plenty of vegetable and fruit dishes that are a perfect match for barbecue's robust taste.

The universal side dishes are beans and slaw. But there are many others that make the perfect complement to barbecue.

SLAW

There are two secrets we hold dear in Tennessee. One, of course, is the secret of charcoal mellowing used to give Jack Daniel's Whiskey its rare flavor. The other is the way we sometimes pile slaw on top of our barbecue.

The first time you have barbecue in Memphis, you think the waitress got your order goofed up. Because there in your sandwich, spooned on top of your pulled pork, is a heap of slaw. But don't despair; give it a try. It's a mighty tasty combination, barbecue and slaw. You can eat it on top of your meat or on the side.

Down East Slaw

1 cup mayonnaise
1 tablespoon sugar
1 tablespoon white vinegar
1 tablespoon mustard
1 medium head cabbage, grated

Combine mayonnaise, sugar, vinegar and mustard and pour over cabbage. Mix well. Refrigerate overnight. Serves 12.

Lexington Red Slaw

1 cup mayonnaise
1 tablespoon white vinegar
1 tablespoon sugar
1 cup your favorite tomato-based barbecue sauce
1 head cabbage, shredded

Combine mayonnaise, vinegar, sugar and barbecue sauce in a mixing bowl. Pour over cabbage and mix well. Refrigerate overnight.

For best results use the same sauce you are using on your meat. Serves 12.

Moody Slaw

1 medium head cabbage, grated
2 carrots, grated
1/2 onion, finely grated
1 cup mayonnaise
1/4 cup milk
1 tablespoon sugar
1 tablespoon vinegar
Salt and pepper to taste

Toss cabbage, carrots and onion together. Mix mayonnaise, milk, sugar, vinegar, salt and pepper. Pour over cabbage mixture and stir. Serves 12.

Pete's Creamy Coleslaw

1 5-ounce can evaporated milk
1/4 cup apple-cider vinegar
2 tablespoons sugar
1 teaspoon salt
1/4 teaspoon celery seed
1/8 teaspoon pepper
1/2 cup mayonnaise
4 cups shredded cabbage
1 medium carrot, shredded
1 rib celery, diced

Stir together milk, vinegar, sugar, salt, celery seed, pepper and mayonnaise. Pour over cabbage, carrot and celery and mix. Chill. Serves 8.

Mary Lee's I Fought the Slaw and the Slaw Won

3 pounds cabbage
3 ribs celery
1 medium onion
1 small green pepper
3 carrots
2 cups sugar

Shred cabbage. Chop celery, onion, pepper and carrots. Sprinkle, then mix in sugar.

1 cup vinegar
1/2 cup vegetable oil
1 teaspoon celery seed
1 teaspoon salt

Bring vinegar, oil, celery seed and salt to a boil. Pour over cabbage mixture. Chill overnight. Serves 12.

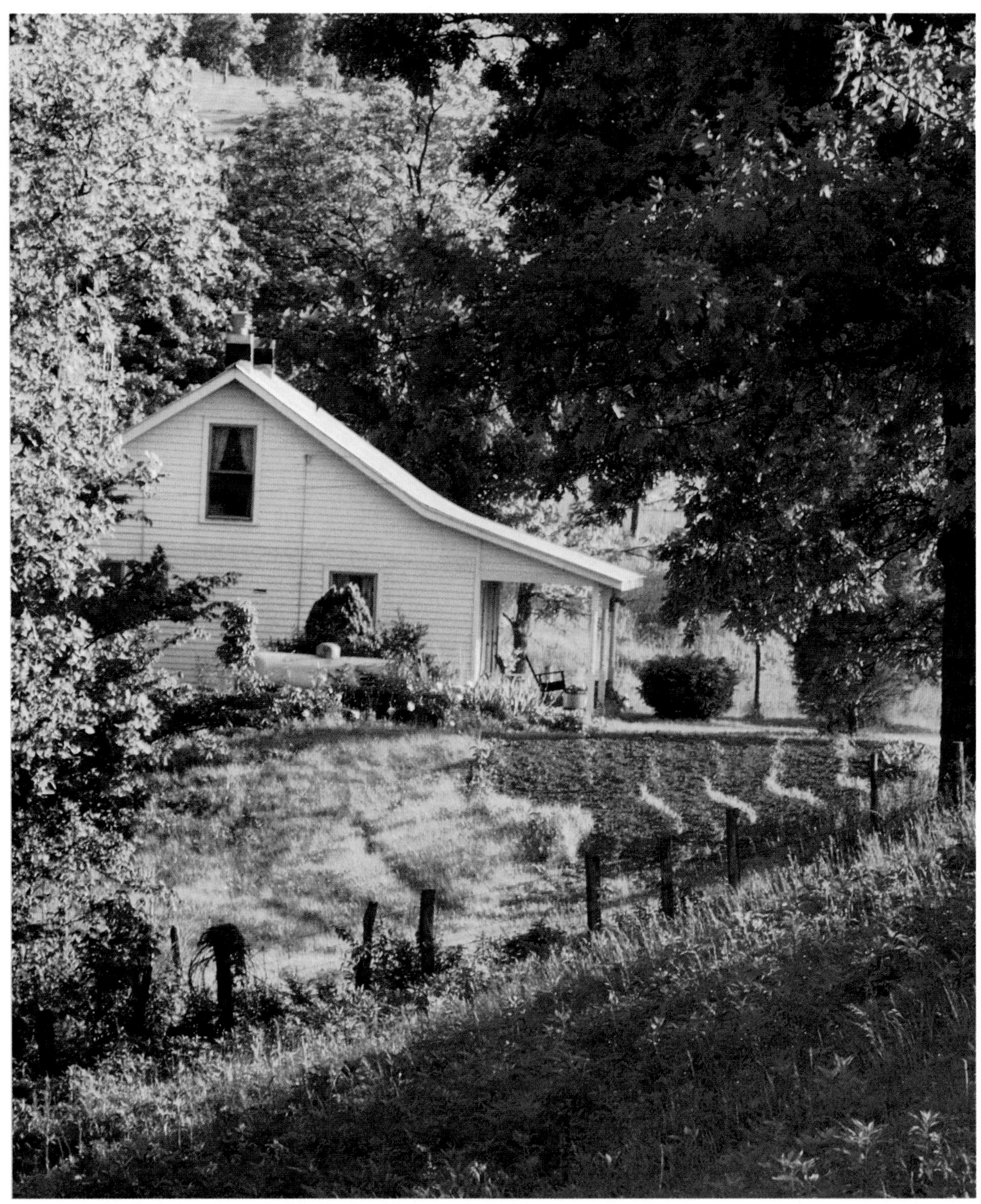

Big River Slaw

1/2 cup white vinegar
1/2 cup vegetable oil
3/4 cup sugar
1/4 teaspoon salt
1 medium head of cabbage, shredded
1 large carrot, peeled and grated

Combine vinegar, oil, sugar and salt in a saucepan and bring to a boil. Simmer for 10 minutes. Toss cabbage and carrot together. Pour sauce over cabbage mixture and let sit 1 hour. Refrigerate in a tightly sealed container.

Serve on top of sandwich. Serves 12.

Texas Slaw

1 medium head cabbage, shredded
1/2 medium onion, shredded
2 tablespoons sweet pickle relish
1/4 cup mayonnaise

Mix cabbage and onion. Add pickle relish and mayonnaise. Refrigerate until ready to serve. Serves 12.

Slick's Slaw

1 medium head cabbage, shredded
2 carrots, grated
3/4 cup sour cream
1 tablespoon red-wine vinegar
1 tablespoon sugar
1 teaspoon salt
1/2 teaspoon pepper
1 1/2 cups mayonnaise

Toss cabbage and carrots in a bowl. Combine remaining ingredients and pour over vegetables. Stir until blended. Cover and refrigerate. Serves 12.

Darnell's Potato Slaw

1/4 cup mayonnaise
1 tablespoon mustard
2 cups cabbage, shredded
1 cup potatoes, diced
1/4 cup green pepper, chopped
1/4 cup cucumber, sliced
1 teaspoon salt

Combine mayonnaise and mustard. Toss remaining ingredients in bowl. Pour in dressing. Toss gently until well-mixed. Chill for at least 1 hour. Serves 4 to 6.

Colonial Coleslaw

1/2 cup heavy cream, whipped
1/2 cup sugar
1/2 cup vinegar
1 medium head cabbage, shredded
1/4 teaspoon salt
1/4 teaspoon pepper

Mix sugar into whipped cream, then stir in vinegar. Pour over cabbage, season with salt and pepper, stir well and chill. Serves 12.

Eine Kleine German Slaw

6 strips bacon, diced
1 large head red cabbage, shredded
1 apple, diced
1/4 cup water
1/4 cup sugar
2 teaspoons salt
1 teaspoon pepper
8 tablespoons vinegar

Brown bacon in saucepan. Add cabbage, apple and water. Cover and steam for 1 hour, stirring frequently. Add sugar, salt, pepper and vinegar and stir. Serve warm. Serves 12.

Bevo's Slaw

1/2 cup sugar
1 tablespoon prepared mustard
1/4 cup vinegar
1 teaspoon salt
3/4 cup salad oil
1 head cabbage, shredded
3 large carrots, grated

Combine sugar, mustard, vinegar, salt and oil and mix well. Pour over cabbage and carrots and mix well. Serves 12.

The Little Bible Teacher's Mustard Slaw

1 head cabbage, shredded
2 onions, chopped
2 green peppers, chopped
1/2 cup mustard
1/2 cup vinegar
1 cup sugar
1 cup vegetable oil
1 tablespoon salt
1 tablespoon celery seed

Mix cabbage, onions and peppers in a large bowl.

Combine remaining ingredients in bowl and stir well. Pour vinegar mixture over cabbage mixture, mix thoroughly. Cover and refrigerate overnight. Serves 12.

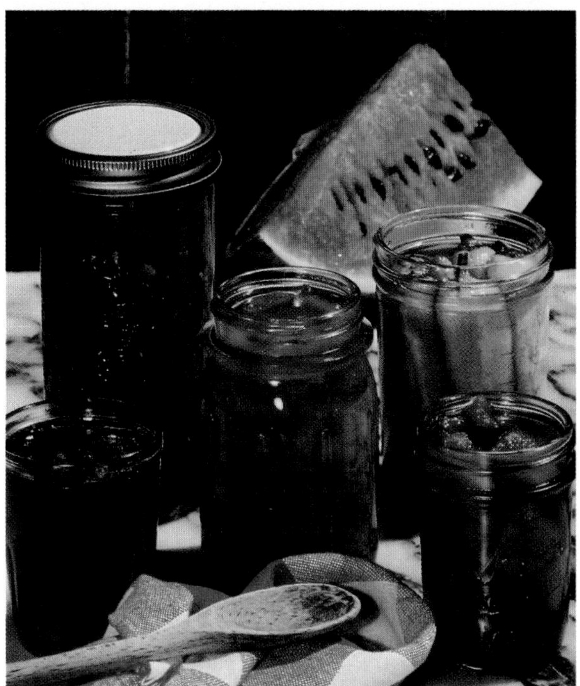

Another Slaw

4 cups cabbage, shredded
1 8-ounce can crushed pineapple, drained
1 8-ounce can sliced water chestnuts, drained
1/4 cup green onion, chopped
1/4 cup mayonnaise
1 tablespoon mustard
1 teaspoon ginger
1/2 teaspoon salt
1/4 teaspoon pepper

Combine cabbage, pineapple, water chestnuts and onion in a bowl. Combine mayonnaise, mustard, ginger, salt and pepper. Pour over cabbage mixture and toss gently. Serves 8 to 12.

Beans

When we have a barbecue at our house, my wife and I divide the cooking duties. She prepares the coleslaw and the dessert; I cook the barbecue and the beans.

My beans always win raves from friends. Invariably someone will ask for the recipe. I usually hem and haw and make some vague suggestion that it's an old family recipe that I've been sworn to keep secret. The truth is I don't have a recipe. I make it up as I go along, tasting frequently to see what it needs.

Here's how I do it.

My Bean Symphony

A can of pork and beans large enough for your crowd
1 medium onion, minced
1 rib celery, chopped
Whatever barbecue sauce I'm using that day
Molasses
Honey
Jack Daniel's Whiskey
A well-stocked spice shelf
Barbecue meat

I never fix my beans the same way twice. I mix the beans, onion, celery and a cup or so of barbecue sauce in a large pot. Next I dribble in about half of an 8-ounce jar of molasses. Then I add in the dry spices: I usually start with black and red pepper. From then on I treat it like a symphony and I'm the conductor: a little of this, some of that. I save the honey and Jack Daniel's for last, adding them to taste. Then I stir it all up and bake at 325 degrees for about 2 hours (depending on the size of the pot). When the barbecue comes off the pit, I stir in some of the meat (about half a pound for every quart of beans).

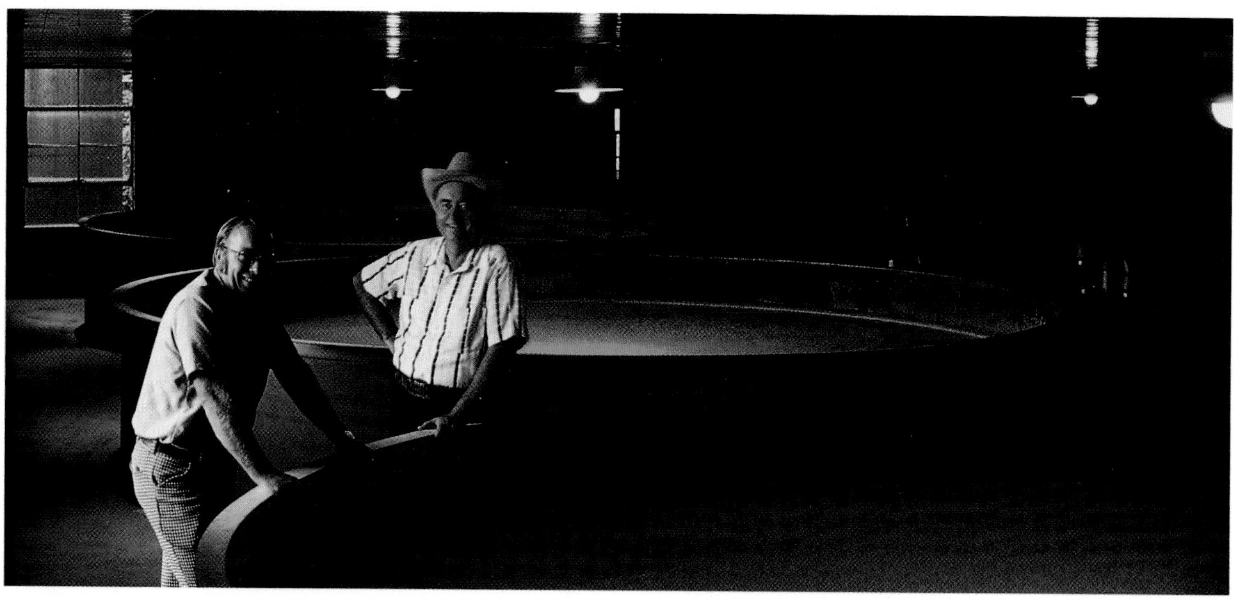

WILL'S BACON BAKED BEANS

1 16-ounce can pork and beans
1 16-ounce can ranch-style beans
1 green pepper, diced
1 medium onion, diced
4 slices bacon
1 4-ounce can mushroom stems and pieces, drained
1/4 teaspoon oregano
2 tablespoons Worcestershire sauce
2 tablespoons wine vinegar
1 tablespoon mustard
1/4 cup brown sugar
1/4 cup your favorite barbecue sauce
1/2 teaspoon celery salt
1/2 teaspoon lemon pepper
1 teaspoon olive oil
1/4 teaspoon garlic powder

Cook bacon until crisp. Crumble.

In a large pot, combine the beans, green pepper and onion. Add crumbled bacon. Then add the remaining ingredients. Bake at 350 degrees for 30 minutes. Serves 8 to 12.

JACK'S BAKED BEANS

1 28-ounce can pork and beans
1/3 cup Jack Daniel's Whiskey
2 tablespoons brown sugar, packed
1 teaspoon instant coffee
1 teaspoon mustard
1 tablespoon lemon juice

Combine beans, Jack Daniel's, brown sugar, coffee, mustard and lemon juice in a large pot. Bake at 350 degrees for 40 to 45 minutes. Serves 6 to 8.

Up-and-Coming Barbecue Man

Newton Vance says he's got barbecue sauce in his blood.

He's probably right. He was cooking barbecue before he could spell it. His daddy was one of the founders of Leigh's Barbecue in Kevil, Kentucky, and Newton was tending the pit there before he could even see over it.

He went away to college in Lexington, Kentucky and worked his way through school cooking at Billy's Barbecue there. Then in 1987 Newton decided he wanted his own pit. So he moved to Frankfort and opened Capital Bar-B-Q in a rustic building across the street from a bowling alley.

Newton is devoted to his art, the art of barbecue. He cooks all his meats at least 24 hours, usually putting them on at 11 in the morning and not taking them off the pit until 11 the next morning. And when he's cooking, he sleeps in a little apartment off the kitchen. "I'm up all night. I bought me a river house two years ago but since I've owned it, I haven't spent 10 nights there."

His specialty is pork shoulder; he cooks it over hickory coals for at least 24 hours, hand pulls the meat, chops it and squirts on a thin red sauce.

Newton's barbecue is as good as any you'll find, but he modestly declines to be ranked with the barbecue masters. He knows too many pitmasters who've been in barbecue for decades. Why, his place only opened in '87. He shrugs his shoulders: "I just like to think of this as an up-and-coming barbecue place."

Capital Bar-B-Q's Bar-B-Q Smoked Beans

1 gallon tomato sauce
5 cups mustard
2 pounds brown sugar
5 1-gallon cans pork and beans
1 pint molasses
1/4 cup black pepper
1/4 cup salt
3 large onions
3 large green peppers
4 cups water

Mix tomato sauce, mustard and brown sugar in a large pan. Add pork and beans, molasses, pepper and salt. Cut up onion and green peppers and add to mixture. Mix thoroughly. Add water and allow it to stay on top. Smoke beans over hickory coals for 10-12 hours.

Roy's Baked Green Beans

$2^1/_2$ cups fresh white bread cubes
$^1/_2$ cup butter, melted
4 3-ounce cans sliced mushrooms, drained
3 15 $^1/_2$-ounce cans cut green beans, drained
$^1/_4$ teaspoon salt
$^1/_8$ teaspoon pepper
2 teaspoons onion, chopped
2 cans cream of mushroom soup
1 cup milk
$^1/_2$ cup toasted slivered almonds

Toss bread cubes with butter. Place half of the cubes in greased casserole dish. Add mushrooms and beans. Sprinkle with salt, pepper and onion. Combine soup and milk and pour over beans. Sprinkle with almonds and remaining bread cubes. Bake at 400 degrees for 30 minutes. Serves 12.

Owensboro Beans

1 21-ounce can pork and beans
$^1/_4$ cup onion, chopped
$1^1/_2$ tablespoons brown sugar
1 teaspoon dry mustard
$^1/_4$ cup ketchup

Place beans in a baking dish. Mix in onion, brown sugar, dry mustard and ketchup. Lay bacon on top of beans. Bake in a 350-degree oven until bacon is done – 30 to 40 minutes. Serves 6.

POTATO SALADS

MAMAW'S GERMAN POTATO SALAD

4 cups cooked potatoes, cubed
8 slices bacon, cooked crisp and crumbled
1 cup celery, chopped fine
3 green onions with tops chopped

Combine all ingredients and put in baking dish.

Topping
1/2 cup mayonnaise
1/4 cup white vinegar
2 teaspoons sugar
1 teaspoon mustard
1 teaspoon salt
1/4 teaspoon black pepper

Combine all ingredients and pour over potato mixture. Bake at 350 degrees for 20 minutes. Serves 8 to 10.

DEE'S POTATO SALAD

6 medium potatoes
3 eggs
1 teaspoon salt
1/2 teaspoon paprika
1/4 teaspoon pepper
6 slices bacon, cooked crisp and crumbled
1/3 cup scallions, chopped fine
2 tablespoons pimentos
1/4 cup French dressing
3/4 cup mayonnaise

Boil potatoes 20 minutes or until tender. Drain, dry, peel and cut. Hard-cook eggs and slice. Add eggs, salt, paprika, pepper, bacon, scallions and pimentos to potatoes and blend. Add French dressing and mayonnaise. Mix until well-coated. Refrigerate. Serves 12.

LEESBURG CHECKER CLUB POTATO SALAD

4 cups potatoes, boiled and cubed
2 tablespoons onion, minced
2 tablespoons pimento, minced
1 cup celery, diced
1/2 cup sweet cucumber pickles, chopped
1 cup toasted slivered almonds
1 teaspoon salt
1/2 teaspoon pepper
1/4 cup mayonnaise

Combine all ingredients and toss gently with a fork. Serves 8.

Kentucky River Potato Salad

5 potatoes
1 rib celery, chopped
1/2 onion, finely chopped

Peel potatoes, cut into bite-size pieces. Cook in boiling water for 15 minutes or until tender (but not soft). Drain. Add celery and onion. Make dressing.

Dressing
3/4 cup mayonnaise
1 teaspoon mustard
1 tablespoon vinegar
1/8 teaspoon pepper
1 1/2 teaspoons salt
1 tablespoon sugar
2 tablespoons milk

Mix well and pour over potato mixture. Blend and refrigerate. Serves 8 to 10.

Walter's Hot Potato Salad

5 slices bacon, diced
1/2 cup onion, minced
1/4 cup vinegar
3 tablespoons sugar
1 1/2 teaspoons salt
1/8 teaspoon crushed oregano
1/4 teaspoon pepper
1 teaspoon mustard
3 cups potatoes, cooked and diced
1/2 cup celery, diced
2 tablespoons green pepper, chopped
2 eggs, hard-cooked and chopped
1/2 cup grated cheese

Fry bacon until brown, then dice. Combine onion, vinegar, sugar, salt, oregano, pepper and mustard in a saucepan. Bring to a boil and hold boil for 2 minutes. Pour hot mixture over potatoes. Stir in remaining ingredients. Serves 6 to 8.

OTHER SIDE DISHES

Leonard Heuberger is generally credited with creating Memphis-style barbecue sandwiches at his tiny restaurant on South Bellevue Boulevard. Leonard's opened in 1922 and immediately began serving his trademark sandwich: barbecued pork, pulled and piled on a bun, sprinkled with a tomato-vinegar sauce and crowned with coleslaw. Teenagers, among them Elvis Presley, flooded the place in the 50s, ordering pig sandwiches with another of Leonard's specialties, onion rings, on the side.

Here's a way to create a similar version at home.

ALMOST LIKE LEONARD'S ONION RINGS

4 large onions
2 cups buttermilk
3 1/2 cups flour
1 cup cornmeal
3 tablespoons onion powder
2 teaspoons salt
2 teaspoons sugar
4 cups milk
2 eggs, beaten
Cooking oil

Peel onions. Slice 1/2-inch thick and separate into rings. Use no ring smaller than a silver dollar, if you can remember how big a silver dollar is. Soak overnight in buttermilk.

Combine flour, cornmeal, onion powder, salt, sugar, milk and eggs and mix well. Pour oil to depth of 2 inches in a saucepan and heat to 375 degrees. Dip each onion ring in batter, then fry about 2 minutes or until golden brown. Drain and serve hot.

MRS. BUCK'S BARBECUE ONIONS

Start with a large whole onion, preferably a big yellow, Vidalia or sweet Washington State onion. Trim off top and outer skin with paring knife. With knife, carve a small well in top of onion. Pour in a tablespoon of your favorite barbecue sauce. Wrap onions individually in heavy aluminum foil. Place onions on top of the grill, in a campfire or in the oven. It usually takes about 45 minutes, depending on the heat of the fire. In the kitchen oven, bake at 400 degrees for 50-60 minutes. Plan on 1 onion per person.

Vert Ego II's Barbecued Potatoes

This recipe came to us while cruising on Vert Smith's Vert Ego II down the Tennessee River. We used a cooker but an oven will do.

4 unpeeled potatoes
3/4 cup French dressing
Salt and pepper to taste

Bake the potatoes in their skins about 50 minutes at 450 degrees or until they are slightly tender. Do not fully cook since they must be sliced. While still warm, quarter the potatoes lengthwise. Place the potatoes in a glass baking dish and cover with the dressing. Let stand 1 hour, turning over. Pour off dressing and place potatoes on the grill. Salt and pepper to taste. Grill the potatoes until golden brown. Serves 6 to 8.

Garibaldi's Rosin Potatoes

Get enough common ordinary rosin to fill an iron cauldron or kettle 3/4 full; the bigger the kettle the better. Melt over a wood fire out in the open. When the rosin has melted, put in the potatoes. They immediately sink, and when done they demurely come bobbing to the surface. Take them out with a wrought-iron fork or ladle, but be careful not to puncture the skins. Have 2 or 3 thicknesses of newspaper cut into squares big enough to roll each potato in, and secure safely with a twist at both ends. The rosin sticks to the paper when it cools, which is at once. Cut straight across through the middle and break open – presto! The skin will pull away, leaving a soft, deliciously mealy affair.

Jack's Sweet Potatoes

2 tablespoons cornstarch
1/2 teaspoon nutmeg
2 teaspoons salt
1/2 cup sugar
1 cup water
1 tablespoon lemon juice
1/3 cup Jack Daniel's Whiskey
6 large sweet potatoes, cooked
Miniature marshmallows

Combine cornstarch, nutmeg, salt and sugar in saucepan. Stir in water. Cook until clear, stirring constantly. Add lemon juice and Jack Daniel's and stir. Peel potatoes and cut crosswise into thick slices. Place in buttered shallow casserole and cover with the above mixture. Cover and bake at 375 degrees for 30 minutes, basting occasionally. Sprinkle with marshmallows and broil until golden brown. Serves 12.

Lem's Sweet Potatoes

4 cups sweet potatoes, boiled and sliced
1/2 cup brown sugar
1/2 cup sugar
Juice of 1/2 lemon
3/4 teaspoon nutmeg
4 tablespoons butter, melted
1/2 cup Jack Daniel's Whiskey

Mix ingredients and mash together. Spoon into a casserole and bake at 350 degrees until piping hot. Serves 8.

Sweetwater Cinnamon Sweet Potatoes

12 (uncooked) sweet potatoes, peeled and sliced
2 sticks cinnamon
Water to cover
1/2 cup butter
1 cup pancake syrup

Place sweet potatoes and cinnamon in saucepan and cover with water. Boil until potatoes are tender. Drain water and reserve. Melt butter with pancake syrup. Pour over sweet potatoes and add reserved cooking liquid. Bake at 350 degrees for 1 hour. Serves 20.

Charlotte's Cheese Potatoes

1/2 cup butter
3 large potatoes, peeled and pared
Salt and pepper
1 medium onion, sliced
1/2 pound sharp American cheese, cubed
4 slices bacon, cooked crisp

Melt butter in a skillet. Slice potatoes and add to skillet. Sprinkle with salt and pepper. Stir in onion and cheese cubes. Crumble bacon over potatoes. Cover and cook on low heat, stirring occasionally. Cook until potatoes are tender. Serves 6.

Unbelievably Easy Scalloped Potatoes

8 medium potatoes, sliced thin
1/4 cup minced onion
1 10 3/4-ounce can condensed cream of mushroom soup
1 cup milk
2 teaspoons salt
Dash pepper

Alternate layers of potatoes and onions in a greased 2-quart casserole dish. Combine soup, milk and seasonings. Pour over potatoes. Cover and bake at 350 degrees for 45 minutes. Serves 12 to 16.

Real Good Potato Puffs

1 8-ounce package cream cheese, softened
4 cups hot mashed potatoes
1 egg, beaten
1/3 cup onion, finely chopped
1/4 cup pimento, chopped
1 teaspoon salt
Dash pepper

Mix cream cheese and potatoes until well-blended. Add remaining ingredients. Bake in 1-quart casserole dish at 350 degrees for 45 minutes. Serves 8.

CURLEY MOREMEN'S GRILLED CORN-ON-THE-COB

6 ears of fresh corn, husk on, or 6 ears frozen corn
Butter, salt and pepper

Wrap the unopened corn (in husk) in heavy aluminum foil and place on top of grill. Turn every 10 minutes for about 1/2 hour. Shuck husk and serve. Some prefer garlic salt but butter is more universal, with salt and pepper to taste. Serves 6.

BARBECUED CORN TENNESSEE-STYLE

Choose tender ears of Golden Bantam or Country Gentleman corn. Without necessarily removing more than the outer layers of husk, plunge 10 minutes into fiercely boiling, salted water. Husk now, and wrap each ear with 3 thin rashers of home-smoked lean bacon skewered with toothpicks. Impale the ear on a long, peeled, rustic wand, paint well with a basting made from 1/2 butter and 1/2 peanut butter, lusciously melted together; then broil over the coals turning to brown on all sides. When at home use the oven broiler, omitting the wands entirely. If corn is not parboiled first, it takes a long time to cook, burns cheeks, hands and bacon; tends to make the corn too tough.

BUFORD LEECH'S CORN PUDDING

4 eggs
2 cups cream-style corn
3 tablespoons flour
1 tablespoon sugar
1 teaspoon salt
1/4 teaspoon pepper
1 cup milk
1 tablespoon melted butter
1/4 cup Jack Daniel's Whiskey

Beat eggs until thick. Add corn. Combine flour, sugar, salt and pepper in mixing bowl. Stir in milk, then butter. Combine with corn mixture, beating well. Stir in Jack Daniel's. Pour into 1-quart buttered casserole. Bake at 325 degrees for 1 hour 20 minutes. Serves 8 to 10.

IRON SKILLET CABBAGE

4 slices bacon
1/4 cup vinegar
1 teaspoon brown sugar
1 teaspoon salt
1 tablespoon onion, finely chopped
1/4 cup water
4 cups cabbage, quartered

Cook bacon until crisp and remove from skillet. Crumble. Combine vinegar, sugar, salt and onion in skillet. Add bacon and heat. Add water and cabbage. Cover and steam until tender. Serves 8 to 10.

JACK MIDDLETON'S MUSTARD OR COLLARD GREENS

Boil hog jowl or bacon (cut in 1/4-inch-thick rashers) in plenty of salted water until about tender. Have pot really boiling when the greens go in, adding a pinch of soda. When the greens are tender, drain well to avoid the strong water; use the sliced jowl or bacon rashers to garnish the heap of greens on the platter.

BETH VISH'S BROCCOLI SIDE

4 10-ounce packages frozen broccoli
2 cans cream of chicken soup
1 cup mayonnaise
1 stick butter
1 package herb-seasoned stuffing mix

Cook and drain broccoli. Mix soup and mayonnaise, then pour over broccoli in a shallow baking dish. Brown butter in skillet and add stuffing mix, stirring often. Put on top of broccoli. Bake at 350 degrees for 30 minutes. Serves 12.

Bobo's Hoppin' Jack

Cover 2 cups of dried peas with 2 quarts of water, slightly salted, and toss in 4 rashers of smoked "side-meat." Bacon and home-smoked country bacon is best with rashers cut in half and 1/4-inch thick. Simmer slowly until peas are not quite done. Pour off all but 3 cups of this cooking water, add 1 cup of brown or white uncooked rice. Put everything in top of a double boiler and draw off when rice is well-steamed and tender.

Pepper seasoning varies with each Southern cook. There may be none, or a cook may put in a small red pepper pod, a redbird pepper, or lots of ground pepper. If dried cow peas are used (fresh are not obtainable in the North), be sure to soak overnight. The bacon usually is laid about the rice-bean blend. If no double boiler is on hand, use very slow fire so the rice won't stick to the pot. Or the rice may be boiled separately, using cooking water from the peas. Serves a whole bunch.

Pat DeChurch's Stuffed Eggplant

1 large eggplant
1/2 pound ricotta cheese
1 6-ounce jar pimentos, drained
1/4 teaspoon garlic powder
1 egg
1/2 cup Italian bread crumbs
6 tablespoons butter
2 tablespoons flour
Salt to taste
1 1/2 cups milk
6 slices Cheddar cheese

Cut off ends of eggplant and peel. Cut in half. Dig out both halves to make boats. Set pulp aside. Microwave eggplant in a dish with a little water, covered, for 12 minutes or until soft. Meanwhile make stuffing.

Mix ricotta cheese, half of pimentos, garlic powder, egg and 1/4 cup bread crumbs. Cook extra pulp in small amount of butter until soft. Add to stuffing.

Remove eggplant from microwave. Drain off excess water. While it cools, make cream sauce.

Melt 3 tablespoons butter in saucepan over low heat. Stir in flour. Salt to taste. Cook, stirring, until bubbly. Stir in milk, stirring until thick. If too thick, add more milk. Stir in remaining pimentos. Stuff cooled eggplant boats. On top put slices of Cheddar cheese, 1/4 cup bread crumbs and dot with butter. Pour sauce around, not over, eggplant. Bake at 350 degrees until brown and bubbly. Serves 6.

MACARONI AND CHEESE, CHEESE, CHEESE (3-Cheese Macaroni)

1 8-ounce package macaroni
3 cups milk
4 tablespoons butter
2 tablespoons flour
1 teaspoon salt
1 teaspoon grated onion
1 cup mozzarella
1/2 cup Cheddar cheese
1/2 cup Parmesan cheese
Pepper to taste

Cook and drain macaroni. Make white sauce with milk, butter, flour and salt. Add onion, cheese and pepper. Stir until cheese is melted. Mix with macaroni. Bake at 350 degrees for 30 minutes. Serves 12.

FRITTER FRIED OKRA

1 cup flour
3 teaspoons baking powder
1/2 teaspoon salt
2 eggs, beaten
1/3 cup milk
5 cups okra, thinly sliced

Sift flour, baking powder and salt together. Combine eggs and milk. Stir in flour mixture until smooth. Add okra and stir gently. Drop by spoonsful into deep-fat fryer. Fry until golden brown. Drain on paper towel and serve while still hot. Serves 12.

CASSEROLE SIDE DISHES

After the barbecue pit, the greatest cooking invention may be the casserole dish. The major advantage of this versatile cooking container is that, if you want, you can mix, cook and serve, all in the same bowl. And that bowl doesn't take up much space on a picnic table. At a barbecue feast, a casserole dish offers a lot of good eating in a small container.

KINGSPORT GARLIC GRITS CASSEROLE

4 1/2 cups boiling water
1 teaspoon salt
1 cup uncooked grits
1 stick butter
1 6-ounce stick garlic cheese
2 eggs, beaten
1/2 cup milk

Bring water and salt to boil and slowly add grits. Cook 3 minutes, until thickened. Add butter and cheese and stir until dissolved. Add eggs and milk. Pour into a greased 2-quart casserole dish. Dot with butter. Bake at 350 degrees for 45 minutes.

SOUPS, STEWS AND SALADS

In North Carolina they call it Brunswick Stew. Down in South Carolina it's simply hash. Over in Kentucky they call it burgoo.

The ingredients differ, as does the taste, but these hearty stews are the soups of the barbecue world.

SOUPS AND STEWS

Kentuckian J.T. Looney was famed all over the country for his burgoo. He crisscrossed the continent cooking up his burgoo for political get-togethers and private parties. His burgoo was so famous, it gave him his nickname, the Burgoo King, a name that would live on forever when a thoroughbred named for Looney, Burgoo King, won the 1932 Kentucky Derby.

Following is his original recipe, as he wrote it down.

The Original Kentucky Burgoo

600 pounds lean soup meat (no fat, no bones)
200 pounds fat hens
2,000 pounds potatoes, peeled and diced
200 pounds onions
5 bushels cabbage, chopped
60 10-pound cans tomatoes
24 10-pound cans puree of tomato
24 10-pound cans carrots
18 10-pound cans corn
Red pepper and salt to taste
Tabasco sauce to taste

Mix a little at a time. Cook 15 to 20 hours in a kettle outdoors. Serves an army.

Oldham County Kentucky Burgoo

2 pounds pork shank
2 pounds veal shank
2 pounds beef shank
2 pounds breast of lamb
1 4-pound hen
8 quarts cold water
1½ pounds onions
1½ pounds potatoes
1 quart tomato puree
6 carrots, diced
2 green peppers, diced
2 cups cabbage, chopped
2 cups whole corn, fresh or canned
2 cups okra, diced
2 cups lima beans
1 cup celery, diced
2 pods red pepper
1 tablespoon salt
1 tablespoon cayenne pepper
1 tablespoon Tabasco sauce
½ cup Worcestershire sauce

Put meat and cold water in large pot and slowly bring to a boil. Simmer until the meat is tender enough to fall from the bones. Remove the meat from the stock. Cool and chop, discarding skin, bones and fat.

Peel and dice potatoes and onions. Return meat to stock and add potatoes and onions. Add remaining vegetables. Allow to simmer until thick. Add seasonings and continue cooking approximately 10 hours, stirring frequently during the first part of the cooking and almost constantly after burgoo begins to thicken.

Note: Burgoo should be soupy, not thick.

South Carolina Chicken Bog

1 chicken (4 to 5 pounds)
1 large onion, chopped
6-8 slices bacon
4 cups rice, uncooked
1 teaspoon salt
1/2 teaspoon pepper

Boil chicken and onion in half gallon of water until tender. Remove chicken from stock. Debone chicken and shred meat. Fry bacon until crisp. Remove bacon and reserve 3 tablespoons grease. Put bacon, chicken meat and bacon grease into chicken stock. Add salt and pepper. Bring to a boil. Pour in rice and simmer until most of liquid is absorbed. Continue to cook until rice is done. If it gets too dry, add a little water.

Barbecue Vegetable Soup

1 cup onions, chopped
1 cup celery, chopped
1 pound barbecued pork or beef, pulled and chopped
1 10-ounce package frozen mixed vegetables
2 quarts water
2 cups stewed tomatoes
1/2 cup tomato juice
1/4 cup whatever barbecue sauce you're using
2 cups diced potatoes
1 teaspoon salt
1 teaspoon sugar
1/2 teaspoon red pepper

In a large stock pot combine onions, celery, meat, mixed vegetables, water, stewed tomatoes, tomato juice and barbecue sauce. Cook 2 hours on medium heat. Add potatoes, salt, sugar and pepper. Cook until potatoes are soft.

Mmmmm Gumbo

2 pounds turtle meat
2 pounds peeled crawfish
1 pound green onions, chopped
1 large green bell pepper, chopped
1 8-ounce can mushrooms, drained
1/4 cup flour
1 tablespoon file powder
1 teaspoon paprika
1 teaspoon cayenne pepper
1 tablespoon black pepper
1/4 cup bacon drippings
3 cups uncooked rice

Parboil turtle for 15 minutes on high heat. Drain and boil in 2 quarts water on medium heat until turtle is tender enough to remove from bones. Bone turtle. Retain 2 cups of broth. Put boned turtle and crawfish in remaining broth. Add onions, bell pepper and mushrooms and cook on low heat.

In a saucepan, brown flour and seasonings in bacon drippings. Add reserved broth. Cook and stir constantly until mixture thickens. Add thickened mixture to turtle and crawfish mixture. Simmer over very low heat for 30 minutes. Cook rice according to instructions on package. Serve gumbo over rice.

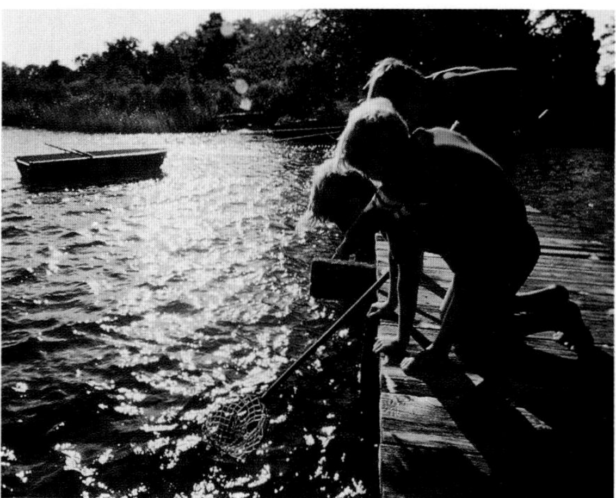

The Brunswick Stew-ard

When Evelyn and Auborn Grogan went hunting for a new home a few years back, their first consideration wasn't the number of bedrooms or the size of the kitchen.

"We wanted to make sure we had a big enough yard for a Brunswick Stew shed," says Evelyn.

Evelyn is known around Reidsville, North Carolina for her Brunswick Stew. When her kids were young and the family needed a little spending money, she'd whip up a pot – a big pot – and send the kids out to sell it. "We had a big family, 7 children, so they could sell a lot of stew."

The stew-selling got started when one of the kids began showing musical ability. "She was so musically inclined that we decided we needed a piano." Evelyn fired up the stew pot, everyone took a turn helping stir, and then the kids fanned out over the neighborhood selling small jars of the stew.

"The kids are all grown now, so I only make up one batch a year to sell." But she still has her 50-gallon pot set up in her stew shed. Now, though, she usually makes only about 15 gallons of stew at a time "for family get-togethers. But I keep some in the freezer all the time."

But every now and then, when the PTA calls, Evelyn will fire up the big pot again, to help out. That's when she misses her kids. "I needed that big family to help stir and fetch and things. Why, it took two at the pot at all times."

Evelyn Grogan's Brunswick Stew

8 pounds of chicken
2 pounds of lean beef

Cook, cool and bone.

8 pounds potatoes, peeled, but not diced
Soak about 3 pounds of onions, chopped
1 pound dried baby lima beans
1 gallon tomatoes

Cook together using broth. When these vegetables begin to cook add:

3 cans baby lima beans
3 cans cream-style corn
1 can whole kernel corn

Add meat. Stir, stir, and never stop stirring.

Add salt, pepper and 3 tablespoons of sugar.

Keep enough water in the pot to equal 4 gallons when the stew is done.

"I usually cook the meat the night before. The potatoes and onions may be peeled then too. Cover them with cold water. Be sure to use all of the broth in the stew.

"And cook over hardwood. We tried gas, but it's not the same atmosphere.

"Serve the stew as a meal by itself or with coleslaw and hush puppies."

GENERAL JOHNSON'S JAMBALAYA

2 cups bread crumbs
1 tablespoon butter
1½ cups rice
2½ cups boiled chicken, minced
1 large onion, minced
Speck crushed garlic
1 cup okra, sliced
2 cups skin-free cooked tomato
1 green pepper, chopped
1 small rib celery, chopped
1 bunch snipped parsley
2 tablespoons butter
3 dashes Tabasco sauce
¼ teaspoon ground mace

Fry bread crumbs in butter for a couple of minutes. Boil rice until almost done. Mix chicken and rice together in saucepan and reserve. Gently saute onion, garlic, okra, tomato, green pepper, celery and parsley in 2 tablespoons butter. When onion colors slightly, mix with chicken and rice; add Tabasco sauce and mace.

Butter a pottery oven dish well, turn everything into it, cover with bread crumbs, and brown at about 350 degrees.

TERRY WEISS' OKLAHOMA BEEF STEW

(She admits it's her mother's recipe.)

2 pounds stewing beef, cut in 1-inch chunks
Salt and pepper to taste
2 tablespoons flour
1 tablespoon vegetable oil
1 teaspoon seasoned salt
5 large celery ribs
1 pound carrots, sliced
5 large potatoes, peeled and cut in chunks
1 onion, diced
1 10½-ounce can condensed tomato soup
1 tablespoon Worcestershire sauce

Season beef with salt and pepper, dust with flour and brown in oil in a heavy skillet. Put browned beef in a dutch oven and cover with water. Add seasoned salt and bring to a boil. Cover and simmer for 2 hours. Add vegetables and more water if necessary. Simmer for another hour. Add tomato soup, Worcestershire sauce, salt, pepper, and simmer for 15 minutes. Stew should sit for at least 1 hour before serving. Better still, refrigerate overnight and serve the next day.

Pop's Beloved's Deep South Fresh Water Turtle Soup Stew

Two turtles
Salt
10 cloves
3 dashes Tabasco sauce
1/4 teaspoon mace
1/2 teaspoon allspice
1 medium onion, diced
Dash crushed garlic
2 tablespoons butter
2 tablespoons flour
2 pinches sweet basil
2 tablespoons sherry
2 scant tablespoons lemon juice
Trifle of grated zest of orange (orange part of peel only)

Two average turtles will serve 6. With a hatchet make a horizontal incision both sides between feet, to separate top of shell from flat lower portion. Reserve eggs, if any, and some of the fat. Scald feet to skin, using pliers for this operation to save temper. Put turtles in kettle, cover with cold water, salt lightly and add cloves, Tabasco sauce, mace and allspice. Simmer slowly and when tender trim off bones, dicing meat crossgrain to avoid strings. Meanwhile, fry onion and garlic in 1 tablespoon butter. When tender add to meat and rich stock. Blend flour with same amount of butter to make brown roux, work smooth with soup, then stir well into the pot. The stew should be like heavy cream.

Meanwhile, scald upper shells. Pour in stew, salted to taste. Add pinch sweet basil to each, 1 tablespoon sherry each, same with 1 scant tablespoon lemon juice and a trifle of grated zest. Spread sliced turtle eggs, or hard chicken eggs, on top. Cover with any good pastry dough, prick to permit steam to escape, and brown in oven at 350 degrees, brushing with a little milk during last 10 minutes to glaze.

Ridgerunner Stew

Mention the word ridgerunner in the South and folks will chuckle. Ridgerunner comes from the South's outlaw past, when manufacturing whiskey was illegal due to Prohibition and moonshining was a way of life. In the hills, where the water came from limestone springs and was iron-free, moonshining was as common as whittling. The moonshiners made their illicit drink back in the hills, high on the ridges so they could see down in the hollers if a stranger approached. An unknown face could send a runner across the ridges faster than fire to sound an alarm.

Someone kept close watch over the still at all times, minding the store so to speak, ever alert for revenuers, the federal agents charged with finding the stills and destroying them. Stew was a natural for the moonshiners, who had long idle periods while tending their stills. There are abundant recipes, of stews that is, that have survived Prohibition. Here is a rendition of one given to me by an elderly gentleman in Franklin County, Tennessee, who admitted to a little moonshining experience on his resumé. In fact, he spent his whole life making whiskey. When the Jack Daniel Distillery started back after Prohibition ended, he went to work for them and worked until he was up in his seventies. His last years were spent as a guide at the tourist center. He used to tell his visitors that the distillery kept him on because they didn't want him to go back into competition with them.

4 pounds top round steak, fat removed and cubed, put in casserole
Add:
1 bunch celery
1 small bunch carrots, chopped
2 medium onions, grated
1 can tomatoes, cut up, with juice
3 slices white bread, cubed fine
3 tablespoons minute tapioca
Salt and pepper to taste
1 16-ounce box frozen peas
Oregano, thyme and fines herbes
1 clove garlic, crushed

Mix all ingredients except peas. Cook in the oven at 225 degrees for 4 hours. Add the peas after 3½ hours.

SALADS

BARBECUE SALAD

Make up a simple salad, just the way you like it: lettuce, tomatoes, carrots, whatever. On top sprinkle a healthy sampling of chopped barbecue meat. Top with your favorite barbecue sauce.

TERRY'S TUNA SALAD

1 9¼-ounce can white tuna, drained
1 10½-ounce package frozen peas, cooked and drained
1 cup celery, thin sliced
1 6-ounce jar cocktail onions, drained
¾ cup mayonnaise
1 tablespoon soy sauce
⅛ teaspoon curry powder
⅛ teaspoon garlic salt
1 tablespoon lemon juice
1 cup Chinese crisp noodles

Combine tuna, peas, celery and onions and chill. Mix mayonnaise, soy, curry, garlic salt and lemon juice and chill. Add noodles to tuna mixture just before serving. Pour mayonnaise mixture over tuna mixture and toss lightly.

JELLICO FRUIT AND CHICKEN SALAD

3 cups cooked chicken, chopped
1 11-ounce can mandarin oranges, drained
1 cup mayonnaise
1 cup chopped celery
1 cup seedless white grapes, halved
½ cup raisins
½ teaspoon salt
¼ teaspoon pepper

Mix all ingredients thoroughly but gently. Chill.

DEE'S CHICKEN SALAD

3 tablespoons lemon juice
4 cups cut-up boiled chicken
1 cup sliced celery
⅓ cup chopped onions
1 teaspoon salt
½ teaspoon pepper
1 2-ounce jar of pimento, drained
¼ cup diced roasted almonds
⅓ cup mayonnaise
1 cup grapes

Pour lemon juice over chicken. Add rest of ingredients and mix.

JAKE'S SALAD

3 cups cabbage, shredded
1 cup crushed pineapple, drained
½ cup pecans, chopped
8 maraschino cherries, chopped
1½ ounces cream cheese, softened
3 tablespoons mayonnaise
3 tablespoons pineapple juice
¼ teaspoon salt

Combine cabbage, pineapple, pecans and cherries in a bowl. In another bowl combine cream cheese, mayonnaise, pineapple juice and salt and mix well. Pour over cabbage mixture and mix well.

JUST A 5-CUP SALAD

1 cup pineapple tidbits, drained
1 cup mandarin orange slices, drained
1 cup miniature marshmallows
1 cup coconut
1 cup sour cream

Mix and chill.

Mayberry Salad

1 head cauliflower, cut in pieces
1 bunch broccoli, chopped
1 red onion, chopped
1 green pepper, chopped
1 2-ounce jar pimentos
Salt and pepper to taste
1 cup mayonnaise
1/2 cup oil
1/3 cup wine vinegar
1/2 cup sugar
Dash dry mustard

Mix cauliflower, broccoli, onion, pepper and pimento. Mix together remaining ingredients and pour over vegetables. Cover and let stand in refrigerator overnight.

Charlie Grant's Cauliflower-Lettuce Salad

1 head lettuce
1 head cauliflower
1 pound bacon, fried crisp and crumbled
1 small onion, chopped
1/2 cup garbanzo beans
2 cups mayonnaise
1/4 cup sugar
1/3 cup Parmesan cheese

In glass bowl layer lettuce, cauliflower, bacon, onion and beans. In another bowl combine mayonnaise, sugar and cheese. Spread on top of salad. Chill overnight and toss before serving.

Judy Pavoni's Broccoli Salad

1 bunch fresh broccoli, cut into bite-size pieces
2 small onions, chopped
1 cup raisins
1/4 cup fresh mushrooms, sliced
1 pound bacon, fried crispy
1 cup mayonnaise
2 tablespoons vinegar
1/4 cup sugar

Combine in a bowl. Chill.

Gone By Supper Salad

1 head lettuce
1 bunch endive
1 14-ounce can artichoke hearts, drained
2 onions, sliced and separated into rings
2 grapefruit, sectioned
French dressing

Make a nest of lettuce and endive. Arrange artichoke hearts, onion and grapefruit in nest. Pour on dressing.

Sweet Baby's Fruit Salad

1 cup cubed cantaloupe
1 cup cubed honeydew
1 cup cubed watermelon
3 bananas, sliced
1 cup mayonnaise
$^{1}/_{2}$ cup strawberries

Combine cantaloupe, honeydew, watermelon and bananas in a bowl. Mix mayonnaise and strawberries in a blender. Pour over fruit.

Fruit Basket Turnover

1 cantaloupe
1 bunch white seedless grapes
1 15$^{1}/_{2}$-ounce can pineapple chunks, drained
2 bananas, chunked
$^{1}/_{4}$ cup honey
$^{1}/_{8}$ cup lime juice

Scoop balls from cantaloupe. Toss fruits. Combine honey and lime juice and beat. Pour over fruit. Toss gently.

Cherry Coke Salad

1 16-ounce can pitted Bing cherries
1 15$^{1}/_{4}$-ounce can crushed pineapple
1 3-ounce package cherry Jell-O
1 3-ounce package strawberry Jell-O
1 8-ounce package cream cheese
1 cup pecans, chopped
2 cups Coca-Cola

Drain juice from cherries and pineapple and heat in saucepan. Dissolve gelatins with hot juices. Let cool. Melt cheese. Add pineapple and nuts. Cut cherries into small pieces and fold gently into cheese mixture. Add this mixture to gelatin-juice mixture. Add Coca-Cola and mix well. Pour into mold and refrigerate.

Vinnie's Vegetable Salad

$^{3}/_{4}$ cup vinegar
$^{1}/_{2}$ cup cooking oil
1 tablespoon water
1 cup sugar
1 teaspoon salt
1 teaspoon pepper
1 16-ounce can English peas, drained
1 16-ounce can French-style green beans, drained
1 12-ounce can shoe-peg white corn, drained
1 pimento, chopped
1 cup chopped celery
1 green pepper, finely chopped
1 bunch green onions, chopped

Combine vinegar, oil, water, sugar, salt and pepper in a saucepan. Stir. Bring to a boil; remove from heat and set aside to cool. In a large bowl mix peas, beans, corn, pimento, celery, green pepper and onions. Add dressing and mix well. Cover and refrigerate for at least 12 hours. (Stir several times during this 12 hour period.)

PINEAPPLE RIGHT SIDE UP SALAD

1 15½-ounce can crushed pineapple, undrained
1 teaspoon vanilla
½ cup sugar
2 tablespoons cornstarch
¼ cup water
2 eggs, beaten
Butter
Cinnamon

Mix pineapple, vanilla and sugar in a casserole dish. In a bowl mix cornstarch and water until smooth and set aside. Beat eggs until thick. Add cornstarch mixture to eggs and stir. Pour this over pineapple mixture. Stir and dot with butter. Sprinkle lightly with cinnamon. Bake at 350 degrees for 1 hour.

AMERICUS' PEANUT-CABBAGE SALAD

2 tablespoons flour
¾ cup sugar
Salt and pepper to taste
2 eggs, beaten
1½ cups water
½ cup vinegar
3 tablespoons mustard
1 head cabbage, shredded
½ cup peanuts, chopped

Sift dry ingredients together. Combine eggs, water, vinegar and mustard and mix well. Pour into dry mixture and stir well. Pour into saucepan and cook until dressing is thick and smooth. Remove from heat and allow to cool. Combine cabbage and peanuts in a bowl. Pour in dressing and toss.

WILL SPICY BARBECUE KILL YOU? NAH.

Next time a friend declines to attend one of your barbecues because "that kind of food isn't good for you," tell him about this recent study conducted at Baylor College of Medicine in Houston.

After noticing stomach-lining damage on two patients who had just eaten spicy food, doctors there decided to test the theory that the temporary damage was caused by the highly-spiced meal.

They enlisted 12 subjects, 8 men and 4 women, and varied their lunch and dinner meals over four days. They used a fiber optic tube to examine the stomach lining of each subject every morning.

One meal, called BLAND, consisted of four ounces of unseasoned T-bone steak, half a cup of unseasoned peas, half a cup of unspiced potatoes and eight ounces of distilled water.

A second BLAND meal was identical except for the addition of three 375-gram tablets of aspirin, which doctors know causes stomach irritation.

A third meal, called SLIGHTLY SPICY, was mozzarella-cheese pizza with 36 grams of pepperoni.

And experimental meal No. 4, SPICY, was a Mexican TV dinner: two beef enchiladas, pinto beans and rice, plus 2½ jalapeno peppers and 1½ tablespoons of spicy picante sauce.

As expected the aspirin-laced meal produced damage to the stomach lining. Only

McClard's Bar-B-Q Fine Foods, Hot Springs, Arkansas

one of the 12 survived it without damage.

The surprise was that none of the other meals damaged the stomach at all on average. A few small spots occurred, but there were as many with the bland diet as with the spicy diet.

If you need to prove this to your friend, the test results were reported in the Dec. 16, 1988, issue of the Journal of the American Medical Association.

However, another study of the effects of Tabasco sauce demonstrated that if ingested in large enough amounts, hot sauce could cause respiratory failure in rats. The catch is in the amount of Louisiana hot sauce required to bring on death.

The scientific journal Toxicon reported in a 1990 edition that the lethal dose works out to about half a cup of sauce per 10 pounds of body weight. That means if you weigh 140 pounds, you shouldn't drink more than a quart and a half of straight Tabasco in any one sitting.

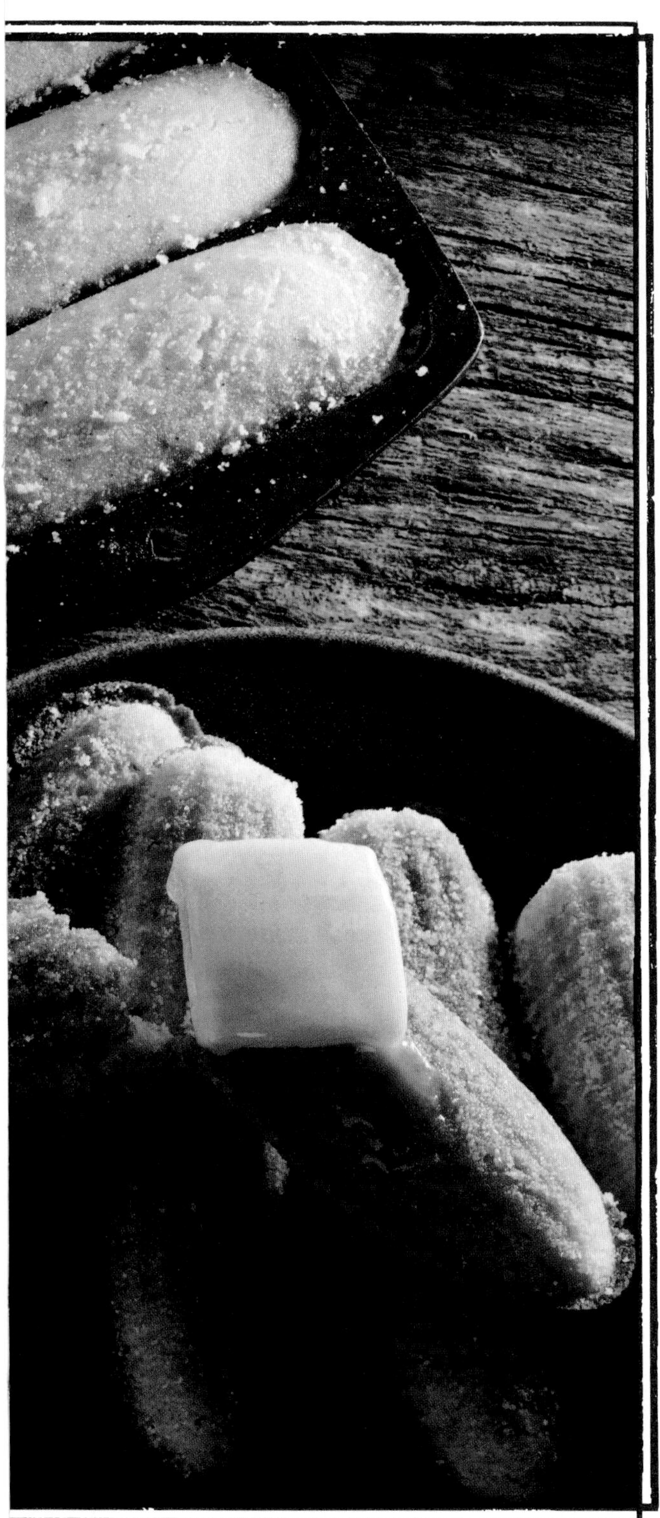

HOME BAKED BREADS

The menu for the first Thanksgiving hasn't survived, but you figure: a successful corn harvest; a ravenous band of colonists; a guest list that just happened to include Indians, the folks who had invented corn bread; and turkey, cooked over a slow fire. It probably wasn't zucchini-nut bread the Pilgrims used to sop up the turkey gravy.

Since then barbecue and corn bread have been a staple of American cooking. I know several barbecue restaurants that go so far as to serve their barbecue on corn bread. It's not a bad idea either. You might give it a try.

And Dolly Loyd at Center Point Barbecue in Hendersonville, Tennessee, just north of Nashville, serves her barbecue on corn bread pancakes. I don't know how to spell the phrase that describes that combination, but "Mmmmmmm gooooooood" is close.

One of the first recorded corn-bread recipes comes from "The Plimoth Colony Cook Book," published 30 years after the first Thanksgiving:

"Scald a quart of milk, pour it to three cups of Indian meal, add a bit of butter. When cool, stir in four eggs, a great spoonful of flour and a half-teaspoon of salt. Bake in small cups for 20 minutes."

Don't try this at home.

This recipe lacks those modern cooking aids, baking powder and baking soda. The recipe predates the use of either and the resultant corn bread

OTHER BREADS

JACK'S WHISKEY BREAD

1 package dry yeast
3¼ cups flour
¼ cup brown sugar
½ cup warm water (about 120 degrees)
2 eggs plus 1 white, beaten
1 teaspoon salt
⅓ cup butter, melted
½ cup warm milk
¼ cup Jack Daniel's Whiskey

Combine yeast, 1 cup flour, brown sugar and water in a bowl. Mix well, then cover. Let dough rise for 1 hour. Beat eggs until light. Add remaining ingredients and mix well. Combine with yeast mixture and beat well. Beat this mixture hard, with your hands, for 5 minutes, until the dough is light but still has body. Put in bowl, cover and allow to rise another hour. Remove and beat hard again for 5 minutes. Place in greased loaf pan and cover, allowing dough to rise to top of pan. Place in cold oven. Bake at 400 degrees for 15 minutes, then reduce heat to 325 and bake another 25 minutes.

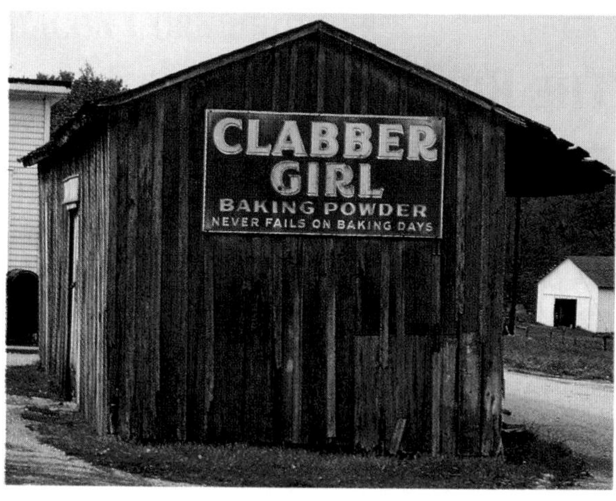

ALMOST WONDER BREAD

2 packages yeast
1 cup warm water (about 120 degrees)
1 pint plain yogurt
½ cup sugar
1 teaspoon salt
¼ cup butter
2 cups boiling water
3 eggs
½ cup wheat germ
12 cups unbleached flour

Add yeast to warm water. In a large bowl combine yogurt, salt, sugar and butter. Mix well with a mixer. Add boiling water and mix until butter melts. Test to make sure mixture is warm, then add yeast solution. Mix well with mixer. Add eggs and wheat germ and mix. Add 3 cups flour and mix well. Add 3 more cups flour and mix well. Add 3 more cups of flour and mix by hand. Add final 3 cups of flour and mix by hand. When dough no longer sticks to side of bowl, turn out to floured board. Knead for 10 minutes, or until dough is easy to handle. Grease mixing bowl and return to bowl. Cover with warm, wet towel. Allow to rise in warm place (at least 90 degrees) until double in size. Punch down and put in 4 greased loaf pans. Allow to rise again. Bake at 400 degrees for 30 minutes. Brush with butter and cool.

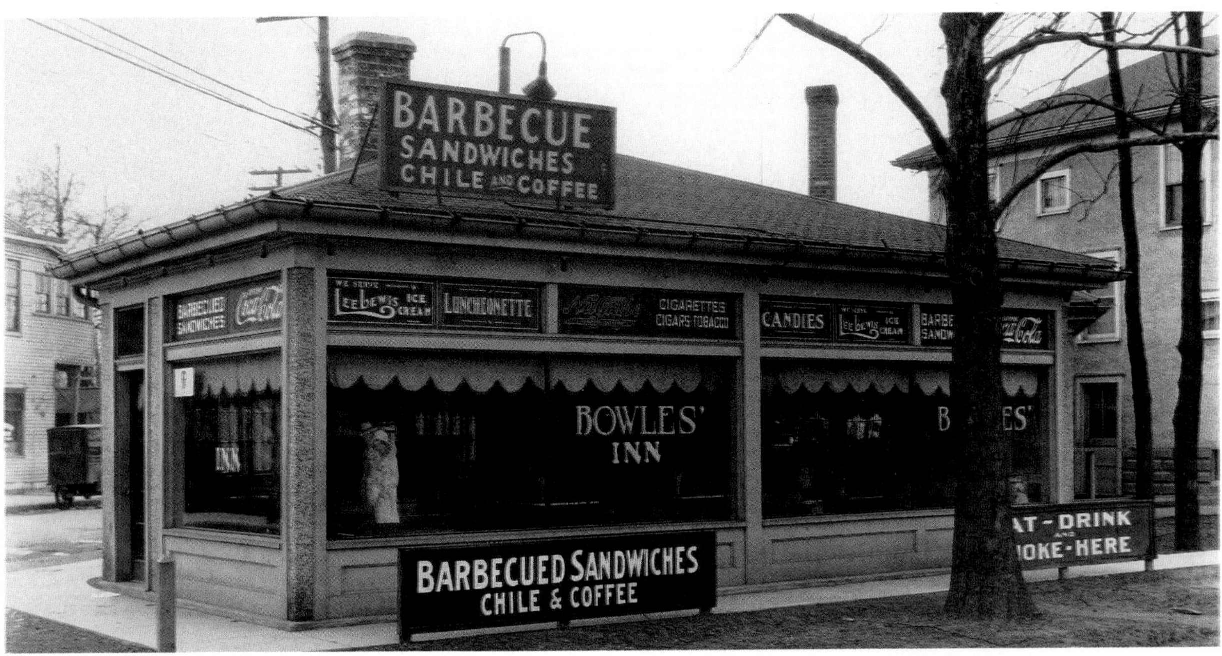

PROFESSIONAL BARBECUE EATER

Bob Moody has a lot of credits after his name. He's Director/Group Programming Services for Nationwide Communications Inc. He's former Billboard Magazine Radio Program Director of the Year. He's president of the Auchinleck (Scotland) Boswell Society and a member of the board of directors of the Country Music Association.

But the title the Arkansas native is proudest of is Professional Barbecue Eater. He never cooks the stuff, but what a time he has had practicing his craft of eating it.

"It is a measure of my respect for true barbecue genius that I don't attempt to imitate the skill that requires years of experience, perfectly adjusted equipment and a stoic disregard for time.

"No matter where I've traveled (with the exception of a few Northeastern states) I've been able to find some displaced Southerner who didn't mind spending all day hovering around a smoker. And I don't mind paying him for his time.

"That's the solemn duty of a dedicated barbecue eater. If you find someone whose pulled pork or pig-sicles inspire your awe, support his art. Show him how to apply for a grant. Buy a house in the neighborhood and move there if you have to.

"And if he walks by while you've got a mouthful, be sure to let your eyes roll back in your head and twitch both legs. It's really payment in full."

Poppy Seed Bread

3 cups flour
$1^1/_2$ teaspoons salt
$1^1/_2$ teaspoons baking powder
$2^1/_4$ cups sugar
3 tablespoons poppy seeds
3 eggs
$1^1/_2$ cups milk
$1^1/_8$ cups oil
$1^1/_2$ teaspoons vanilla
$1^1/_2$ teaspoons almond extract
$1^1/_2$ teaspoons butter extract

Mix all ingredients together and beat with mixer 2 minutes. Pour into 2 greased and floured loaf pans. Bake at 350 degrees for 1 hour. Let cool 5 minutes, then glaze in pan.

Glaze
$^1/_2$ teaspoon butter extract
$^1/_2$ teaspoon almond extract
$^1/_2$ teaspoon vanilla
$^1/_4$ cup orange juice
$^3/_4$ cup powdered sugar

Mix and pour over warm bread.

Whole-Wheat Bread

$^1/_3$ cup honey
1 cup milk
$^1/_4$ cup butter
2 eggs
1 teaspoon salt
$1^1/_2$ cups whole-wheat flour
1 cup all-purpose flour
1 tablespoon baking powder

Combine honey, milk and butter in a saucepan and cook over low heat, stirring constantly, until blended. Beat in remaining ingredients. Pour into greased loaf pan and bake at 350 degrees for 1 hour. Cool in pan 15 minutes before removing.

Angel Biscuits

1 package active dry yeast
2 tablespoons warm water (about 120 degrees)
5 cups all-purpose flour
1 teaspoon baking soda
3 teaspoons baking powder
2 tablespoons sugar
$1^1/_2$ teaspoons salt
1 cup shortening
2 cups buttermilk

Dissolve yeast in water. Sift dry ingredients into a large bowl. Cut in shortening with a pastry blender. Add buttermilk, then yeast mixture. Stir until thoroughly moistened. Turn onto a floured board and knead for 2 minutes. No rising is required.

Roll out to desired thickness and cut into rounds with a milk glass. Brush with melted butter and bake on an ungreased pan at 400 degrees for 12 minutes.

Mayonnaise Biscuits

1 cup self-rising flour
$^2/_3$ cup milk
2 tablespoons mayonnaise
4 tablespoons cooking oil

Slowly add milk to flour. Beat in mayonnaise. Put 1 teaspoon of cooking oil into each cup of muffin tin. Drop batter by spoonsful into each muffin cup until cup is half full. Bake at 350 degrees for 15 minutes.

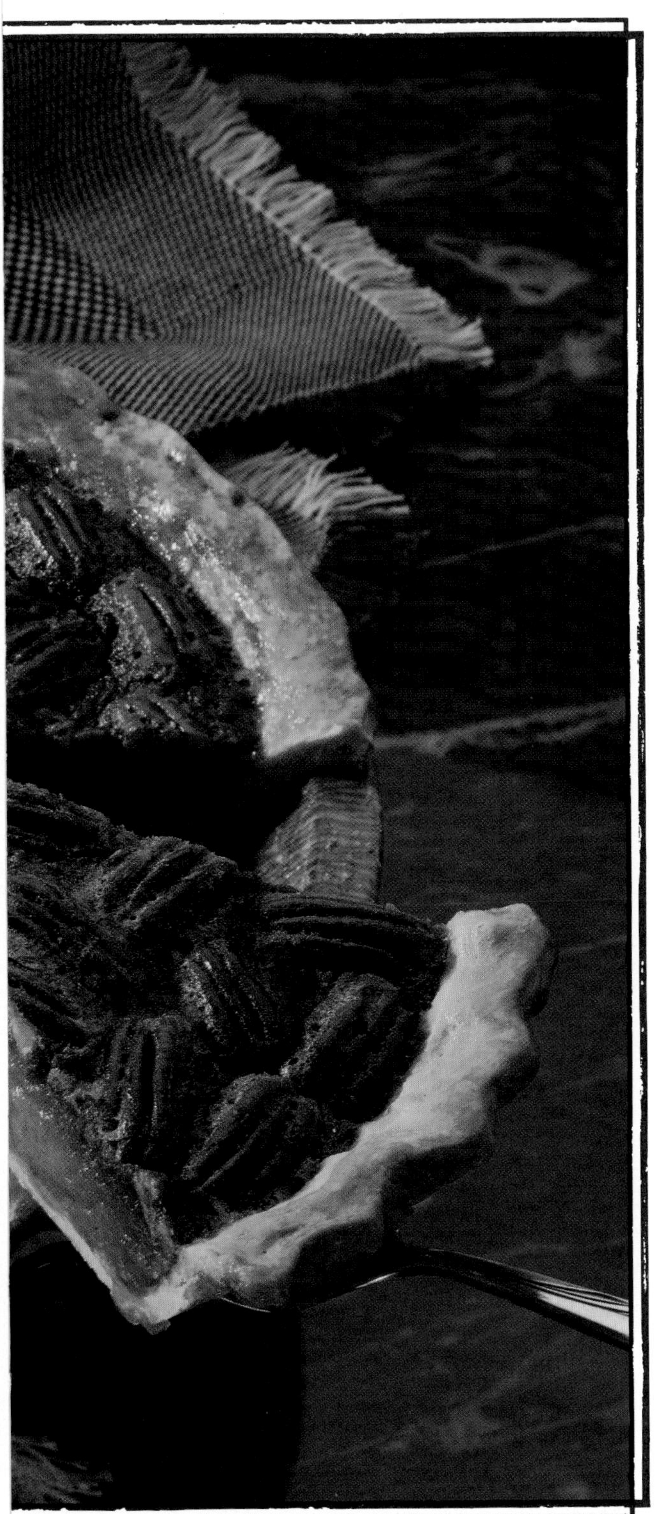

THE GREAT AMERICAN SLICE

It's out there, you know. The perfect pie. Homemade and cut in great big pieces by a little old lady, it's resting under a glass cover, glistening in its glass prison, almost willfully lascivious, dripping with sweetness and the concentrated essence of Mother Nature's bounty, resting atop a butter-rich crust that begs for the edge of a fork. It is a truly wondrous pie, steeped in nostalgia and yet still warm from the oven, a pie that in its making has, like Jack Daniel's Whiskey, translated years of care and tradition into a meltingly sensual mouthful. It would be the perfect pie, except for one serious problem.

You're not eating it.

You see, a perfect pie is lost without an appreciative audience, and that's where you come in: Barbecue lovers are the biggest connoisseurs of pie going. It's impossible to find a great barbecue joint that doesn't have a pie of some kind at the bottom of its menu. At Scott's in Goldsboro, North Carolina, it's lemon pie. Mark's Feed Store in Middletown, Kentucky, features buttermilk pie. Goldie's Trail Bar-B-Que in Vicksburg, Mississippi, offers pecan pie. Ollie's in Birmingham, Alabama, specializes in chocolate meringue. At Charlotte's Rib in St. Louis it's chocolate chess.

And just because pie is at the bottom of the menu doesn't mean it is a third-rate concoction. Pie is the last item on the menu because it is the perfect cap to a barbecue meal.

Graham Cracker Pie Crust

1½ cups graham cracker crumbs
¼ cup sugar
½ cup butter, melted

Mix well. Press firmly into 9-inch pie plate. For cooked crust bake at 375 degrees for 8 minutes. For uncooked crust, chill for 1 hour.

Cookie Pie Crust

½ cup chilled, unsalted butter, cut into pieces
¼ cup plus 1½ teaspoons sugar
1 tablespoon egg, beaten
1 cup plus 2 tablespoons flour

In a food processor, mince butter with sugar using on/off turns. Add egg and blend until combined. Add flour and blend using on/off turns until mixture resembles coarse meal. Gather dough into a ball. Flatten into a disk. Wrap in plastic and refrigerate at least 30 minutes. (Pastry can be prepared a day in advance. Let dough soften at room temperature before continuing).

Heat oven to 350 degrees. Roll dough out on heavily floured surface to ¼-inch thickness. Transfer dough to a 9-inch pie pan. Pat into place, being sure to cover inside of pan completely.

Butter a large piece of foil. Place foil buttered side down on dough. Fill with dried beans or pie weights. (This is very important. Dough around the edges will melt down into the bottom of the pan if this step isn't taken.) Bake until sides set, about 12 minutes.

Carefully remove weights and foil. Pierce dough with fork. Bake until pale golden brown, about 5 minutes. Cool on rack. (This crust tastes like a delicious sugar cookie.)

Pies

Willie Boy's Cherry Pie

1 9-inch unbaked pie shell and top crust
3 cups pitted cherries
1½ cups sugar
¼ cup flour
Dash salt
2 tablespoons butter
1 teaspoon almond extract
1 tablespoon Jack Daniel's Whiskey

Combine cherries, sugar, flour and salt and pour into unbaked pie shell. Dot with butter. Sprinkle with Jack Daniel's. Add lattice top crust. Bake at 425 degrees for 40 minutes.

Tifton Pecan Pie

1 9-inch unbaked pie shell
4 tablespoons butter
4 eggs
3/4 cup sugar
1 1/4 cups white corn syrup
1 tablespoon vanilla
1 cup pecans, chopped
1/4 cup Jack Daniel's Whiskey

Melt butter. Beat eggs and stir in sugar and syrup. Add melted butter, vanilla and pecans. Pour into unbaked pie shell. Bake at 325 degrees for 25 minutes.

Checkmate Chess Pie

1 9-inch unbaked pie shell
3 tablespoons flour
3 cups brown sugar
3 tablespoons butter, melted
3 eggs, beaten
1 cup evaporated milk
1 1/2 teaspoons vanilla

Mix flour and sugar. Add melted butter, beaten eggs, milk and vanilla. Pour into unbaked pie shell. Bake in 325-degree oven for 30 minutes or until done.

Savannah Peach Pie

1 9-inch unbaked pie shell
3/4 cup sugar
3 tablespoons flour
1/4 cup cinnamon
Dash salt
5 cups sliced fresh peaches
2 tablespoons butter
1 tablespoon Jack Daniel's Whiskey

Combine sugar, flour, cinnamon and salt. Add to peaches. Mix lightly. Fill unbaked pie shell. Dot with butter. Add top crust and crimp edges. Bake in 400-degree oven for 40 minutes.

Debbie's Key Lime Pie

1 9-inch baked pie shell
1 13-oz. can sweetened condensed milk
4 eggs, separated
1/2 cup lime juice
6 tablespoons sugar
1/2 teaspoon cream of tartar

In a mixing bowl combine condensed milk, egg yolks and lime juice. Beat 1 egg white until stiff. Fold into mixture and pour into baked pie shell. Beat 3 egg whites and slowly add sugar and cream of tartar. Spread meringue over filling.

Bake at 350 degrees for 20 minutes, or until egg whites turn golden brown. Chill before serving.

Sidewalk Lemonade Chiffon

Graham cracker crust (for 9-inch pie)
2/3 cup sugar
1 envelope unflavored gelatin
1/4 teaspoon salt
3 eggs, separated
1/2 cup cold water
1 6-ounce can frozen lemonade concentrate
1/2 cup whipping cream, whipped

Combine 1/3 cup sugar, gelatin and salt in medium saucepan. Add egg yolks and water and mix well. Cook over low heat until gelatin dissolves and mixture thickens slightly. Add lemonade and stir until dissolved and well-blended. Refrigerate until slightly thickened. Beat egg whites until foamy and add remaining 1/3 cup sugar gradually, beating until stiff peaks form. Fold into lemonade mixture. Fold in whipped cream. Pour into crust and chill until set, about 3 hours.

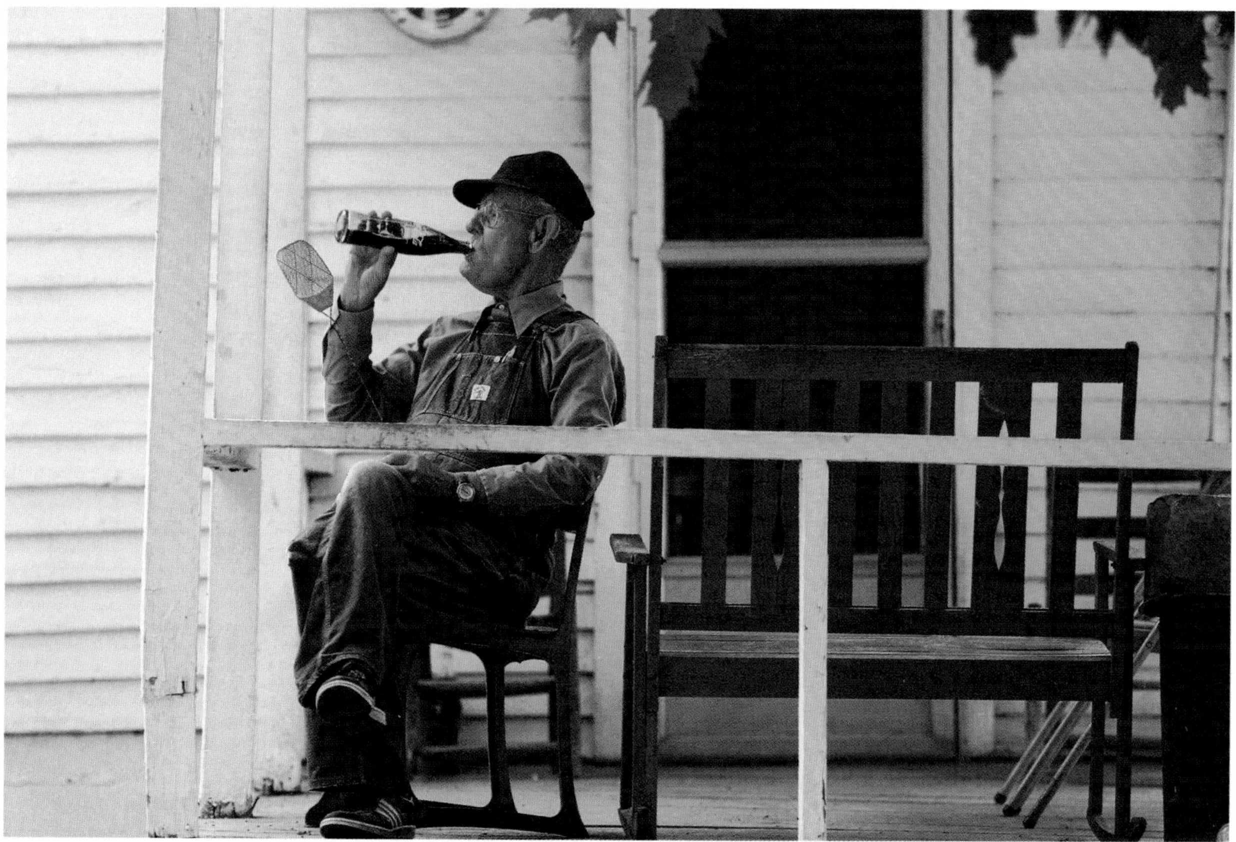

BUFORD LEECH'S BUTTERMILK PIE

3 9-inch unbaked pie shells
1/2 cup butter, melted
3 cups sugar
3 eggs
1/4 cup flour
1/2 teaspoon baking soda
1/2 teaspoon lemon juice
2 cups buttermilk
1/2 teaspoon vanilla

Cream butter, sugar and eggs thoroughly. Add flour and blend well. Mix soda, lemon juice, buttermilk and vanilla. Blend into the first mixture. Pour into an unbaked pie shell and bake at 450 degrees for 10 minutes. Reduce heat to 300 degrees and continue to bake for 30 minutes.

PLAINS' PEANUT BUTTER PIE

1 9-inch baked pie shell
1 8-ounce package cream cheese
1 cup confectioners' sugar
1/2 cup peanut butter
1/2 cup milk
1 8-ounce container frozen whipped topping

Using an electric mixer beat the cream cheese, confectioners' sugar and peanut butter until well-blended. Stir in milk. Then add frozen whipped topping and beat until fluffy. Pour into baked crust. Place in refrigerator or freezer until ready to serve. Serve frozen.

Dear Mother Butterscotch Pie

1 9-inch baked pie shell
1 stick butter
1/2 cup light brown sugar
4 egg yolks
5 1/2 tablespoons flour
1 1/2 cups milk
1 teaspoon vanilla

Melt butter in top of double boiler. Add brown sugar. Remove from heat.

Add egg yolks, flour and milk.

Bring to a boil. Then place over boiling water for 15 minutes. Remove from heat and add 1 teaspoon vanilla. Mix well. Pour into baked pie shell.

Meringue
4 egg whites
1/2 cup sugar

Beat until stiff. Spread meringue on top and bake at 350 degrees for 10 minutes or until golden brown.

Granny Good's Boston Cream Pie

1/3 cup shortening
2/3 cup sugar
2 eggs
1 cup flour
1 teaspoon baking powder
Dash salt
1/2 cup milk
1/4 teaspoon vanilla extract

Cream shortening. Slowly add sugar, beating until light and fluffy. Add eggs, 1 at a time, beating well after each.

Combine flour, baking powder and salt. Add to creamed mixture alternately with milk, starting and finishing with flour mixture. Stir in vanilla. Pour batter into a greased and floured 9-inch round cake pan. Bake at 325 degrees for 25 minutes. Cool in pan 10 minutes. Remove from pan and cool completely.

Split cake layer in half horizontally to make 2 layers. Spread cream filling between layers and spread chocolate glaze on top. Refrigerate.

Cream filling
1/2 cup sugar
1/4 cup cornstarch
1/4 teaspoon salt
2 cups milk
4 egg yolks, slightly beaten
1/2 teaspoon vanilla extract

Combine sugar, cornstarch and salt in a saucepan. Slowly add milk. Stir with wire whisk until blended. Cook over medium heat, stirring constantly until mixture comes to a boil. Boil, stirring constantly, until thickened (about 1 minute). Remove from heat.

Slowly stir 1/4 of hot mixture into egg yolks. Add to remaining hot mixture, stirring constantly. Return to medium heat and bring to a boil, stirring constantly. Boil, stirring constantly, until thickened and smooth (about 1 minute). Stir in vanilla. Cool. Spread between layers.

Chocolate glaze
2 tablespoons butter
2 tablespoons cocoa
1 cup confectioners' sugar
3 tablespoons boiling water

Combine butter and cocoa over boiling water in top of double boiler. Cook until chocolate melts. Cool slightly. Add sugar and water and beat until smooth. Spread over cake.

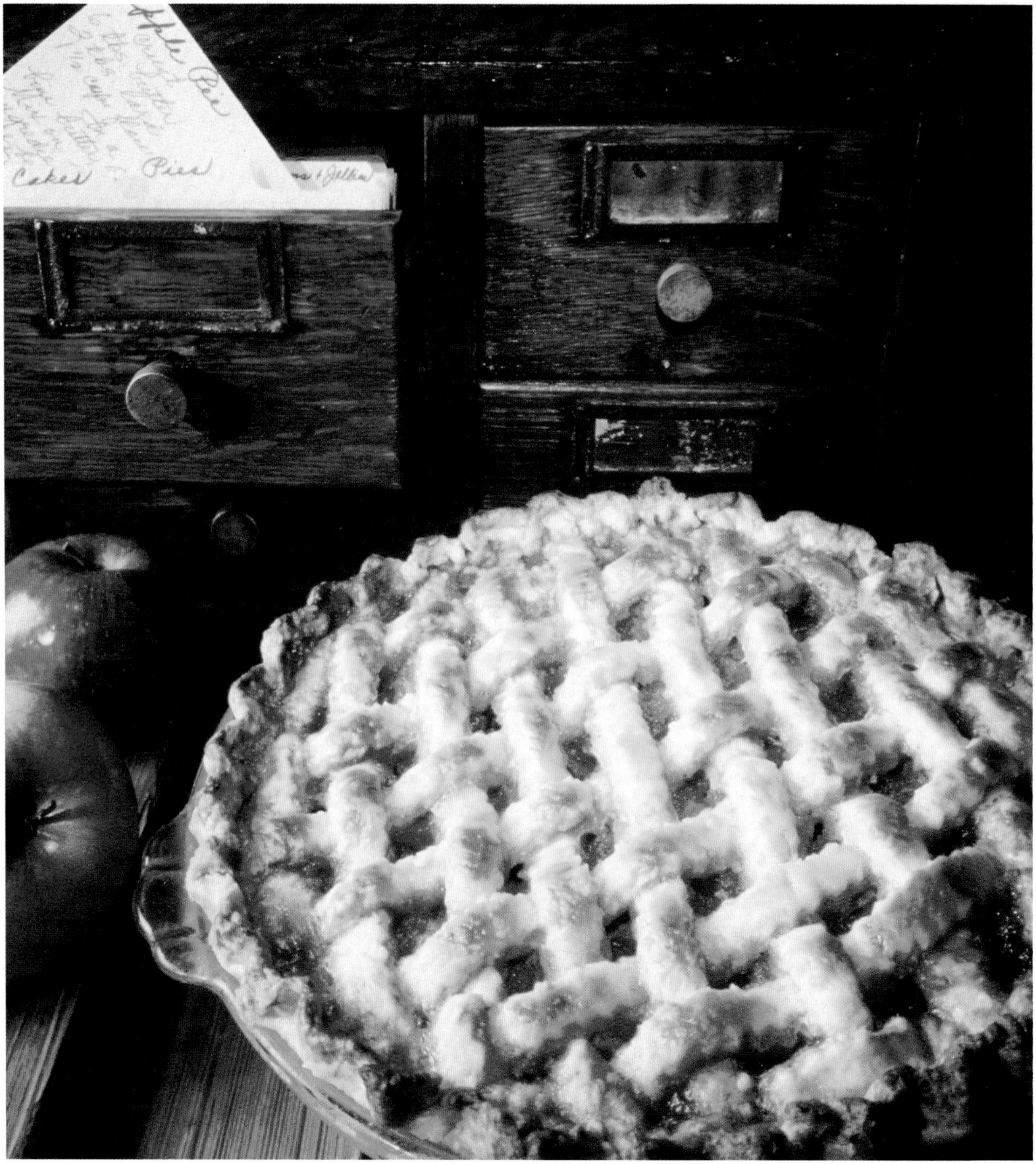

Company's Coming Apple Pie

1 9-inch unbaked pie shell and top crust
6 apples
1 cup sugar
2 tablespoons flour
1 teaspoon cinnamon
Dash nutmeg
Dash salt
2 tablespoons butter

Pare apples and slice thin. Combine sugar, flour, spices and salt and mix with apples. Pour into pie shell. Dot with butter. Add top crust and sprinkle with sugar. Bake in 400-degree oven for 45 minutes.

Mammy's Double Peanut Butter Pie

1½ cups milk
1 package regular vanilla pudding mix (4-serving size)
⅓ cup peanut butter

Slowly stir milk into pudding mix. Microwave 5 to 6 minutes on high, stirring after 3 minutes. Stir in peanut butter. Cool slightly and pour into peanut butter-graham cracker crust. Cover with waxed paper or clear plastic wrap. Chill.

Peanut Butter Graham Cracker Crust
3 tablespoons butter
1¼ cups crushed graham crackers
¼ cup peanut butter
2 tablespoons sugar

In 9-inch glass pie plate, microwave butter for 30 seconds or till melted. Add graham cracker crumbs, peanut butter and sugar. Mix well. Press mixture onto bottom and sides of pie plate. Microwave 1½ to 2 minutes. Set aside to cool.

Oh Baby Chocolate Pie

1 9-inch unbaked pie shell
1 stick butter, melted
¼ cup flour
¼ cup cocoa
1 cup sugar
¼ teaspoon vanilla
2 eggs

Mix ingredients and pour into unbaked pie shell.

Bake 25 minutes at 350 degrees.

Laura Maiura's Shoo Fly Pie

1 9-inch unbaked pie shell
2 cups flour
1 cup sugar
½ teaspoon ginger
½ teaspoon allspice
2 tablespoons shortening
2 tablespoons Jack Daniel's Whiskey
1 teaspoon baking soda
¾ cup boiling water
4 tablespoons dark Karo syrup

Sift flour, sugar, ginger and allspice together, then add shortening. Mix with a pastry blender or fork and make crumbs. Take out a handful to use as topping on pie.

Put baking soda in boiling water and add to Karo. Blend liquids with flour mixture and pour into unbaked pie shell. Top with reserved topping. Bake at 350 degrees for about 1 hour.

Banana-ma Jack Cream Pie

1 9-inch baked pie shell
$^{3}/_{4}$ cup sugar
$^{1}/_{3}$ cup flour
Dash salt
2 cups milk
2 slightly beaten egg yolks
2 tablespoons butter
2 teaspoons Jack Daniel's Whiskey
1 cup miniature marshmallows
3 bananas

Combine sugar, flour and salt in a saucepan. Slowly stir in milk. Cook over medium heat, stirring constantly, until mixture boils and thickens. Cook 2 more minutes; remove from heat. Stir small amount of hot mixture into egg yolks. Pour egg yolk mixture into hot mixture. Cook 2 minutes, stirring constantly. Remove from heat. Add butter, Jack Daniel's and marshmallows. Stir until marshmallows are dissolved. Cool to room temperature. Slice 3 bananas and put on baked pie shell. Pour in cream filling. Add meringue.

Meringue
3 egg whites
$^{1}/_{4}$ teaspoon cream of tartar
1 teaspoon Jack Daniel's Whiskey
6 tablespoons sugar

Beat egg whites with cream of tartar and whiskey until soft peaks form. Slowly add sugar, beating until stiff peaks form and all sugar is dissolved. Spread over pie, sealing to pastry. Bake at 350 degrees for 12 minutes or until meringue is golden brown. Cool.

Lynchburg Checker Club Chocolate Chip Pie

1 9-inch unbaked pie shell
2 eggs, beaten
$^{1}/_{2}$ cup butter, melted and cooled
$^{1}/_{2}$ teaspoon salt
1 cup sugar
$^{3}/_{4}$ cup flour
$^{3}/_{4}$ cup chocolate chips
$^{3}/_{4}$ cup pecans, chopped
1 teaspoon vanilla
2 tablespoons Jack Daniel's Whiskey

Mix ingredients in order. Pour into unbaked pie shell. Bake at 325 degrees for 1 hour or until done.

Maggie's Coconut Cream Pie

1 9-inch baked pie shell
3/4 cup sugar
1/3 cup flour
Dash salt
2 cups milk
2 slightly beaten egg yolks
2 tablespoons butter
2 teaspoons Jack Daniel's Whiskey
1 cup miniature marshmallows
1 1/3 cups flaked coconut

Combine sugar, flour and salt in a saucepan. Slowly stir in milk. Cook over medium heat, stirring constantly, until mixture boils and thickens. Cook 2 more minutes, remove from heat. Stir small amount of hot mixture into egg yolks. Pour egg yolk mixture into hot mixture. Cook 2 minutes, stirring constantly. Remove from heat. Add butter, Jack Daniel's and marshmallows. Stir until marshmallows are dissolved. Stir in 1 cup flaked coconut. Cool to room temperature. Pour into baked pie shell. Add meringue.

Meringue
3 egg whites
1/4 teaspoon cream of tartar
1/2 teaspoon vanilla
6 tablespoons sugar

Beat egg whites with cream of tartar and vanilla until soft peaks form. Slowly add sugar, beating until stiff peaks form and all sugar is dissolved. Spread over pie, sealing to pastry. Sprinkle 1/3 cup flaked coconut over meringue before browning. Bake at 350 degrees for 12 minutes or until meringue is golden brown. Cool.

Wampler's Chocolate Meringue Pie

1 9-inch baked pie shell
1 cup sugar
1/3 cup cocoa
1/3 cup flour
Dash salt
2 egg yolks
2 cups milk
1/4 cup butter
1/4 teaspoon vanilla extract

Combine sugar, cocoa, flour and salt in saucepan, stirring to remove lumps. Reserve egg whites for meringue. Combine egg yolks and milk in a mixing bowl. Mix well. Slowly add milk mixture to cocoa mixture, stirring until blended. Cook over medium heat, stirring constantly, until mixture thickens and comes to a boil. Cook 1 minute, stirring constantly. Remove from heat. Add butter and vanilla, stirring until butter melts. Pour into baked pie shell.

Meringue
2 egg whites
1/4 teaspoon vanilla extract
1/4 cup sugar

Combine egg whites and vanilla. Beat until foamy. Slowly add sugar, 1 teaspoon at a time, beating until stiff peaks form. Spread over pie, sealing to edge of pastry shell. Bake at 400 degrees for 10 minutes.

MOUTH-WATERING DESSERTS

Barbecue is a heavy meal. Many a fellow has been known to head for a comfortable sofa and a soft pillow after consuming a full meal of barbecue.

Nothing wrong with that. A couple of sandwiches of great barbecue's enough to put a bear to sleep. But if you can fight off those forty winks for a few minutes, you'll find your reward well worth it.

In Tennessee we like to call it dessert. And it was dessert that spawned that old saying: saving the best till last.

AUNT IDA'S APPLE CRISP

1 20-ounce can apple pie filling
1/4 cup flour
1 cup old-fashioned oats
1 cup brown sugar
1/4 teaspoon salt
1 teaspoon cinnamon
1/4 teaspoon nutmeg
6 tablespoons butter

Pour apple pie filling in shallow 1-quart baking dish. In bowl combine flour, oats, sugar, salt and spices. Add butter and mix well. Spread topping evenly over pie filling. Bake at 375 degrees for 30 minutes.

Aunt Myrtle's Angel Food Cake

1 cup flour
1 1/4 cups confectioners' sugar
12 egg whites
1 1/2 teaspoons cream of tartar
1/4 teaspoon salt
1 1/2 teaspoons vanilla
1/4 teaspoon almond extract
1 cup sugar

Sift flour with confectioners' sugar 3 times. Beat egg whites with cream of tartar, salt, vanilla and almond extract until soft peaks form. Beat in sugar, 2 tablespoons at a time. Continue until meringue holds stiff peaks. Sift 1/4 of flour mixture over whites. Fold in lightly with up-and-down motion, turning the bowl. Fold in remaining flour mixture by fourths. Bake in ungreased 10-inch tube pan at 375 degrees for 30 minutes.

Buffalo Mountain Sweet Potato Pudding

3 cups grated sweet potatoes
1 1/2 cups sugar
3/4 cup buttermilk
1/4 cup sweet milk
1/4 cup Jack Daniel's Whiskey
1/2 teaspoon cinnamon
1/2 teaspoon cloves
1/2 stick butter, melted
1/2 cup chopped pecans
1/2 teaspoon salt
2 eggs, well-beaten
Grated orange zest (orange part of rind only)

Mix ingredients in order and bake in 9x13-inch pan at 300 degrees for 1 hour.

Dinner-on-the-Ground Coconut Cake

1 cup shortening
2 cups sugar
3 cups flour
1 teaspoon salt
1/2 teaspoon baking soda
1 teaspoon baking powder
1 cup buttermilk
1 teaspoon vanilla
1 teaspoon lemon extract
1 teaspoon coconut extract
5 egg whites, unbeaten

Cream shortening and sugar. Sift together remaining dry ingredients and add to sugar mixture alternately with buttermilk. Add vanilla, lemon and coconut extracts. Add egg whites last and beat. Makes 3 layers. Bake at 325 degrees for 20 minutes.

Filling
1 cup sugar
1 1/2 cups water
1/2 teaspoon vanilla
1/2 teaspoon lemon extract
1/2 teaspoon coconut extract
2 cups fresh or flaked coconut

Heat sugar and water until soft boil. Remove from heat and add vanilla, lemon extract and coconut extract. Add coconut. Let sit while making icing.

Icing
2 1/2 cups sugar
1/2 cup corn syrup
1/2 cup hot water
2 egg whites
2 tablespoons confectioners' sugar

Combine sugar, corn syrup and water in saucepan and boil until mixture begins to thicken. Remove from heat. Beat egg whites until stiff. Slowly pour syrup over egg whites until mixture begins to thicken. Add confectioners' sugar to stiffen. If too stiff add hot water one drop at a time.

Put bottom layer on plate. Pierce cake with fork tines. Spread coconut filling over cake. Spread a small amount of icing on bottom of next layer before putting it on. Do top layer same way. Ice entire cake and sprinkle coconut on top.

Carrie's Chocolate Pound Cake

3 cups sugar
2 sticks butter
5 eggs (room temperature)
3 cups flour
5 tablespoons cocoa
1/2 teaspoon salt
1/2 teaspoon baking powder
1 cup milk
1/2 cup cooking oil
1 tablespoon vanilla

Mix sugar and butter. Add eggs one at a time. Mix the remaining dry ingredients. Alternately add dry ingredients and milk to sugar mixture. Add cooking oil and vanilla last. Mix well. Bake in a greased and floured tube pan or bundt pan at 300 degrees for 1 hour and 20 minutes.

Icing
1 16-ounce box confectioners' sugar
1 8-ounce package cream cheese (room temperature)
1 stick butter (room temperature)
1 teaspoon vanilla
5 tablespoons cocoa

Mix well. Ice cake when cake is completely cool.

Reunion Rhubarb Coffee Cake

1/2 cup sugar
1 cup brown sugar
1/2 cup butter
1 large egg
1 cup buttermilk
2 cups flour
1 teaspoon baking soda
1 1/2 cups uncooked rhubarb (cut fine and sprinkle with flour)
3/4 cup pecans

Beat sugar, brown sugar, butter and egg. Add the buttermilk, flour, soda, rhubarb and nuts. Pour into 2 9-inch cake pans or 1 9x13-inch pan, greased and floured. Sprinkle with topping. Bake at 350 degrees for 30-40 minutes.

Topping
1/3 cup sugar
1/2 teaspoon cinnamon

Mix and sprinkle on top of batter.

Bess & Maude's Quick Cobbler

1/2 stick butter
1 cup flour
1 teaspoon baking powder
Dash salt
1 cup sugar
2/3 cup milk
1 quart any kind of fruit (sweetened)

Melt butter in pan. Mix flour, baking powder, salt and sugar. Mix with butter and milk. Pour into pan. Put fruit on top of batter. Bake at 350 degrees for 30-40 minutes.

Little Alton's Apple Dumplings

2 cups flour
2 teaspoons baking soda
1 teaspoon salt
2/3 cup shortening
1/2 cup milk
6 apples, peeled and cored

Sift together dry ingredients. Cut in shortening until mixture looks like crumbs. Add milk and stir until flour is moist.

On a lightly-floured surface roll dough until about 1/4-inch thick. Cut into squares. Put whole apple in each square. Sprinkle with sugar, cinnamon and nutmeg; dot with butter. Moisten edges of squares and fold in to center. Pinch edges together. Place in an ungreased baking pan. Pour syrup (recipe follows) over dumplings, then sprinkle with sugar. Bake at 375 degrees for 35 minutes.

Apple dumpling syrup
1 1/4 cups sugar
2 cups water
1/2 teaspoon cinnamon
1/4 cup butter

Mix sugar, water and cinnamon and cook 5 minutes but do not boil. Add butter.

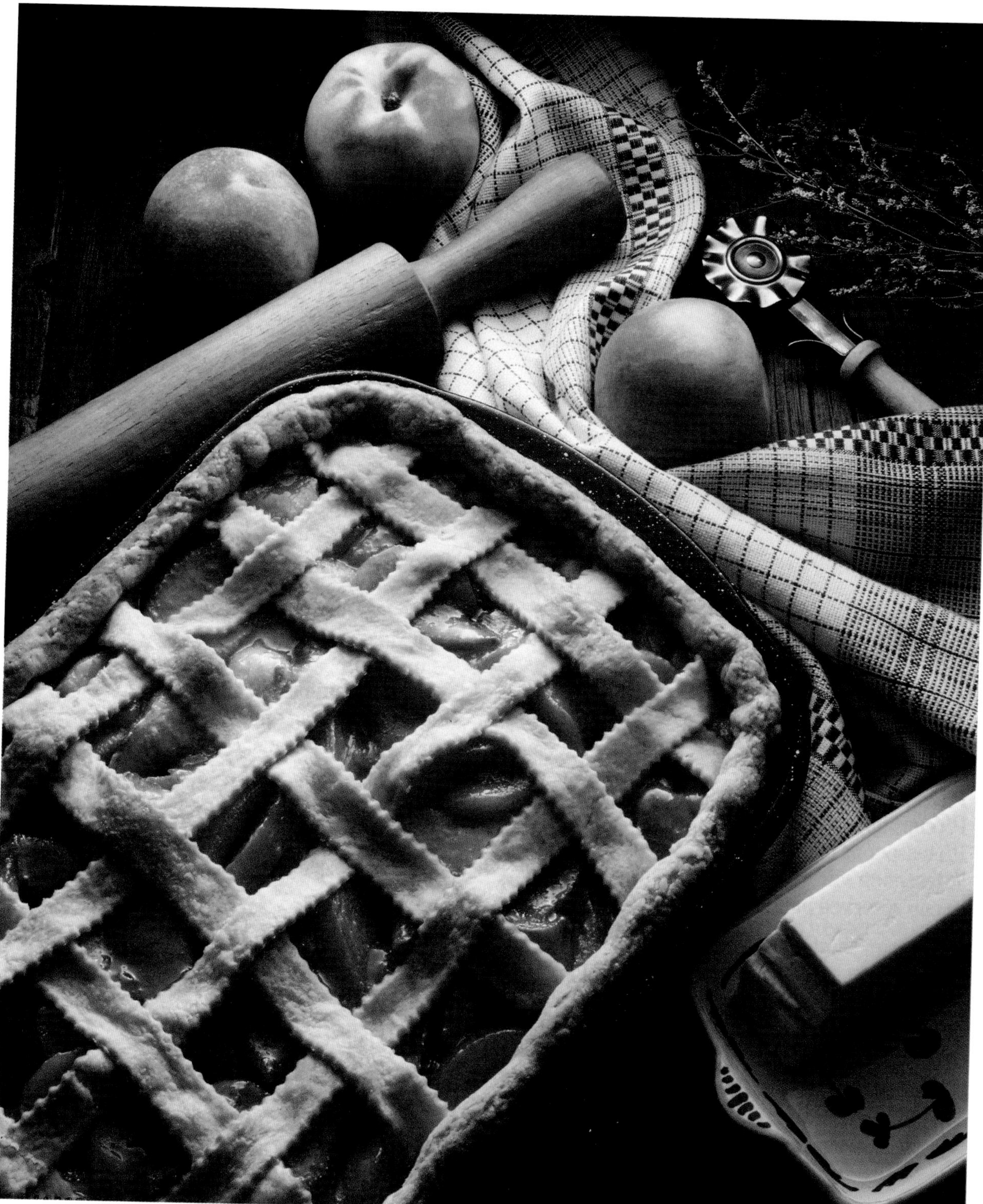

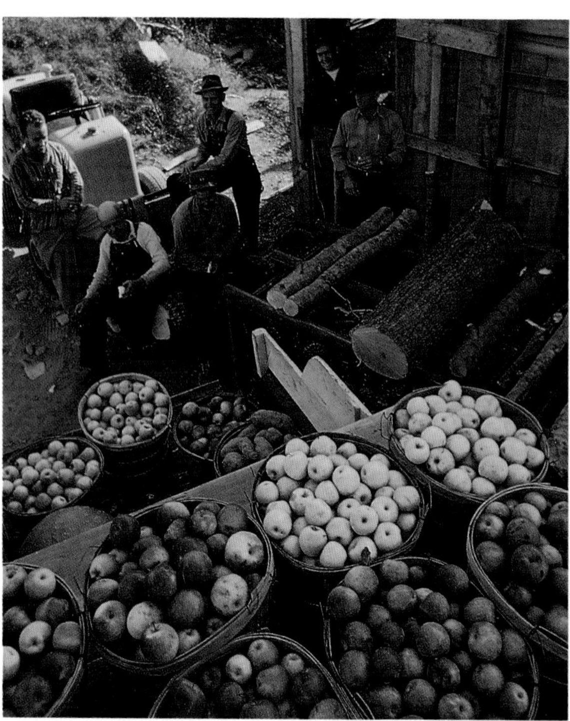

Viney's Cheesecake

1 8-ounce package cream cheese, softened
1 pint sour cream
1 cup sugar
2 eggs, beaten
1 teaspoon vanilla

Crust
1½ cups graham cracker crumbs
½ cup butter
1 teaspoon cinnamon

Mix cream cheese and sour cream. Beat until smooth. Add sugar, eggs and vanilla. Beat well. Butter 9-inch springform pan and add mixture of crumbs, butter and cinnamon, patting them down to form a crust. Pour cheese mixture over top. Bake at 350 degrees for 45 minutes.

Poe Family Apple Cake

1 cup vegetable oil
3 eggs
2 cups sugar
3 cups flour
½ teaspoon salt
1 teaspoon baking soda
2 teaspoons baking powder
1 tablespoon cinnamon
3 cups apples, peeled and chopped
¼ cup Jack Daniel's Whiskey
½ cup chopped pecans

Mix oil, eggs and sugar and beat until creamy. Sift dry ingredients and add to mixture. Add apples, Jack Daniel's and pecans. Mix well. Bake in a greased and floured tube pan at 350 degrees for 1 hour and 20 minutes.

Glaze
¼ cup brown sugar, packed
2 tablespoons butter
1 tablespoon evaporated milk

Combine ingredients in saucepan. Bring to a boil and cook, stirring constantly, for 2 minutes. Reduce temperature. Drizzle lukewarm mixture over cake.

Uncle Ron's Fruit and Cream

4 fresh peaches, peeled and sliced
2 tablespoons sugar
1 14-ounce can sweetened condensed milk
¼ cup lemon juice
¼ cup heavy cream, whipped
2 tablespoons Jack Daniel's Whiskey

Sprinkle peaches with sugar and set aside.

Beat sweetened condensed milk with the lemon juice until thick. Add in peaches, whipped cream and Jack Daniel's.

SPLATTER CREEK BREAD PUDDING

1 cup sugar
2 cups cream or milk
2 cups bread crumbs
2 whole eggs plus 3 egg yolks
Few grains of salt
1/4 teaspoon cinnamon
1/4 teaspoon allspice
2 teaspoons vanilla
4 tablespoons butter, melted
1 cup raisins

Mix together and bake in a 325-degree oven for 30 minutes or until done.

Jack Sauce
2 sticks butter, melted
2 cups confectioners' sugar
2 large eggs
1 ounce Jack Daniel's Whiskey

Melt butter. Whip in confectioners' sugar. Fold in eggs. Add whiskey. Serve warm over bread pudding.

JACK'S BROWNIES

3/4 cup sifted flour
1/4 teaspoon baking soda
1/4 teaspoon salt
1/2 cup sugar
1/3 cup shortening
2 tablespoons water
1 6 ounce-package chocolate chips
1 teaspoon vanilla
2 eggs
1/3 cup Jack Daniel's Whiskey
1 1/2 cups nuts

Sift flour, soda and salt together. Combine sugar, shortening and water and cook over low heat to boiling point, stirring constantly. Remove from heat. Add chocolate chips and vanilla. Stir until smooth. Add eggs, 1 at a time, beating well. Add flour mixture and nuts. Stir well. Pour into greased 9-inch pan. Bake at 325 degrees for 30 minutes. Sprinkle with Jack Daniel's. Frost with white frosting and chocolate glaze.

White Frosting
1/2 cup butter
1 teaspoon vanilla
2 cups confectioners' sugar

Combine butter and vanilla. Beat until creamy. Slowly add sugar. Beat until smooth. Spread on cooled brownies.

Chocolate Glaze
1 6-ounce package chocolate chips
1 tablespoon butter

Melt chocolate chips and butter over hot water. Spread over white frosting. Chill until firm. Cut into 1-inch squares.

CHURCH HILL CHOCOLATE SHEET CAKE

2 cups flour
2 cups sugar
1 cup butter
5 tablespoons cocoa
1 cup water
1/2 cup buttermilk
2 eggs
1 teaspoon baking soda
1 teaspoon vanilla

Sift flour and sugar in mixing bowl. In a saucepan bring butter, cocoa and water to a boil. After it boils pour over sugar and flour mixture. Add buttermilk, eggs, soda and vanilla and mix well. Pour into well-greased jellyroll pan and bake at 400 degrees for 20 minutes. Test at 18 minutes.

Icing
1/2 cup butter
1/4 cup water
2 tablespoons cocoa
6 tablespoons sugar
1 box confectioners' sugar
1 teaspoon vanilla
1 cup chopped pecans

Start 5 minutes before cake is done.

Mix butter, water, cocoa and sugar and bring to a boil. Pour hot mixture over confectioners' sugar. Add vanilla and pecans.

Pour on while cake is hot.

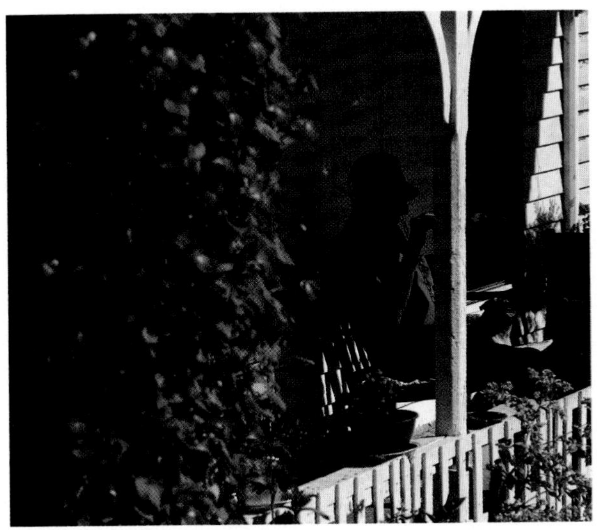

Tennessee Mud Cake

2 sticks butter
1/2 cup cocoa
2 cups sugar
4 eggs, slightly beaten
1 1/2 cups flour
Pinch of salt
1 1/2 cups chopped pecans
1 teaspoon vanilla
Miniature marshmallows

Melt butter and cocoa together. Stir in sugar and eggs. Mix well. Add flour, salt and chopped pecans. Beat in vanilla. Mix well. Spoon batter into a greased 13x9x2-inch pan and bake at 350 degrees for 35 minutes. Sprinkle miniature marshmallows on top of warm cake. Cover with chocolate frosting.

Chocolate frosting
1 16-ounce box confectioners' sugar
1/2 cup milk
1/3 cup cocoa
1/2 stick butter

Mix until smooth and spread over hot cake.

Red & Fred's Red Velvet Cake

1 1/2 cups sugar
1 cup shortening
2 eggs
2 tablespoons cocoa
1 2-ounce bottle red food coloring
2 1/4 cups flour
1 teaspoon salt
1 cup buttermilk
1 teaspoon vanilla
1 teaspoon baking soda
1 tablespoon vinegar

Cream sugar and shortening. Add eggs and beat well. Make a paste of cocoa and food coloring. Blend into creamed mixture. Combine flour and salt. Add alternately to creamed mixture with buttermilk and vanilla. Add soda alternately with vinegar. Bake in 2 round 9-inch layer pans which are well-greased and floured. Bake at 350 degrees for 20 minutes. When cool, slice layers horizontally and frost. Makes 2 layers.

Frosting
3 tablespoons flour
1 cup milk
1 cup butter
1 cup sugar
1 teaspoon vanilla

At low heat cook flour and milk, stirring constantly until thick. Cool. Cream butter, sugar and vanilla until fluffy. Add to flour mixture and beat until consistency of whipped cream. Spread between each layer and on top of cake. Sprinkle with coconut or nuts.

Joyce's Tennessee Toddy Cake

1 pound box white raisins
1/2 pound box chopped dates
2 cups Jack Daniel's Whiskey
1 cup brown sugar
2 cups granulated sugar
3 sticks butter
6 eggs, beaten separately
5 cups sifted flour
2 teaspoons nutmeg
1 teaspoon baking powder
1 pound bag shelled pecans

Soak raisins and dates in Jack Daniel's Whiskey and cover overnight. Grease a 10-inch tube pan. Line the bottom only with brown paper and grease again. Cream sugars and butter until fluffy. Add egg yolks and beat well. Add the soaked fruit and remaining liquid.

Reserve a small amount of flour for the nuts and add remaining flour to mixture. Add the nutmeg and baking powder. Beat egg whites until stiff but not dry. Fold into batter. Add the floured pecans last. Pour into prepared pan. Bake at 275 degrees for about 3 1/2 hours or until cake tester comes out clean. Do not overcook. Cool thoroughly on a wire rack. Remove from pan and stuff the center hole with a whiskey soaked cloth. Wrap in heavy foil and store in the refrigerator. Let mellow for 3 weeks before serving. Slice thin to serve.

Jack's Jam Cake

2 cups sugar
1½ cups butter, softened
6 eggs
3 cups flour
1 teaspoon baking soda
4 teaspoons cocoa
1 teaspoon cinnamon
1 teaspoon allspice
1 teaspoon cloves
½ cup buttermilk
1 teaspoon vanilla
2 cups blackberry jam (seedless)
¼ cup Jack Daniel's Whiskey

Cream the sugar and butter. Add eggs, 1 at a time, beating after each. Sift together flour and baking soda. Stir into flour mixture cocoa, cinnamon, allspice and cloves. Add flour mixture and buttermilk alternately to butter mixture. Stir in vanilla, jam and Jack Daniel's. Bake in 9-inch pan at 350 degrees for 30 minutes. Makes 6 layers.

Filling
2 8-ounce packages figs, chopped
1 cup sugar
1½ cups water

Cook until thick. Cool and spread between layers with icing.

Caramel Icing
½ cup butter
1 cup brown sugar
¼ teaspoon salt
¼ cup evaporated milk
2½ cups confectioners' sugar
1 teaspoon vanilla

Melt butter in saucepan. Blend in brown sugar and salt. Cook over low heat 2 minutes, stirring constantly. Add evaporated milk. Continue stirring until mixture comes to a boil. Remove from heat. Blend in confectioners' sugar. Add vanilla. Thin with milk if needed. Spread on cake and between layers.

Jack's Spice Cake

2 cups brown sugar
½ cup oil
2 eggs
2 teaspoons cinnamon
1 teaspoon baking soda
1 teaspoon allspice
1 teaspoon nutmeg
½ teaspoon ginger
¾ cup buttermilk
1 teaspoon salt
2 cups flour
¼ cup Jack Daniel's Whiskey

Mix together and bake in a greased and floured tube or bundt pan at 350 degrees for 40 minutes.

Jack Daniel's Glaze
2 cups confectioners' sugar
1 tablespoon butter
2 teaspoons Jack Daniel's Whiskey
Enough milk to make a thin glaze

Mix ingredients together and pour over cooled cake.

Cousin Brenda's Pineapple Cake

2 eggs
2 cups sugar
1 teaspoon vanilla
1 16-ounce can crushed pineapple, undrained
2 teaspoons baking soda
2 cups flour
1/2 cup chopped pecans

Beat eggs in mixing bowl until foamy. Add sugar, vanilla and pineapple. Mix soda with flour and add slowly to above mixture. Add nuts. Pour into 9x13-pan and bake 40 minutes at 350 degrees.

Frosting
1 8-ounce package cream cheese, soft
1/2 stick butter
1 3/4 cups confectioners' sugar
1 teaspoon vanilla

Mix and spread over warm cake. (Can be beaten with beater.)

Dean Holler Fudge Sauce

(for ice cream)

1 stick butter
1/2 cup cocoa
3 cups sugar
1 13-ounce can evaporated milk
1 teaspoon vanilla

Melt butter in saucepan. Add cocoa, then milk and stir constantly. Mix in sugar until well blended and mixture begins to boil. Remove from heat and add vanilla. Cover until cool.

Coca-Cola Cake

2 cups sugar
2 cups flour
1 stick butter
1 1/2 cups miniature marshmallows
1/2 cup shortening
3 tablespoons cocoa
1 cup Coca-Cola
1/2 cup buttermilk
1 teaspoon baking soda
2 eggs, beaten
1 teaspoon vanilla
1 cup chopped pecans

Sift together sugar and flour. Bring to a boil the butter, marshmallows, shortening, cocoa and Coca-Cola. Mix together with the sugar and flour and add the rest of the ingredients. Pour into greased and floured 9x13-inch pan. Bake at 350 degrees for 40 minutes.

Icing
1 stick butter
3 tablespoons cocoa
6 tablespoons Coca-Cola
1 teaspoon vanilla
1 cup marshmallows
1 16-ounce box confectioners' sugar
1 cup pecans

Melt butter and add rest of ingredients, except nuts. Beat and add nuts. Spread on cake.

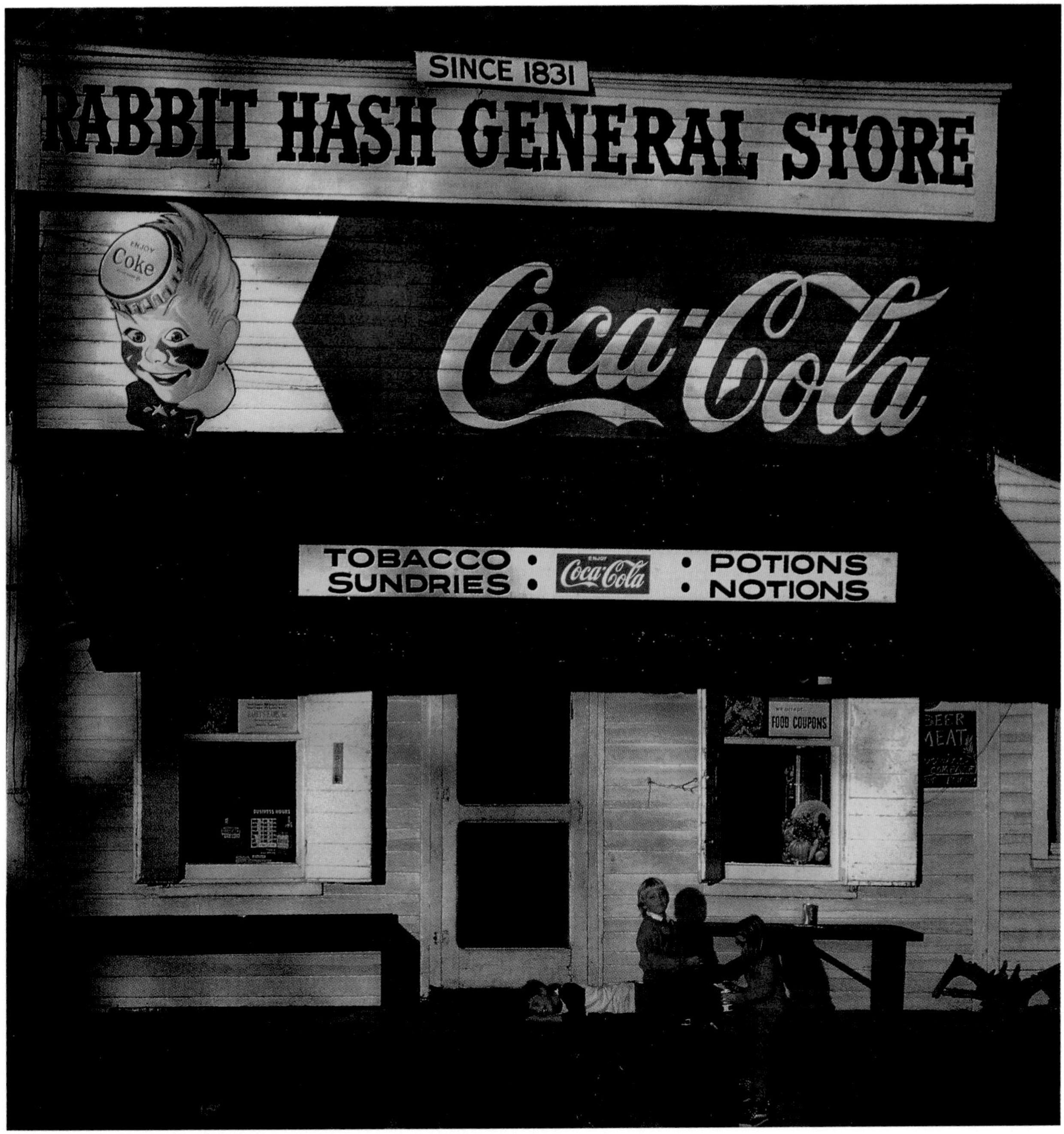
SINCE 1831
RABBIT HASH GENERAL STORE
ENJOY Coke
Coca-Cola
TOBACCO • SUNDRIES •
ENJOY Coca-Cola
• POTIONS • NOTIONS
FOOD COUPONS
BEER
MEAT

Summer Pound Cake

3 cups sugar
1 pound butter, softened
6 eggs, room temperature
4 cups flour
$^3/_4$ cup milk
$^1/_4$ cup Jack Daniel's Whiskey
1 teaspoon vanilla extract

Combine sugar and butter. Cream until light and fluffy. Add eggs 1 at a time, beating well after each addition. Add flour to creamed mixture, alternately with milk, beating well after each addition. Stir in Jack Daniel's and vanilla extract. Pour batter into a well-greased and floured 10-inch tube pan. Bake at 300 degrees for 1 hour and 40 minutes.

Judy's Banana Pudding

3 3-ounce boxes instant vanilla pudding
5 cups milk
1 9-ounce container frozen whipped topping
1 8-ounce container sour cream
5-6 bananas
1 box vanilla wafers

Add pudding mix to milk. Stir until thick. Add whipped topping and sour cream. Layer wafers in the bottom of a large bowl. Cover with 2 bananas, sliced. Pour in $^1/_3$ of the pudding mix. Repeat twice. Chill.

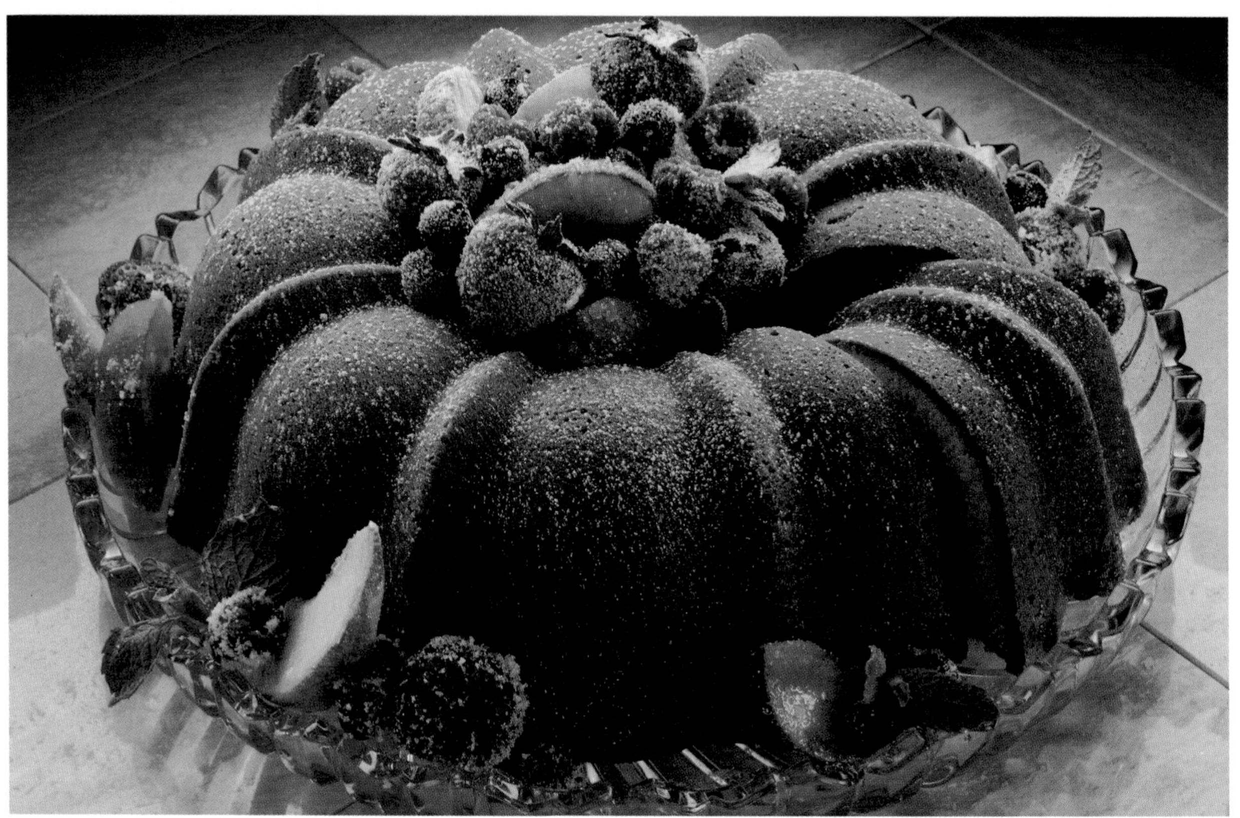

Leesburg Banana Cake

1/2 cup shortening
1 cup sugar
2 eggs
1 cup mashed bananas
1/4 cup milk
1/4 cup Jack Daniel's Whiskey
2 1/4 cups flour
2 teaspoons baking powder
1/4 teaspoon baking soda
1/2 teaspoon salt

Cream shortening. Slowly add sugar, beating until light and fluffy. Add eggs 1 at a time, beating after each. Add bananas, milk and Jack Daniel's to cream mixture. Beat well. Combine flour, baking powder, soda and salt. Stir into banana mixture.

Pour into 2 greased and floured 9-inch pans. Bake at 350 degrees for 30 minutes or until wooden toothpick inserted in center comes out clean. Cool in pan 10 minutes. Remove from pan. Cool completely on wire rack. Frost.

Frosting
2 tablespoons butter, softened
1 small ripe banana
1 16-ounce box confectioners' sugar
1 tablespoon Jack Daniel's Whiskey

Cream butter. Add banana. Beat well. Add remaining ingredients and beat well. Spread over cake.

Mamaw's Carrot Cake

1 3/4 cups sugar
1 cup vegetable oil
4 eggs
2 cups flour
2 teaspoons baking powder
2 teaspoons baking soda
1 teaspoon salt
2 teaspoons cinnamon
3 cups grated raw carrots
1/3 cup Jack Daniel's Whiskey
1/2 cup chopped pecans

Cream sugar and oil. Add eggs. Sift flour, baking powder, baking soda, salt and cinnamon. Add to creamed mixture. Fold in carrots, Jack Daniel's and nuts. Pour into 3 greased and floured 9-inch cake pans. Bake at 350 degrees for 25 minutes.

Frosting
1 8-ounce can crushed pineapple
1/2 cup butter
1 8-ounce package cream cheese
2 teaspoons vanilla
1 16-ounce box confectioners' sugar
2 tablespoons pineapple juice

Drain pineapple, reserving 2 tablespoons juice. Cream butter, cream cheese, vanilla and sugar. Add pineapple juice. Spread frosting and pineapple between each layer. Frost cake with remaining mixture.

COOL AND REFRESHING DRINKS

You don't need a degree in thermal engineering to know it gets terrifically hot around the barbecue pit. The traditional cooling method used by pitmen is the red bandanna: slowly wipe across brow as needed.

A side trip under the shade tree also helps. But for this kind of hot, not even air conditioning is a solution. The only way to cool down a pitman or pitwoman is with a refreshing, cold beverage.

A good rule of thumb is to make a new drink every time you check the meat. Another good rule of thumb is to check the meat frequently.

Bar-B-Q Delight

1 6-ounce can frozen limeade concentrate, thawed
6 ounces Jack Daniel's Whiskey
6 ounces beer

Combine all ingredients. Serve over ice in stemmed glass.

Cold Red Dog Saloon Punch

1 tablespoon confectioners' sugar
Juice of half a lemon
2 ounces Jack Daniel's Whiskey

Dissolve sugar in a small amount of water. Fill 12-ounce bar glass with shaved ice. Pour in ingredients. Shake well and garnish with 2 thin slices of lemon. Serve with a straw.

Art's Barn Burner

2 ounces Jack Daniel's Whiskey
Juice of half a lemon
3 drops Tabasco sauce
$^1/_2$ teaspoon Worcestershire sauce
$^1/_2$ teaspoon chili sauce

Frappe hard and serve in any fireproof glass.

Wyooter Hooter

1 part Jack Daniel's Whiskey
4 parts Sprite
Dash of Grenadine

Mix and serve over ice.

Sundown Cocktail

4 dashes simple syrup
2 dashes bitters
2 ounces Jack Daniel's Whiskey
1 lemon peel

Fill 10-ounce bar glass one-third full of ice. Add ingredients. Shake and strain into glass.

Simple syrup recipe:

Dissolve 1 teaspoon sugar in $^1/_2$ cup boiling water. Let cool.

Jack Daniel's Mint Julep

Sugar
Fresh mint sprigs
2 ounces Jack Daniel's Whiskey
2 tablespoons apricot brandy

Make syrup by bringing to a boil 4 parts sugar and 1 part water until thickened. Crush 1 mint sprig in a 12-ounce glass. Add 1 ounce whiskey and 3/4 ounce syrup. Stir. Partially fill glass with ice. Stir again and finish filling glass with ice. Float 1 tablespoon of apricot brandy on top. Garnish with wet mint sprinkled with sugar.

Jack Daniel's Punch

2 750-ml bottles Jack Daniel's Whiskey
1 18-ounce can pineapple juice
6 ounces lemon juice
24 ounces orange juice
2 14-ounce bottles ginger ale
Sugar
Orange, lemon and pineapple slices

Combine Jack Daniel's Whiskey, pineapple juice, lemon juice and orange juice over block of ice in punch bowl. Add ginger ale and sugar to taste. Garnish with orange, lemon and pineapple slices.

Jack Daniel's Sling

1 teaspoon confectioners' sugar
1/2 cup water
2 ounces Jack Daniel's Whiskey
Nutmeg

Dissolve the sugar in the water. Add the whiskey and ice. Stir thoroughly with a spoon. Grate nutmeg on top and serve.

Jackiri

1 6-ounce can frozen limeade or lemonade concentrate
1 6-ounce can water
1 tablespoon sugar
1/2 cup Jack Daniel's Whiskey
Ice

Combine all ingredients in an electric blender. Process. Cracked ice will produce a smoother consistency. For a thicker drink, add more ice. Serve in a stemmed glass.

Jack Collins

1 6-ounce can frozen lemonade concentrate
1/3 cup Jack Daniel's Whiskey
Soda water or tonic water
Maraschino cherries and orange wedges

Stir lemonade concentrate with Jack Daniel's Whiskey until melted and well-mixed. Pour into pitcher. Add soda or tonic water to taste. Serve in tall glasses filled with ice cubes. Garnish with cherries and orange wedges.

Sazerac

Pernod
1 sugar cube
3 to 4 drops bitters
Strip of lemon zest
Strip of orange zest
Crushed ice
2 ounces Jack Daniel's Whiskey

Pour enough Pernod into a low glass to coat the interior completely. Place the sugar cube in the bottom of the glass and drop the bitters onto it. Crush the sugar with the back of a spoon. Add lemon and orange zest. Fill glass two-thirds full with crushed ice. Pour Jack Daniel's Whiskey over ice and stir once.

THE CAMARADERIE OF THE PIT

For thousands of years man has been drawn by fire. It is a trait so inborn, so established that anyone seeking attention – a college football team, a political candidate, a Boy Scout leader – can count on it. It is a given.

That is why it is so pathetic to see a solitary figure hunched over a barbecue fire, sopping meat, stoking coals.

Barbecue was not meant to be cooked alone. A barbecue fire, like a full bottle of Jack Daniel's Whiskey, begs for company.

So the first thing to do when getting ready to cook barbecue, before ordering the meat, before preparing the sauce, before chopping the wood, is to get on the phone and call over your friends. You need mention only two words – barbecue and fire – to be assured of company.

The ideal time to begin cooking barbecue is just as the sun is going down. The heat of the day is dissipating. Vocal cords are just getting lubricated.

Divide the responsibilities equally, making sure each member of the cooking team has an important job. Remember: busy hands are happy hands.

Every crowd is assured of including a few night owls and a few early birds. Let the night owls take the late shift, until say 3 or 4 in the morning. Mix them up a pitcher of Lynchburg Lemonade and you'll be surprised what a competent job they can do sopping meat and keeping the fire burning.

The early birds, the people who are usually impatient with the paper boy, can take up the slack at about 5. They'll probably fix up some breakfast on the fire.

And, most important, as the cooked meat is coming off the pit, make sure the members of your team get the first cuts. That is barbecue chivalry. And besides, who knows? You may want those guys back again for another all-night cookout. Next time they'll probably bring the Jack Daniel's.

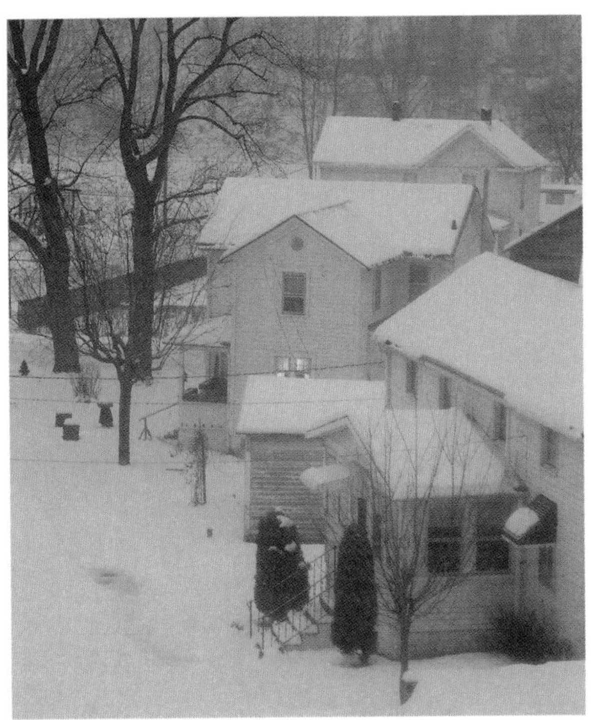

Jack Frost

2 tablespoons Jack Daniel's Whiskey
1 tablespoon Drambuie
2 tablespoons cherry juice or Grenadine
$^1/_4$ cup orange juice
$^1/_4$ cup bottled sweet-and-sour mix
Maraschino cherries

Combine Jack Daniel's Whiskey, Drambuie, cherry juice, orange juice and sweet-and-sour mix over ice in tall glass. Garnish with a cherry.

Snow Shoe

2 parts Jack Daniel's Whiskey
$1^1/_2$ parts peppermint schnapps

Pour over crushed ice and stir.

Authentic Jack Daniel's Moore County Mist

Lemon twist
$2^1/_2$ ounces Jack Daniel's Whiskey

Pack 6-ounce tumbler with finely crushed ice. Rub rim with lemon twist and place twist on top of ice. Pour Jack Daniel's Whiskey over ice. Sip slowly as your glass frosts.

Tennessee Tom and Jerry

12 eggs, well-beaten
1 cup sifted confectioners' sugar
6 jiggers ($1^1/_2$ ounces each) Jack Daniel's Whiskey
6 cups boiling water
Nutmeg

Combine eggs and sugar in a blender until thick. Add a jigger of whiskey to each of 6 glasses. Pour $^2/_3$ cup boiling water into each glass. Add several tablespoons of the sugar mixture to each. Garnish with a dash of nutmeg. Serve hot.

Action Jackson's Spicy Icy Vodka Martini

Fill glass with ice. Pour in 2 ounces of imported Icy vodka. A dash of distilled or spring water is optional. Add 3 or 4 very thin slices of jalapeño pepper.

Gobbler's Cobbler

2 ounces Jack Daniel's Whiskey
1 tablespoon sugar
3 slices of orange

Fill 12-ounce tumbler with ice. Shake well. Imbibe through a straw.

Lynchburg Lemonade

1 part Jack Daniel's Whiskey
1 part triple sec
1 part bottled sweet-and-sour mix
4 parts Sprite
Lemon slices
Maraschino cherries

Combine Jack Daniel's Whiskey, triple sec, sweet-and-sour mix and Sprite. Add ice and stir. Garnish with lemon slices and cherries.

Lynchburg Slush

2 cups water
$\frac{1}{3}$ cup sugar
1 6-ounce can frozen lemonade concentrate
$\frac{1}{2}$ cup Jack Daniel's Whiskey
1 quart ginger ale
1 lemon, thinly sliced

In blender, combine water, sugar, lemonade and Jack Daniel's Whiskey. Process until the sugar is dissolved. Transfer to covered container and freeze (mixture will remain slushy). To serve pour frozen mixture into 2-quart pitcher and add ginger ale. Float lemon slices on top.

Uncle Tub's Shrub

Thin rinds of 2 lemons
Juice of 5 lemons
2 liters Jack Daniel's Whiskey
1 liter sherry
2 pounds cube sugar

Mix lemon rinds, lemon juice and Jack Daniel's. Cover for 3 days, then add sherry and sugar. Run through a jelly bag and bottle.

Lynchburg Country Club Punch

$\frac{1}{2}$ jigger rum
$1\frac{1}{2}$ ounces Jack Daniel's Whiskey
1 teaspoon sugar
1 lime, peel and juice

Combine ingredients and shake with ice. Turn into goblet. Garnish with sprigs of mint or a stick of fresh pineapple.

White Rabbit Smash

$\frac{1}{2}$ tablespoon sugar
1 tablespoon water
2 ounces Jack Daniel's Whiskey

Fill 10-ounce bar glass two-thirds full of shaved ice. Stir in ingredients and garnish with 2 sprigs of mint.

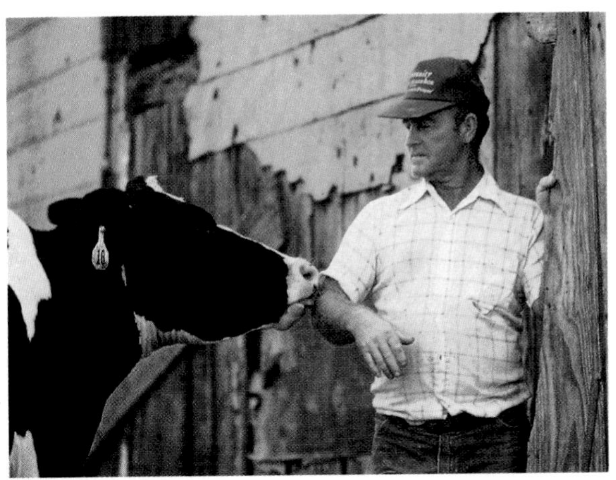

Milk Punch

2 ounces Jack Daniel's Whiskey
1 ounce rum
1/2 ounce brandy
2/3 cup vanilla ice cream
1/4 cup half-and-half
Nutmeg

Process all ingredients except nutmeg in a blender until thick. Sprinkle a dash of nutmeg on top before serving.

Moo Juice Punch

1 cup Jack Daniel's Whiskey
2 cups cold milk
6 tablespoons confectioners' sugar
1/2 teaspoon vanilla
6 ice cubes, coarsely crushed
Nutmeg

Pour all ingredients into blender except nutmeg. Blend well. Pour into glasses or cups and sprinkle with nutmeg.

Lynchburg Coonhunter's Punch

6 lemons or 10 limes, sliced thin
1 fresh pineapple, cored and sliced fine
1 750-ml bottle Cognac brandy
1 375-ml bottle Jamaican rum
1 quart green tea
3 cups sugar
1 750-ml bottle Jack Daniel's Whiskey
4 liters dry champagne
2 quarts club soda

Slice lemon and pineapple and marinate, tightly covered, overnight with brandy. At noon of the evening when you intend to serve it, add rum, tea, sugar and Jack Daniel's Whiskey. Blend well. Just before serving mix in champagne, then club soda. Chill cups for best results.

MULESKINNER #1

2 ounces Jack Daniel's Whiskey
1 piece lemon peel

Fill a 10-ounce bar glass half full of boiling water. Stir in Jack Daniel's. Garnish with lemon peel.

MULESKINNER #2

1 lump sugar
2 ounces Bushmill Irish Whisky
1 piece lemon peel

Fill a 10-ounce bar glass half full of boiling water. Stir in Bushmill Irish Whisky. Garnish with lemon peel.

OLD LYNCHBURG DANDELION WINE

2½ gallons water
6 quarts (dry measure) dandelion blooms
6 lemons
6 oranges
1 tablespoon ginger
1 cup sugar
3 cups chopped raisins
1 tablespoon brewer's yeast

Mix dandelions with water and boil for 30 minutes. Peel and juice lemons and oranges, reserving juice. Grate peels. Mix ginger, sugar and grated lemon and orange peels into boiling mixture. Simmer for 30 minutes. Pour into stoneware crock and add lemon and orange juice. When lukewarm stir in brewer's yeast.

Scald out a 2½ gallon keg. Pour in raisins.

When fermentation of hot mixture has stopped, siphon and strain off into keg. Rack off after 4 months or so and bottle.

GARIBALDI TWINS' CHERRY BOUNCE

This is from the fresh fruit giant of old Chicago, John Garibaldi, and is fit for a nuptial or anytime sip.

1 liter Jack Daniel's Whiskey
Small, wild cherries
½ cup granulated sugar

Pour the whiskey into a pitcher. Fill the empty bottle half full with cherries. With a funnel pour in sugar. Pour the Jack Daniel's Whiskey back into the bottle. Place cheesecloth over top of bottle to allow it to breathe. Place bottle in a dark closet for one month. If patience is a virtue, you'll have a drink sensation that will make a dark winter night come alive. Also perfect for after barbecue.

THE HOGARITA

A few years back George Larrimore, a Memphis native, packed up and moved to Los Angeles. But although he was gone from his hometown, he never lost his love of Memphis barbecue. Almost every spring he leads a team of West Coast barbecue fanatics and party animals, mostly party animals, back home to compete in the Memphis in May International Festival World Championship Barbecue Cooking Contest.

Larrimore calls his team the Hollywood Hogs Barbecue Experience. Decked out in Hawaiian shirts and baggies, they look good. In 1987 the Hogs won first place in the showmanship category. The judges were impressed with the beachhead they established in their cooking area: a real beach with sand, surfboards, beach music and moving waves.

Larrimore and his teammates concocted a drink for quaffing with the barbecue they cooked: the Hogarita. It'll keep you cool by the pit; just be careful not to fall in.

3 parts fresh-squeezed lime juice
2 parts tequila
1 part triple sec
Dash of grapefruit juice (for bite)
Dash of grape juice (for nice pink color)

Blend until perfect.

Mrs. Butts' Boiled Custard

2 quarts whole milk
$1^1/_2$ cups sugar
6 large eggs
2 teaspoons vanilla
Whipped cream
Jack Daniel's Whiskey

Warm milk over low heat. Mix sugar and eggs together. Add 1 cup warm milk to sugar-egg mixture. Stir and add to rest of warm milk. Heat on low until mixture coats spoon. Strain mixture into a bowl. Add vanilla. Keep covered in refrigerator and serve cold. Serve in punch cups with a dollop of whipped cream and a lacing of Jack Daniel's.

Original Tennessee Toddy

1 teaspoon sugar
$^1/_4$ cup water
2 ounces Jack Daniel's Whiskey
1 small lump ice

Stir with a spoon in a 10-ounce bar glass.

Holler Holiday Hot Toddy

Jack Daniel's Whiskey
1 tablespoon sugar
$^1/_2$ lemon
Boiling water

Use heavy glass tumbler. Fill half full with Jack Daniel's Whiskey. Add sugar. Squeeze lemon and drop into glass. Stir until sugar dissolves. Fill glass with boiling water.

Tims Ford Toddy

2 ounces Jack Daniel's Whiskey
1 teaspoon simple syrup
1 teaspoon Curacao
1 jigger cognac
3 dashes orange bitters or Angostura bitters
1 teaspoon Pernod

Stir in a bar glass with ice and strain into a whiskey glass.

Old Fashioned

Pinch of sugar dissolved in $^1/_2$ teaspoon of water
2 drops bitters
1 slice orange, halved
1 maraschino cherry
Jack Daniel's Whiskey

Combine sugar, water, bitters, orange and cherry in an old-fashioned glass. Top with Jack Daniel's to taste.

Hot Shot Sling

3 ounces Jack Daniel's Whiskey

Fill a 10-ounce bar glass one-third full of boiling water. Pour in Jack Daniel's Whiskey. Grate nutmeg on top.

JACK O'MELON

This isn't a Halloween trick, it's a barbecue treat: a watermelon spiked with Jack Daniel's Whiskey.

The hard part isn't getting the Jack Daniel's inside the watermelon. That's easy: all you have to do is cut out a 2-inch plug in the top of the melon. Turn it upside down and allow the water to drain out. Insert an inverted 750 ml. bottle of Jack Daniel's Whiskey, opened, of course, in the hole. After the bottle has drained, replace the plug. Rotate the watermelon and then let it sit for 1 hour to allow the whiskey to flow to all sections of the fruit. Jab holes in the watermelon at strategic drinking spots with an ice pick. Insert straws and yell "Come and get it."

Oh yeah, the hard part. The hard part is in selecting the melon. You want it at the peak of ripeness, when its fruit is sweetest. You can find the best candidate by thumping the melons at the fruit stand. Curl your middle finger into your palm and pull your thumb back over it. Now shoot the finger out in a flipping motion. When it strikes the melon, listen closely. If it is a deep, resonant sound, like an echo, the melon is ready.

This method of melon selection requires some practice, so you may have to do this every night for a couple of weeks until you get it exactly perfect.

TENNESSEE SPIRIT PUNCH

1 12-ounce can frozen lemonade concentrate
1 6-ounce can limeade concentrate
1 6-ounce can orange juice concentrate
6 cups water
1 cup sugar
2 cups Jack Daniel's Whiskey

Combine all ingredients. Place in freezer. Just before it freezes, process in a blender. Serve in stemmed glasses.

TENNESSEE-STYLE APPLE CHERRY LIQUEUR

5 16-ounce cans tart red cherries, drained and pitted
2 fresh apples, cored and quartered but not peeled
2 cups sugar
1½ teaspoons whole allspice
1½ teaspoons whole cloves
1 cinnamon stick
4 cups Jack Daniel's Whiskey

Combine all ingredients in a 4-quart glass jar. Stir and cover. Place in a cool, dark place for at least 8 weeks. Stir daily or several times a week. Strain before serving. Serve in liqueur glasses.

Tennessee Julep

2 teaspoons sugar
Dash of water
5 sprigs fresh mint
2 ounces Jack Daniel's Whiskey
Pineapple cubes
Maraschino cherries
Confectioners' sugar
1 tablespoon peach brandy

To a 12-ounce mint julep glass, add sugar, dash of water and 4 sprigs of fresh mint. Bruise mint thoroughly and fill glass half full with finely cracked ice. Add Jack Daniel's Whiskey. Stir, and fill glass with ice. Garnish with sprig of mint, pineapple cube and maraschino cherry. Dust mint with confectioners' sugar; add to glass. Float 1 tablespoon of peach brandy on surface of drink.

Tennessee Volunteers Punch

3/4 cup sugar
2 tablespoons bitters
Juice of 5 lemons
1 750-ml bottle Jack Daniel's Whiskey
1 750-ml bottle claret
1 750-ml bottle brandy
1 750-ml bottle sherry

Mix sugar, lemon juice and bitters until dissolved. Mix in liquor.

Red Dog Saloon Punch

2 ounces Jack Daniel's Whiskey
2 cups boiling water
Sugar to taste

Dissolve the sugar with 1 cup of water. Pour in Jack Daniel's and add remainder of water. Sweeten to taste. Garnish with thin slice of lemon.

Tennessee Mud

Coffee
Jack Daniel's Whiskey
Amaretto

Pour coffee into cup. Add Jack Daniel's Whiskey and Amaretto to taste.

Mr. Jack's Jr. Julep

1 teaspoon sugar
2 ounces Jack Daniel's Whiskey
Mint extract

Put sugar in a julep cup. Pour Jack Daniel's Whiskey on top. Add mint extract to taste, 4 to 10 drops. Half fill with ice. Stir to dissolve sugar. Fill remainder with ice.

MOORE COUNTY FLIP

1 teaspoon sugar
2 ounces Jack Daniel's Whiskey
1 egg yolk

Dissolve the sugar in a little hot water. Add the Jack Daniel's and egg. Shake up thoroughly. Pour into a 12-ounce bar glass and fill one-half full of boiling water. Grate nutmeg on top and serve.

BOBO'S FIX

1 teaspoon confectioners' sugar
Juice of half a lemon
1 lemon peel
2 ounces of Jack Daniel's Whiskey

Dissolve the sugar in a small amount of water. Fill the glass about two-thirds full of shaved ice. Pour in whiskey. Stir well and garnish with lemon peel.

JACK SOUR

1 part Jack Daniel's Whiskey
2 parts bottled sweet-and-sour mix
Maraschino cherries
Orange slices

Combine Jack Daniel's Whiskey and sweet-and-sour mix. Serve over cracked ice. Garnish with a cherry and an orange slice.

DUSENBERRY'S DAISY

3 dashes corn syrup
2 dashes almond extract
Juice of half a lemon
2 ounces Jack Daniel's Whiskey

Fill glass one-third full of shaved ice. Add ingredients. Shake thoroughly. Strain into large cocktail glass and fill up with club soda.

FESTIVALS!

Jack Daniel's association with barbecue is as old as the hills of Moore County, and as new as the Jack Daniel's World Championship Invitational Barbecue contest, which made its debut in 1989.

Although the contest is young compared to other barbecue festivals, it is already the premier barbecue cooking competition, the event that barbecue cooking teams aim for. You see, the Jack Daniel's contest is a championship of champions, a Super Bowl of Barbecue. Every one of the 32 competing teams has won at least one regional contest in the preceding year and many display scores of trophies from previous contests. Champions travel hundreds of miles, from Washington state, from Texas and Oklahoma and Virginia, from all over in fact, to compete shoulder-to-shoulder, and rib-to-rib, in Lynchburg, Tennessee.

While the champions are slaving over their pits, leaving no bone unturned in an effort to take home the Grand Championship trophy, local Lynchburg clubs and civic organizations are keeping the crowd of barbecue lovers occupied with craft displays and food stands on the town square.

If you go to only one barbecue contest in your life, this is the one to attend. In Lynchburg everyone seems to know everyone else, and if you're a stranger, they introduce you around. There's pig racing, a cake walk, a rolling-pin-throwing contest, a lawn-tractor pull, all the kinds of events you'd expect at a small-town fair. And, of course, the best thing about a barbecue contest: the barbecue.

At the Jack Daniel's contest, lines seem to form magically, first at one tent, then at

another, as the cooks send in their entries. These barbecue fanatics know that once the competition meat has gone to the judge's tent, the competitors are ready to turn their attention to another trophy, the People's Choice Award, given to the barbecue deemed tops by vote of the festival attendees. One piece of advice: there is no wrong line. All the contestants are winners and so are their barbecue meats.

SUBJECT INDEX

APPETIZERS

BARBECUE SAUCES

Beans

Beef

Breads

Casseroles

Chicken

Coleslaw

Cooking Techniques

Corn

Desserts

Drinks

Game

Lamb

Pie Crusts

Pies

Pork

Potatoes

Potato Salads

Salads

Seafood

Soups and Stews

Vegetables

ALPHABETICAL INDEX

G

H

I

J

K

L

M

ACKNOWLEDGEMENTS

Book design by Julie Breeding/Paul Plaschke Studio, Louisville, Kentucky.

Chapter heading photographs by Warren Lynch & Associates, Louisville, Kentucky. Food styling by Karen Lynch and Sally Ann Ladd.

Photographs on pages 79 and 113 by the Maryland Tourism Office.

Photographs on pages 50, 73, 74, 75, and 81 by Alaska Seafood Marketing.

Photographs on pages 80 and 115 (left) by Louisiana Seafood Marketing.

Photograph on page 14 by the Florida Department of Commerce, Division of Tourism.

Photographs on pages 66, 69 (left), and 115 (right) by the National Livestock and Meat Board.

Photograph on page 23 by © Texas Highways and reprinted by permission.

Photographs on pages 31 and 177 by the North Carolina Division of Travel and Tourism.

Photographs on pages 20 and 51 by the National Pork Producers Council.

Photographs on pages 34 (left), 37, 38 (left and right), and 140 by the Texas Department of Commerce.

Photographs on pages 56, 128, 132, 139, 153, and 154 by © Martha White Foods, Inc., Nashville, Tennessee and reprinted by permission.

Photographs on pages 25 and 67 by the South Carolina Department of Agriculture.

Photographs on pages 8, 16, 19, 22, 26, 40, 43, 44, 49, 54, 59, 61, 68, 72, 85, 90, 93, 94, 98, 107, 116, 117, 120, 127, 130 (right), 137, 141, 142, 150, 155, 157, 159, 163, 168, 171, and 180 by James Archambeault. © Graphics Art Center Pub. Co.

Photographs on pages 33, 55, 60, 76, 88, 100, 108, 143, 160, and 175 by © Richard Nugent and printed by permission.

Photographs on pages 10 and 11, 27, 28 and 29, 32, 52, and 53, 64 and 65, 82 and 83, 101, 102, and 103, 104, 110 and 111, 119, 121, 124 and 125, 134 and 135, 148 and 149, 166 and 167, and 176 by Warren Lynch and Associates.

Photographs on pages 15, 45, 46, 58 (left), 78, 87, 92, 106, 112, 144, 173 (left), and 174 by © *The Courier-Journal.* Reprinted with permission.

Photographs on pages 62 and 131 by the University of Louisville Photographic Archives.

Photographs on pages 36, 109, and 123 by Vince Staten.

Photographs on pages 180 (left), and 181 by Tom Barnett.

Recipe testing by Judy Staten.

Typesetting by Advertising Production Service, Louisville, Kentucky.

Proofreading by Ann Lane, Paul Plaschke Studio, Louisville, Kentucky and Jenna Monohan.

DRUG DANGERS

Joan Vos MacDonald

Enslow Publishers, Inc.
40 Industrial Road
Box 398
Berkeley Heights, NJ 07922
USA

PO Box 38
Aldershot
Hants GU12 6BP
UK

http://www.enslow.com

To my daughter, Amy

Library of Congress Cataloging-in-Publication Data

MacDonald, Joan Vos.
Tobacco and nicotine drug dangers / Joan Vos MacDonald.
p. cm. — (Drug dangers)
Includes bibliographical references and index.
Summary: Examines the history of tobacco and nicotine use, as well as the social and medical aspects of smoking, and offers suggestions on how to quit.
ISBN 0-7660-1317-0
1. Tobacco—Physiological aspects Juvenile literature.
2. Nicotine—Physiological aspects Juvenile literature.
3. Children—Tobacco use—Prevention Juvenile literature.
[1. Tobacco habit. 2. Smoking. 3. Nicotine.] I. Title.
II. Series.
RC567.M17 2000
613.85—dc21 99-36405
CIP

Printed in the United States of America

10 9 8 7 6 5 4 3 2 1

To our Readers:
All Internet addresses in this book were active and appropriate when we went to press. Any comments or suggestions can be sent by e-mail to Comments@enslow.com or to the address on the back cover.

Photo Credits: American Cancer Society, pp. 8, 11; *American Heritage New Illustrated History of the United States*, vol. 1 (both), p. 33; Cleo Freelance Photo/New England Stock Photo, p. 14; Clifford Keeney/New England Stock Photo, p. 34; Díamar Interactive Corp., p. 49; John and Diane Harper/New England Stock Photo, p. 25; Karen Dodge/New England Stock Photo, p. 29; National Library of Medicine, p. 43; Skjold Photos, p. 22.

Cover Photo: Corel Corporation

contents

Titles in the **Drug Dangers** series:

Alcohol Drug Dangers
ISBN 0-7660-1159-3

Amphetamine Drug Dangers
ISBN 0-7660-1321-9

Crack and Cocaine Drug Dangers
ISBN 0-7660-1155-0

Diet Pill Drug Dangers
ISBN 0-7660-1158-5

Ecstasy and Other Designer Drug Dangers
ISBN 0-7660-1322-7

Herbal Drug Dangers
ISBN 0-7660-1319-7

Heroin Drug Dangers
ISBN 0-7660-1156-9

Inhalant Drug Dangers
ISBN 0-7660-1153-4

LSD, PCP, and Hallucinogen Drug Dangers
ISBN 0-7660-1318-9

Marijuana Drug Dangers
ISBN 0-7660-1214-X

Speed and Methamphetamine Drug Dangers
ISBN 0-7660-1157-7

Steroid Drug Dangers
ISBN 0-7660-1154-2

Tobacco and Nicotine Drug Dangers
ISBN 0-7660-1317-0

Tranquilizer, Barbiturate, and Downer
Drug Dangers
ISBN 0-7660-1320-0

one

Hooked

Julia is fifteen. She started smoking "as a habit" when she was twelve, but the first time she and her baby-sitter's daughter tried a cigarette, they were nine or ten.

"My baby-sitter's daughter told me that she started smoking, and at one of our Girl Scout meetings or something, we went back to her house to smoke," said Julia.

Now Julia smokes between half a pack and a pack a day. It took about two years for her to work up to smoking that much.

Why did she get started?

"It's stupid and cheesy, but I guess I still think smoking makes me look cool. You know, cigarettes are like forbidden fruit and I feel all rebellious when I'm smoking. Also, it's weird, but all my smoker friends agree, I like the feeling I get when I haven't had a cigarette in a couple of hours, and I finally get to have one. It's like a huge relief, when I get to satisfy the craving," said Julia.

There are, however, some things Julia does not like about smoking. She does not like spending money on cigarettes, and she also does not like being addicted to something. "Sitting in English class and fiending for a cigarette," she said, is not her idea of a good thing. Julia is also not fond of the smoker's cough she now has in the morning.

"Me and my friends all joke about having emphysema when we start coughing."

Julia plans to quit when cigarettes cost over three dollars per pack or before she has children.

"I definitely will quit once I get pregnant or plan on getting pregnant, because I wouldn't want to raise a child around a smoker. I believe that I probably wouldn't have started smoking so young [or at all] if I hadn't grown up seeing my mother and my grandmother always smoking, because I guess it kind of made me think, 'If its such a bad thing to do, why would they be doing it?' "

In the few years she has smoked, Julia has already tried to quit twice.

"The first time I just decided to go cold turkey, but it didn't work. I bought a pack of cigarettes within the day. The second time I tried to lower my intake of nicotine by switching from Marlboro Lights to Ultra Lites, but I just started smoking more cigarettes to compensate. Lowering the amount of nicotine in cigarettes doesn't work. I suppose if I had real incentive to quit, I would, like if I was planning to have a child, but I am not, so I doubt I will be quitting soon."[1]

Drew does not smoke, but at thirteen she knows more than she ever wanted to about quitting smoking. She has seen her father try to quit many times and never succeed for very long.

Almost three years ago, Drew's father had a heart transplant. People get this kind of operation when their heart is so damaged it cannot be fixed by taking medication or making repairs. Their only chance of survival is to have an operation in which they get a new heart donated by the family of someone who has died.

Part of the reason Drew's father got so sick was that he had smoked a pack of cigarettes a day since he was about sixteen. Drew was very happy when her father had a successful heart transplant, but within a few months he started smoking again, putting his new heart and his health at serious risk. Drew was sad, disappointed, and angry that after all the worrying she had done about him, he was doing something he knew would make him sick again.

Even though smoking was one of the reasons that Drew's father had had several serious operations and spent months in the hospital, he has found it difficult to stay away from tobacco for more than a few weeks. When Drew's father started smoking in the 1950s, people did not know how dangerous cigarettes were for their health.[2] It was not until the 1960s that scientists established that smoking tobacco products—especially cigarettes—could cause lung cancer, heart disease, emphysema, and other diseases.

The list of health risks associated with smoking continues to grow, and many of the risks endanger girls in particular.

When Liv started smoking at age fifteen, she knew it was dangerous, but she figured it would be a long time before any of the health risks would affect her. Like many girls her age, she was sure she would be able to quit when she wanted to.

At age twenty-three, when she became pregnant, she decided it was time to quit smoking, because smoking during pregnancy can harm a baby. A mother who smokes might suddenly lose her baby, the baby might not gain a healthy amount of weight before it is born, or the baby might be born too early. Also, babies whose mothers smoke are more likely to die of sudden infant death syndrome (SIDS).[3]

It was so important to Liv that she have a healthy baby that she stopped smoking for nine months. After her baby was born, Liv found herself having an occasional cigarette again. When the baby took a nap, she would sit on the porch and smoke. She did not want to smoke in the house because she wanted to spare her baby the health risks of secondhand smoke—what happens when you inhale another person's smoke. These risks can

Women who smoke while they are pregnant are passing along all of the problems associated with smoking to their unborn child. Babies born to smoking mothers are smaller and exhibit more health problems than babies born to nonsmoking mothers.

include asthma, an increased number of colds and middle-ear infections, and eventually even cancer. The Environmental Protection Agency (EPA) estimates that secondhand smoke causes up to 300,000 cases of pneumonia and bronchitis every year in children under eighteen months old.[4]

Liv also does not want her baby to see her smoking. She does not want her baby to grow up thinking it is acceptable to smoke. She is trying very hard to quit, but like many people who started smoking young, she has learned that this is not as easy as it seems.

The Best Way to Stop Is Not to Start

For most people, it is much easier to start smoking than it is to stop. Not starting would have been the easiest way for all of these smokers and the people around them to live healthier lives.

Most people who start smoking at a young age think they will be able to quit any time they want to. As part of a recent study to find out why young people smoke, scientists asked some high-school seniors who smoked if they thought they would still be smoking five years later. More than half of those seniors said they would either definitely or probably quit.[5]

Five years later, 60 percent of those teens were still smoking the same number of cigarettes or even more. They still wanted to quit but found it too difficult.

Smoking Is a Bad Idea

It is estimated that unless teen smoking rates are cut immediately, more than 5 million young people under age eighteen, who are alive today, will live shorter and

Did You Know?

The diseases caused by tobacco use kill more Americans each year than alcohol, cocaine, crack, heroin, homicide, suicide, fires, car accidents, and AIDS combined.[6]

more unhealthy lives than they would have if they had never smoked.[7]

- One out of three young people who become regular smokers will die of a smoking-related disease.
- More than half of those smokers continue to smoke up to one year before their deaths.

Why is smoking so dangerous? Smoking has been described as slowly poisoning yourself. The habit has been described as drawing smoke, fire, and toxic (poisonous) substances into your lungs for the purpose of giving the body a dose of nicotine, a highly toxic and addictive drug.[8] Does slowly poisoning the body sound like something a person would want to do?

Tobacco smoke has more than four thousand chemicals in it, including nicotine, cyanide (rat poison), and formaldehyde. None of these chemicals is good for the body, and if any were in the air we breathe, we would consider them dangerous pollutants.

At least forty-three of the chemicals in cigarettes are known to cause cancer, a disease in which cells begin to grow in an uncontrollable, unusual and dangerous way.[9] The chemicals found in cigarettes include the following:

- nicotine, a highly addictive drug that works like a stimulant. Nicotine is actually a poison, which, taken in large doses, can kill a person by paralyzing breathing muscles.
- tar, a thick, dark liquid formed when tobacco burns. It coats the lungs and prevents them from getting needed oxygen.
- carbon monoxide, a poisonous gas that is also found in car exhaust.
- cyanide, benzene, formaldehyde, methanol (wood alcohol), and acetylene (the fuel used in welding torches).

Despite these facts, nearly 4 million teens in the United States start smoking every year. Not becoming one of these smokers may be the healthiest decision you ever make.

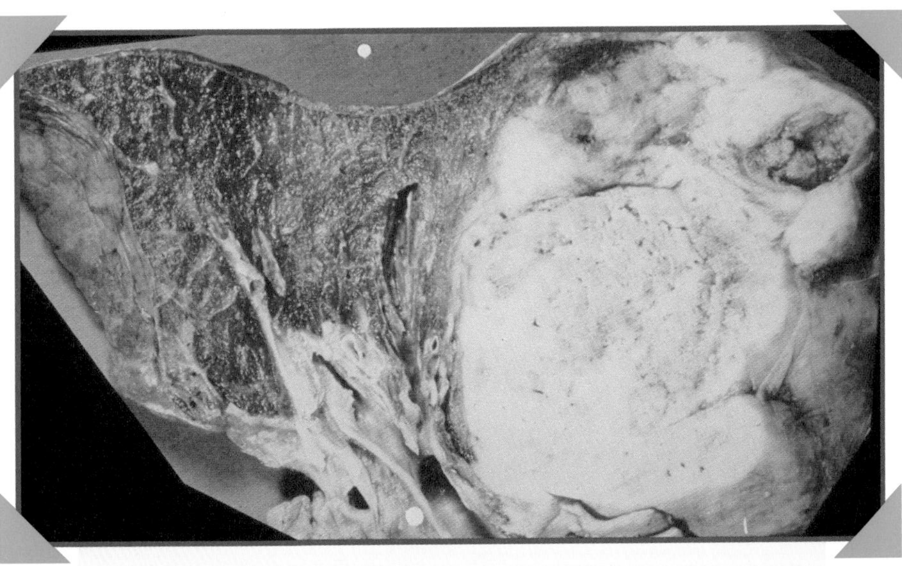

The nicotine and tar found in cigarettes are just a few of the hundreds of chemicals that will damage a smoker's lungs. These unhealthy lungs are showing signs of lung cancer.

two

Social Issues

Most young people start smoking because they are offered a cigarette by someone they know, usually someone their own age. What many young people who start smoking often do not know is exactly how addictive nicotine can be and how quickly it can become addictive.

Making an Informed Choice

If you can answer the following question, you may have a better idea of what is involved and why not to get involved. Which is more addictive, crack/ cocaine, alcohol, or nicotine? Anyone who guessed nicotine is right and will probably have a better idea how to respond if he or she is offered a cigarette.

Nicotine is a legal drug for anyone eighteen or over. However, the risk of becoming addicted to nicotine is greater than the risk of becoming dependent on alcohol or even crack/cocaine.[1]

Once someone develops a nicotine habit, it can be very hard to quit.

Becoming addicted can also happen very quickly. Seven out of ten high-school seniors who smoke wish they had never started. Almost half have tried unsuccessfully to quit.[2] The younger someone is when he or she starts smoking, the harder it may be for that person to quit.

The bad news is that every year about three thousand teens try their first cigarette.[3] The good news is that if a teen does not start smoking by the time he or she graduates from high school, that person probably never will start. Most people who smoke (89 percent) started as teenagers.[4]

There are many reasons young people start smoking. Some do so because other people in their family smoke. Some mistakenly believe smoking can help them lose weight or deal with stress. Some start out of curiosity.

Popular Poison

Let's cut through the excuses and examine how valid these reasons for starting to smoke are. Some teens begin

Why People Smoke

Popular reasons young people start smoking include:

- wanting to fit in
- wanting to seem more grown up
- not believing smoking can really hurt their health

the habit because they want to fit in, but consider this: Is a group in which a member is expected to change his or her values just to fit in worth joining? If people will only spend time with someone when that person smokes, is that acceptable? Real friends make their own decisions, and let friends make their own decisions, about not smoking.

After people become addicted to nicotine, they often discover that smoking does not really improve their social life. It can actually *limit* their social life. Only one in ten teens actually smokes, but many nonsmokers choose to spend less time with people who smoke. Many nonsmokers find smokers less attractive. Eighty-six percent of all teens who answered a 1995 survey said

While smoking may seem like a cool and glamorous thing to do, people who become addicted to nicotine often discover that smoking actually limits their social life. Many nonsmokers choose to spend less time with people who smoke.

they would not date anyone who smoked.[5] The yellowed fingernails and bad breath caused by smoking and the smell of smoke in hair and clothing were considered definite turnoffs.

Sixty-eight percent of teens in another survey said they do not even like hanging around people who smoke.[6]

Sandra, who started smoking eight years ago, at age fourteen, said she was motivated to quit because her boyfriend found her habit "gross."[7]

"My boyfriend, Jason, despised the stench and was freaked about my health," said Sandra, who originally started smoking to fit in.

Smokers are also becoming less popular as people learn about the dangers of secondhand smoke. Inhaling someone else's smoke can cause nonsmokers to develop some of the same health problems smokers get. That means a nonsmoker may be the first choice for someone selecting a roommate or traveling companion.

Smoking Is a Handicap

Being a smoker can make it harder for someone to get a good job. In 1985, 27 percent of all companies banned or restricted smoking inside their buildings. Now the number is up to 56 percent and includes such companies as *Newsday*, the United States Postal Service, and New York Telephone. Even the White House is now smoke-free.[8]

Smoking can also make it harder for workers to work to their full potential, since smokers have to take frequent breaks to satisfy their nicotine addiction.

Smoking is also very expensive. Someone who

Costly Habit

Here's what could be done with the money it costs to fund a nicotine addiction for one year:

- take a trip
- rent hundreds of videos
- go to the movies about 100 times
- get the best seats at more than a dozen top-rate concerts
- buy in-line skates
- buy a racing bike or a canoe
- get several pairs of top-of-the-line sneakers
- get a new hair style and a makeover at a salon

smokes a pack a day at about $3.00 a pack will spend almost $1,100 on cigarettes every year.[9]

Older and Wiser

Some teen smokers think that smoking makes them seem older. Eventually, smoking *will* make a smoker seem far older than he or she is. Smoking causes skin to wrinkle more and at an earlier age. Smoking causes teeth to yellow and hair to become dull.

Many teens start smoking because it seems like an adult thing to do, but as the health risks become better known, the number of adults who smoke continues to drop. In 1964, the year the Surgeon General first announced that smoking causes lung cancer, almost half the adult population smoked (42 percent). Since then it has fallen to 26 percent, and most of those adult smokers (83 percent) wish they had never started smoking.[10]

It Can't Happen to Me

Many young people cannot imagine that smoking could ever hurt them. Only about half of all eighth-graders think that smokers run a greater risk of hurting themselves by smoking a pack or more of cigarettes a day.[11] They are wrong. Not only does smoking put people at a greater risk for life-threatening diseases, but the damage starts with the first cigarette.

Within seconds of the first drag, the stimulant drug nicotine is carried from the lungs to the brain. It releases chemicals in the brain that cause the smoker to want more nicotine and become addicted—dependent on nicotine's effects in order to prevent unpleasant

No Hollywood Glamour

Although models in advertisements may look glamorous while smoking, in real life smoking makes people unattractive by giving them:

- bad breath
- yellow teeth
- yellow fingers
- brittle nails
- dull skin and hair
- a lot more phlegm and an annoying cough
- wrinkles at an early age

withdrawal symptoms. When most people have their first cigarette, they cough and feel dizzy and nauseous.

Some people continue smoking because they like the little rush of energy that nicotine gives them at first. That reaction does not last. Eventually smokers start to suffer withdrawal symptoms—such as irritability, cravings, headaches, dizziness, depression, or sleepiness—when they are not smoking. The immediate danger to the lungs can quickly result in more colds and bronchitis attacks. Smoking can also aggravate asthma and allergies.

Not Starting Is Smart

The young people who *do* smoke tend to be the ones who get lower grades in school and have lower self-esteem. This lowered self-esteem may be part of the reason they have trouble saying no to a habit that is so obviously bad for them.[12]

three

A Dangerous Experiment

"When you smoke you have to throw away all your beliefs," said Michael, age nineteen, who quit smoking three months ago. Fitting in becomes so important, said Michael, that many kids forget about how unhealthy smoking is. When he still smoked, if he had seen a commercial about a kid offering another kid a cigarette, he would have thought, "It's not that way at all."

"But now I think that smoking is all about a kid offering another kid a cigarette. You want to be down, to fit in. Little kids don't really think about why they start smoking. They don't really think through the decision," he said. Michael is now a college sophomore and drama major. He smoked for three years.

Michael knew he was smoking too much when he found himself lighting up before he approached a crowd, but he never wanted to admit he was smoking to look cool. The price for looking cool, however, proved to be too high.

Michael eventually stopped smoking because of sports. "I couldn't stand gasping," he said. "As far as life goes, I don't get real paranoid about things, but I would look at the other people I was playing with and they would be running past me and I would be gasping." He also noticed it had a negative effect on his voice when he acted.

Neither of Michael's parents smokes. He first started smoking to see what it was all about. "It was an experiment," he said. "Like little kids will jump off anything, fall off chairs."

It took him about a year to get to the point of smoking an entire pack a day. "That was the day I realized that I had to calm down," he said. He smoked a pack a day for about a year and then started trying to quit. His first tries were not successful.

"I was lying to myself, making up new techniques to come off. I would smoke only one cigarette, or only smoke in the afternoon after 5:00 P.M. The whole time that I was not smoking, I was thinking about smoking. *I gotta have a cigarette. I gotta have one*. When I got angry, I wanted a cigarette. It was not about the nicotine. I never had a craving for the nicotine. I had a craving for the habit. For a kid, the act of smoking starts out being more important than smoking," said Michael.

Eventually he did quit. Although he started smoking at the same time as his friends, many of them still smoke and do not want to give it up yet. "They don't do anything that requires their lungs," said Michael.

What eventually worked for Michael was going cold

turkey, which means quitting all at once. "I started jogging, started having an incentive to breathe," he said.

"Recently someone had a cigarette in front of me and I couldn't stand the smell of it," said Michael. "I couldn't imagine smoking. As far as friends and family, today I ask friends why they smoke cigarettes. No explanation. No reason. If you don't know why you smoke, you won't know why you want to stop. If you don't have a reason, why are you doing it? I try to get friends not to smoke. Their breath stinks. I wouldn't go out with someone who smokes or share a place with them."[1]

Tobacco Companies Want Your Money

Can you imagine persuading millions of people to do something that costs a lot of money, is dirty, makes them smell bad, makes them cough, offends other people, is a messy nuisance, and might kill them?[2]

That is what tobacco advertising is all about. Every day the cigarette companies must find four thousand new smokers to replace the ones who have quit or died—or they will soon be out of business.[3] Tobacco companies have known about the link between smoking and cancer since 1953. Tobacco company research found that giving tobacco to mice would cause tumors to grow on their backs. Nonetheless, the tobacco industry has continued to work hard at attracting young customers.[4]

The people running tobacco companies assume that young people are too inexperienced to know how bad smoking really is. Once young people smoke a few cigarettes, reason the cigarette makers, they will be addicted enough to buy their product and supply income to the tobacco companies for the rest of their lives.

"Today's teenager is tomorrow's potential customer,"

said a 1981 interoffice memo written at Philip Morris, Inc. That was twenty-eight years after the experiment in which tobacco smoke caused tumors to sprout on mice. It was seventeen years after the 1964 Surgeon General's Report declared that smoking causes diseases.[5]

To interest young people and make them think of cigarettes as innocent fun, the tobacco companies created cartoon characters such as Joe Camel (now retired). Research showed that children as young as three could easily recognize this character.[6] In one recent survey, more six-year-olds recognized Joe Camel than Mickey Mouse.[7]

Cigarette companies also try to make smoking look

Cartoon characters such as Joe Camel (now retired) were created by tobacco companies to interest young people and make them think of cigarettes as innocent fun.

glamorous by using beautiful young models in their advertisements and by paying film companies hundreds of thousands of dollars to use their brands of cigarettes in movies with popular stars.[8] In places where tobacco advertising is allowed, free items such as mugs and T-shirts feature pictures that young people identify with cigarettes (such as Joe Camel) in vivid colors. In countries where cigarette advertising is not allowed, cigarette companies open up teen nightclubs that have cigarette brand names; give away tickets to rock concerts in exchange for empty cigarette packs; give away kites or notebooks with cigarette brand names on them; or sell fashionable clothing with their brand names on it.[9]

Advertising Myths

There are three common myths cigarette advertisers use to attract young people, but the facts behind them show that believing them can be a mistake.

Myth 1: Smoking tobacco is flavorful and satisfying; it can be mild, light, mellow, gentle, cool, fresh, and delicious.[10]

Fact: Such descriptive words *are* used in cigarette advertisements. But do not be fooled. There is nothing delicious or fresh about the taste of tobacco, and it is anything but mild, light, or mellow on your throat. Smoking can cause the throat to bleed.

Myth 2: Smoking will give a smoker desirable qualities, such as youth, beauty, popularity, strength, ruggedness, or talent at a sport.

Fact: Most beautiful models do not smoke. It keeps hair and skin from getting the oxygen they need to shine. "Cigarettes—yuck! I think smoking is disgusting in every way," said actress and model Brooke Shields.[11] Many nonsmokers do not want to hang out with smokers, which can cut into a person's popularity.[12] About half of the teens responding to a 1994 survey said they thought smoking made smokers look insecure.[13]

Smoking can diminish even a trained athlete's ability to perform well in a sport.[14] The male cigarette models chosen to advertise cigarettes make male smokers seem strong, rugged, or tough, but David Millar, the first Marlboro Man model, died of emphysema, and Dave Gorelitz, a Winston model, quit his three-pack-a-day habit when his brother, also a smoker, developed lung cancer.[15]

Myth 3: Smoking is an activity that is free from hazard.

Fact: Even the tobacco companies know this statement is not true. In fact, tobacco companies that own life insurance companies charge smokers almost double the amount of money for life insurance than they charge nonsmokers.[16] More than 5 million children living today will die prematurely because they decided to smoke.[17]

Targeting Girls

Special efforts have been made by cigarette companies to recruit girls to smoke. Ad campaigns tell girls that smoking can help them lose weight, seem more glamorous, be more powerful, and be more lovable. The makers of Misty cigarettes use a "slim and sassy" logo to make girls think that if they smoke they will be slimmer and more popular.[18]

Although these ads have been very successful in getting more girls aged fourteen to seventeen to smoke,

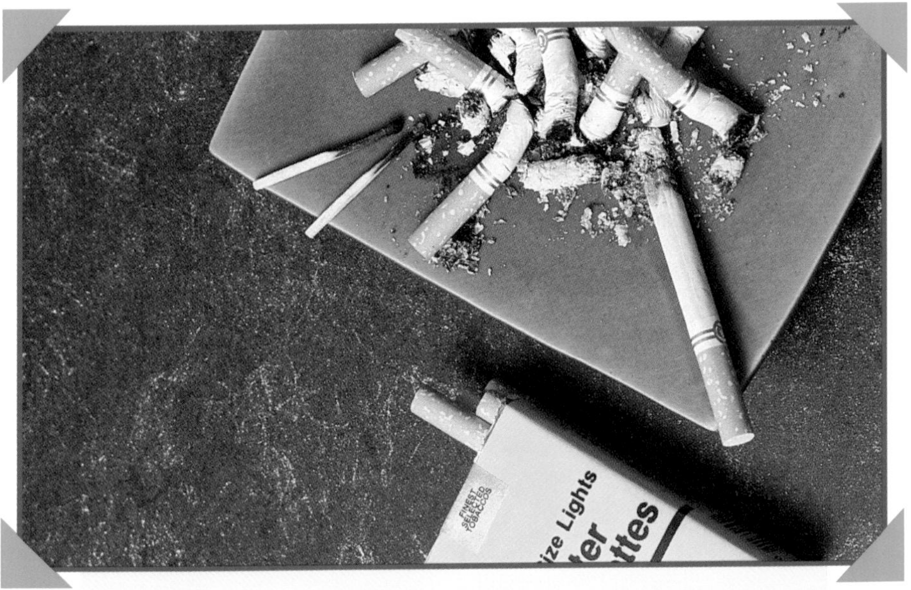

Smoking may be portrayed as glamorous in movies and television, but in reality it does more harm than good.

What Is Your Tobacco IQ?

True or False: (Answers on page 26.)

1. Smoking is an effective way to lose weight.
2. Deciding to smoke shows how independent a person is.
3. Smokers do fun things like go boating, swimming, skiing, and hiking.
4. Smoking can solve personal problems.
5. Smoking is cool because famous people smoke.
6. Smoking makes a person popular.
7. Some people smoke and nothing ever happens to them.

Answers to Tobacco IQ Quiz

1. False. Although smokers do tend to be thinner than nonsmokers, the difference is usually less than five pounds. Most models and actors prefer healthier ways to lose weight, such as eating healthier, low-fat foods or exercising. **2. False.** By the time a person has tried a few cigarettes and decided that he or she is a smoker, that person is probably addicted, which means he or she has become a slave to cigarettes. That can mean having to go out in a blizzard to buy cigarettes, spending money on cigarettes rather than food, and feeling bad when there is no nicotine fix. **3. True.** They just do not do them as well as nonsmokers (who have more energy and better breathing ability). Smokers also probably cannot afford to do those things as often as they might like because smoking is expensive. **4. False.** Going for a smoke may give a person a few moments to think about a problem, but a person can do that without a cigarette by, for example, going for a walk. Smoking will only create financial, health, and social problems to add to existing problems. **5. False.** People in movies smoke because they are paid large sums of money to play a character who smokes. Many of the people you see smoking in movies do not smoke in real life. Not only are ordinary people not paid to smoke, but smoking will give them more medical bills than not smoking. **6. False.** In a room full of adults, 75 percent will not smoke.[19] **7. True.** Some people walk in traffic and nothing ever happens to them. The odds, however, are heavily stacked against smokers.

the only other "more" they actually deliver is that cigarette companies earn more money from a habit that will make more girls sick.[20]

In 1964, when the Surgeon General's first report on smoking came out, men were six times as likely as women to die of lung cancer; but then twice as many men as women smoked. Those numbers have changed. Partly because of advertising directed at them, teenage girls are taking up smoking at higher rates than boys, and, if this continues, more women than men will soon smoke.[21]

Women are already getting more smoking-related diseases, especially lung cancer, which is now the number-one cancer killer of women.[22] This type of cancer is up to three times more likely to develop in women smokers than in men who have the same smoking habits.[23]

"You've come a long way," said the advertising campaign for Virginia Slims, a cigarette marketed directly to women. Although women have come a long way, when it comes to smoking, they may be going in the wrong direction.

four

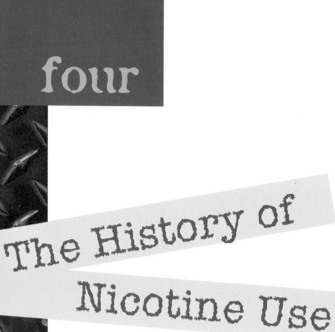

The History of Nicotine Use

The tobacco used to make cigarettes, cigars, pipe tobacco, and smokeless tobacco, such as snuff and chewing tobacco, comes from the leaves of a plant named *Nicotiana tabacum*. The tobacco plant was named after Jean Nicot, a French diplomat who introduced the use of tobacco in France in 1560, believing the plant could be used as a medicine.[1]

Where Tobacco Comes From

Tobacco plants, which are related to the flower known as the petunia and the vegetable known as the eggplant, grow from two to eight feet tall and are a major crop in several states. Before tobacco can be smoked, it has to be cured in one of several ways: by using heat pumped through a flue (a passageway for carrying a current of air or smoke from one place to another), by wood-fire smoke, or naturally in the sun or in open barns. Different methods are used for different types of tobacco. The flue-cured leaf, for example, is used in cigarettes and chewing tobacco.[2]

Perhaps people mistakenly arrived at the idea that smoking has medicinal value because they could feel the strong effect smoking has on the body. In seconds, inhaled smoke and nicotine can start a person's heart pounding an extra fifteen to twenty-five beats per minute, raise blood pressure by twenty points, lower skin temperature as much as six degrees by cutting off circulation, cause a sharp drop in blood sugar, and create physical stress. Although smokers may think cigarettes make them feel better or calm them down, tobacco is hardly a medicine. These effects diminish quickly as the

Tobacco plants such as the ones shown here grow from two to eight feet tall and are a major crop in several states.

body get used to smoking and the smoker becomes addicted.[3]

From the first drag, damage is being done to almost every part of the body by the thousands of chemical substances found in cigarettes, such as nicotine, tar, and carbon monoxide. Nicotine alone is so strong a poison that one drop can kill a bird.[4]

Although nicotine stimulates the brain and seems to heighten awareness, it also paralyzes and destroys important body tissues. Every drag of a cigarette leaves habit-forming nicotine in the lungs, destroying the cilia (small hairs) there. Normally, these tiny hairs brush mucus out of the lungs, but when nicotine kills them, they cannot do that anymore. Lack of cilia is the reason that smokers are more likely to develop coughs, colds, bronchitis, and asthma. The tar in cigarettes sticks to the lining of the lungs and makes it hard to breathe.[5] Carbon monoxide takes much-needed oxygen away from the body, starving the heart and other organs that need oxygen to function well.[6]

How Different Parts of the Body Are Affected by Smoking

Brain:

Smoking keeps oxygen from the brain. When blood vessels in the brain get narrow, the likelihood of a stroke increases.

Lungs:

Besides bringing cancer-causing substances to the lungs and making it harder for the lungs to clear them, smoking increases the risk of catching colds.

Heart:
Nicotine raises heart rate and blood pressure, increasing the odds of a heart attack. It also leads to the buildup of deposits in the arteries, which causes heart disease.

Stomach:
Smoking encourages the secretion of stomach acid, which can lead to ulcers.

Intestines:
Smoking can also cause ulcers in the intestines.

Digestive tract:
Besides ulcers in the stomach and intestines, smoking can cause cancer in the mouth, throat, esophagus, and bladder.

Reproductive tract:
Smoking increases cancer risk for women, especially in the breasts and reproductive organs. A pregnant woman who smokes is more likely to have a miscarriage, a premature baby, or a baby who dies of sudden infant death syndrome (SIDS).

Ears:
Smokers have a 70 percent higher risk of hearing loss.[7]

Tobacco Reaches Europe

Jean Nicot probably got the idea that tobacco was medicinal from the American Indians, who smoked pipe tobacco in religious ceremonies and used it as a medicine long before Christopher Columbus sailed to the New World in 1492. Different tribes used it for different reasons, including dulling the pain of rattlesnake bites, treating colds and headaches, and keeping people from feeling hungry and thirsty.[8]

When Christopher Columbus sailed to the New World in 1492, his crew had never seen anyone smoking. When they first saw American Indians inhaling and exhaling smoke, they thought the Indians were perfuming themselves with the herb.[9]

Columbus also brought tobacco seeds back to Europe, where farmers grew the plant for use as a medicine that helped people relax.[10] The habit of smoking looked so odd that it took a while for people to accept it. When Sir Walter Raleigh first smoked a cigarette on his return from the American colonies, his servant was so upset that he threw a tankard of ale on Raleigh's head to put out the smoke.[11]

The growing of tobacco crops began in North America after an English colonist brought tobacco seeds from South America to Virginia.[12] Since Virginia's climate and growing conditions were well suited to tobacco, it became an important crop there.

Before the Revolutionary War, most of the tobacco grown in the American colonies was sent to England. After the war, it was used in the United States primarily to make snuff, cigars, and pipe tobacco. Although some people smoked hand-rolled cigarettes, it was not until the invention of the cigarette-rolling machine in the early 1880s that cigarette smoking became affordable enough to be very popular.[13]

Smoking as a Health Hazard

Smoking has always had some powerful critics, but until recently the critics were no match for nicotine addicts. The Puritans considered tobacco a dangerous narcotic. King Louis XIV decreed that tobacco could be sold only by prescription, but that unpopular law was overturned.

When Christopher Columbus (left) sailed to the New World in 1492, his crew had never seen anyone smoking a cigarette. When Sir Walter Raleigh (right) first smoked a cigarette on his return from the American colonies, his servant threw ale at Raleigh's head to put out the smoke.

King James I of England forbade the planting of tobacco in England and Wales, but people grew it anyway. Queen Victoria of England tried to outlaw smoking in the British Army, without much effect.[14]

Although people had suspected all along that smoking was not healthy, it was not until 1960 that the American Cancer Society concluded "beyond reasonable doubt" that cigarettes cause lung cancer. In 1964, the United States Surgeon General's Advisory Committee released a report saying that smoking causes

Tobacco is hung out to dry in this tobacco barn. It was not until the invention of the cigarette-rolling machine in the early 1880s that cigarette smoking became affordable enough to become very popular.

lung cancer, emphysema, chronic bronchitis, and heart disease.[15]

Since 1966, federal laws have stated that cigarette makers have to include a warning on cigarette labels stating that cigarettes can negatively affect the health of users. In 1971, radio and television commercials advertising cigarettes were banned. Since 1972 cigarette makers have also had to include a health warning on all printed cigarette advertising.[16]

Ever since people have been made aware of the health risks involved in smoking, they have looked for supposedly safer ways to smoke, such as adding filters to cigarettes or making cigarettes with less tar. So far, all forms of smoking, chewing, or inhaling nicotine have been proven to be unsafe.

Types of Tobacco

Comparing the different types of tobacco shows there is no safe form of smoking.

Cigars

Cigars are denser than cigarettes, because they use whole leaves, and often have a stronger flavor. Recently, smoking cigars or "stogies" has been portrayed as more glamorous and somehow less harmful than smoking other tobacco products because some celebrities said they smoked them. As a result, about 6 million fourteen- to nineteen-year-olds tried a cigar once in the past year. However, cigars may be even more harmful than cigarettes. They contain between 10 and 44 milligrams of nicotine per smoke, compared to 6 to 11 milligrams in an average cigarette.[17]

Pipes

Tobacco can be smoked in pipes, and pipe tobacco is sometimes flavored. People who smoke pipes have the same risk as cigarette smokers for developing cancers of the mouth, throat, larynx (voice box), esophagus (the part of the body that connects the mouth to the stomach), and bladder.[18]

Snuff

Smokeless tobacco is called snuff. One way people use finely ground snuff is by inhaling a pinch through the nose. Coarsely ground moist snuff is held in the mouth, between the lip or cheek and the gum, sometimes in a type of paper casing that is similar to that of a tea bag. Chewing tobacco is made from whole leaf tobacco. It can be chewed by placing a wad between the cheek and the teeth and sucking on it. A flavor may be added.

Smokeless tobacco is just as addictive as smoking tobacco, and it can cause cancerous spots in the cheeks and sores in the stomach. It also causes bad breath, stains the teeth, damages gums, causes tooth decay, and results in people losing their sense of taste and smell.[19]

Smoking Laws and Young People

In many states it is now against the law to sell tobacco products to anyone under eighteen, and in those states salespeople have to ask for identification to make sure the person buying the cigarettes is old enough. However, in most states children can still buy cigarettes from vending machines. Tobacco company salespeople advise store owners that the best place to put cigarette vending machines is at children's eye level and next to merchandise children can legally purchase.[20]

Fortunately, an increasing number of restaurants and other public places are becoming smoke-free. Some people believe that raising the price of cigarettes by increasing the sales tax may be another way to discourage young people from smoking. Because of the low tax on cigarettes in the United States, cigarettes are less expensive here than in many other countries.

Did You Know?

From 1990 to 1993, more Americans died from smoking-related illnesses than were killed in all the major wars in the history of the United States.[24]

Raising the tax on cigarettes has been successful in Canada, where cigarette sales dropped by almost 40 percent in ten years, because the added tax almost doubled the price.[21]

In Massachusetts, the tax was raised on cigarettes and the money the state earned was used to educate young people about the dangers of smoking.[22]

The high cost of smoking in the United States is already the number-one reason young smokers quit. For every 10 percent increase in price, demand among children declines by about 7 percent.

"Maybe it will stop some smoking, but I highly doubt it," said fifteen-year-old Sarah, a student at White Plains High School in New York, in a recent newspaper interview about the effect of a price hike.

"The price is nothing," said her friend, sixteen-year-old Diane, as she puffed on a cigarette.[23]

The real price of smoking cigarettes, however, is higher than most people really want to pay.

five

Smoke No More

Deciding not to smoke is the smartest way to avoid nicotine addiction. However, if someone smokes, the good news is that it is possible for that person to quit. People quit smoking every day, and the minute they stop smoking, the damage done by smoking starts to heal.

Why Is It Important to Quit?

An important first step for anyone who wants to quit smoking is to decide why it is important to quit. There are lots of valid reasons, but they have to be important reasons to the smoker. It has helped some ex-smokers to write these reasons down on an index card and keep them nearby for easy reference.[1]

Here are a few of the reasons most young smokers give for wanting to quit:

- They want fresher breath.
- They do not like yellow fingernails.
- They do not want to smell like an ashtray.
- They want to be better at swimming, cycling, tennis, and other sports.
- They want better all-around health; fewer colds and coughs.
- Food tastes better.
- Flowers and perfumes smell better.
- Holes burned in clothes or furniture are an expensive nuisance.
- No more overflowing ashtrays or picking through unsmoked cigarette butts.
- They would like more money to have fun with.[2]

What Does It Take to Quit?

It is helpful to learn about withdrawal symptoms and what to expect. Not all people have severe withdrawal

Be a Quitter!

Here are three questions to which smokers should be able to answer yes in order to successfully quit.[3]

- Do they want to stop smoking?
- Are they willing to make some changes in their daily routine?
- Are they willing to put up with a period of some uneasy moments after stopping?

symptoms, but most people can expect to feel crabby or tired, have trouble sleeping, want to eat more, have a cough or dry mouth, or feel depressed. Smokers cannot expect to quit without some negative effects, no matter which method they use. They are overcoming an addiction to a serious drug. It is important to remember that these symptoms do not last. The worst usually last a week or two.[4] After the first few days the "crazies" get easier to bear. Most symptoms will go away completely after a while.

To combat withdrawal symptoms, people who are trying to quit should be extra nice to themselves. They should breathe deeply, take relaxing hot baths, drink lots of water, eat healthy meals, take long walks, call a friend when they feel the urge to smoke, and avoid stimulants such as coffee and alcohol. They should also steer clear of people who smoke and places where they expect that other people will smoke.

Reasons for Smoking

It is important for smokers to think about when and why they smoke. Do they smoke around other people? Do they always smoke while sitting in the same chair or after a meal? Nicotine and the routine of smoking are things that the body craves. If a person always smokes at the same time of day, it may be smart to rearrange a daily schedule. If someone always smoke with his friends after lunch, it might be a good idea to go straight from lunch to another class or hang out elsewhere.

Thinking about what kinds of feelings make people want to smoke can help them stop before they react to those feelings and reach for a cigarette. If people smoke when feeling frustrated, it might be a good idea to think about what made them feel that way. It is also a smart idea to find a healthier way to deal with frustration or anger or sadness or lack of energy. If they feel frustrated, they can try running or taking a brisk walk, shooting a few hoops of basketball, hitting a punching bag, taking a long bubble bath, or talking to a friend about the problem.

Smokers can create mental pictures to associate with smoking and not smoking. For example, the image of a nonsmoker as a person whose skin glows and who beams with pride is a good image that smokers can use every time they want a cigarette.

When smokers think of smoking, they can imagine someone with wrinkles; dull, matted hair; and yellowed teeth. They can think of a person who is weak and wheezing. They can think of an ashtray overflowing with cigarette butts or of scrounging through the garbage for cigarette butts (something many smokers do). By reviewing these mental pictures, smokers can decide which images appeal to them.

Deciding How to Quit

Here are a few different methods people use to help them quit smoking.

Nicotine replacement.

Nicotine gum delivers small amounts of nicotine, which is absorbed through the gums. The nicotine patch, which people wear on their bodies like a small bandage, delivers nicotine through the skin. These are both available without a doctor's prescription. They reduce withdrawal symptoms but are most effective when used together with a program that helps people change the way they behave.[5] Smoking cigarettes while using these products could make a person very sick, because that person will be getting too much nicotine in his or her system.

Cold turkey.

Every year many smokers just go cold turkey, which means they give up smoking altogether, all at once, and suffer through any withdrawal symptoms. When some smokers do this, they throw out all their ashtrays, cigarettes, and matches. Some systems for quitting say the best way to avoid feeling deprived is to keep a cigarette around. Some people find it helpful to keep a jar full of cigarette butts or pin up a picture of someone with a smoker's disease to remind them why they are quitting.

Smoking less.

Some people prefer to smoke less and less so that they get used to a lower level of nicotine. People can start by not smoking in their cars, in their houses, or at work. Eventually they give up the last few cigarettes.

Support groups.

Groups such as SMOKENDERS and Smokers Anonymous or groups run by the American Cancer Society or American Lung Association help people change their behavior and understand why they smoke. They also give people the support they need to quit. The groups are usually led by people who used to smoke and know how hard it is to quit.

Alternative methods.

Two other methods that work for some people are hypnosis, in which people allow themselves to be hypnotized into not wanting to smoke, and acupuncture.

Acupuncture is a method of medicine that originated thousands of years ago in China. During treatment, needles are used to puncture the skin at particular pressure points to treat disease, relieve pain, or reduce cravings.

Deciding When to Quit

When it comes to quitting smoking, timing is important. Although many people just quit when they feel they have had enough, it helps other people to pick a special day. A few days before the big exam or a time when there are major problems at home is probably not the best time.[6]

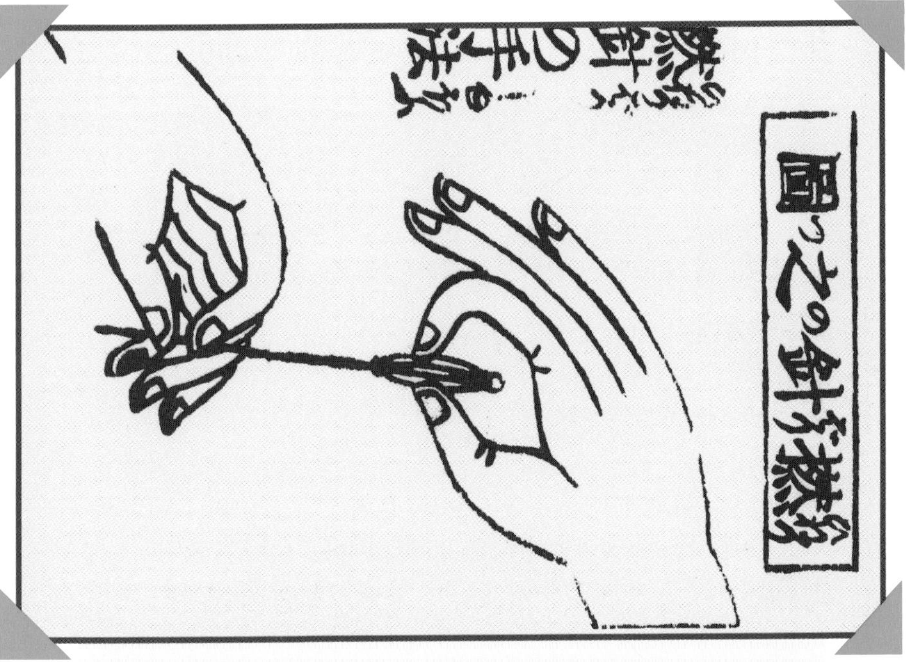

Some people trying to quit smoking may try acupuncture, a method of medicine that originated thousands of years ago in China. During treatment, needles are gently inserted into the skin at specific pressure points to reduce cravings.

The distraction of another problem means there is less attention to give to the serious business of quitting. Some people choose a meaningful day, like Valentine's Day or New Year's Day or a birthday. There is also National Smokeout Day, which is the third Thursday in November, and Kick Butts Day, which falls on April 2 every year.

No Smoker Has to Quit Alone

A person who is trying to do something as difficult as quitting smoking needs support from friends, family, and experts. There are many support groups available. There are also Internet sites, such as The Quit Net <http://www.quitnet.com>, and telephone hot lines, on which smokers can talk to other people about how hard quitting

The Good News About Quitting

- Within only twenty minutes of having the last cigarette, blood pressure and pulse rate return to normal.
- Within eight hours, the oxygen and carbon monoxide in a person's blood reach normal levels.
- Within three months, lung functioning increases by up to 30 percent.
- Within a year, the extra risk of heart disease is cut by half.
- Within five years, stroke risk is reduced to that of a nonsmoker.
- Within ten years, lung cancer death rates are similar to those of nonsmokers.
- Within fifteen years, risk of heart disease is the same as that of a nonsmoker.[7]

is. It is a good idea to tell friends and family so that they know what the smoker is going through and can be supportive.

Smokers should not become discouraged if they cannot quit the first time. Quitting is a very difficult thing to do, and they should feel proud for having the courage to try. For many people, quitting often takes several tries. Each time a person tries to quit, he or she learns something about the smoking habit that may make it easier to succeed the next time.[8]

Supporting a Friend Who Wants to Quit

Nobody can make a smoker quit, but smokers can get the facts, both about what smoking does to them and how they can stop. Smokers can be told how bad smoking is for their health, and they can be assured that they will have the support of friends when they decide to quit.

Here are a few things to do for smokers who want to quit:

- Be there for them if they want to talk. Do not be negative if they fail. Encourage them to try again.
- Let them know you care. Send cards, call, treat them to something special.
- Tell them what a good thing not smoking is. Express pride in their effort.
- Get them out and moving. Get them to sign up for activities. Plan fun stuff to do together.[9]

What You Can Do

By now you know that the best answer to the question "Do you want a cigarette?" is no. However, saying no is much easier after practicing some refusal skills. No matter how someone chooses to say no, it is wise to remember the following:

1. Real friends will still like someone who says no.
2. Many of the kids who smoke now will want to quit before they leave high school.
3. Smokers may enjoy company when they are smoking, but will they be around when other smokers are getting sick more often?

Good Comebacks

Here are a few things to say if someone asks about smoking:

1. I can't. I'm allergic to cigarette smoke.

2. No, sorry, I'm trying out for track (tennis, the swim team, soccer team, etc.).
3. No thanks, I don't like the way it tastes/smells.
4. I don't think smoking is right for me.
5. It's easier for me to act (sing) if I don't smoke.
6. Thanks, but I just quit.

Self-esteem is the key to saying no. There are many healthy ways to feel good and they are all fun to try. These esteem boosters and mood lifters include speed walking, hiking, running, swimming, playing tennis, acting, singing, playing an instrument, writing poetry, playing chess, exploring the Internet, reading, learning to bake great desserts, and lifting weights.

Research shows that young people who are involved in organized sports or other types of regular physical activity find it easier to say no not only because they feel good about themselves, but also because they are concerned about performing well.[1]

Young People Need to Speak Up

Many young people who do not smoke are concerned about not only their own health and safety. They are also concerned about other young people who might start to smoke. Some young people may wonder why cigarette companies are making money off other young people without any regard for the damage smoking can do to them. They may also wonder why there are not more laws to protect young people's health.

With the support of organizations such as C.O.S.T. (Children Opposed to Smoking Tobacco), STAT (Stop Teenage Addiction to Tobacco), Kick Butt (the Campaign for Tobacco-Free Kids), and the Smoke-Free Class of 2000, created by the American Lung Association, the American Cancer Association, and the American Heart Association, some young people are working to change the laws that govern how easy it is for young people to get cigarettes.

Some young people are surprised to discover that they can change laws and that lawmakers will listen to them. But lawmakers do listen, because young people are future voters and they have parents or friends who already can vote. Opinions of young people do count, and if enough young people get together, they can change laws.

Taking Action

Ways in which young people can influence public opinion and help create or change laws include staging antismoking demonstrations, writing lawmakers, and writing to newspapers. Examples of laws that young people are already working to change include

- adding a higher tax on each package of cigarettes so that young people will be discouraged from buying them.
- making the use of vending machines illegal in their state. For example, vending machines are illegal in Massachusetts because they offer young people easy access to cigarettes.[2]
- banning lawmakers from taking campaign money from the tobacco industry, because this might influence the way they vote.

Writing to lawmakers can be easy. Organizations such as the Smoke-Free Class of 2000 can provide a form letter and a list of representatives through its Web site,

Research shows that young people who are involved in organized sports or other types of regular physical activity find it easier to say no to cigarettes. This ability to say no comes not only because the young people feel good about themselves, but also because they are concerned about performing well.

<www.smokescreen.org>, as does C.O.S.T. at its Web site, <www.costkids.org>.

Young people have found creative ways to demonstrate against tobacco, such as those staged by the Campaign for Tobacco-Free Kids on April 2, Kick Butts Day. In Virginia, a group of teens took a well-aimed kick at butts by canceling magazine subscriptions for any magazines that contained cigarette advertisements. In New York, teens brought out a coffin and buried tobacco merchandise inside. In Iowa, a student marching band wore antitobacco uniforms to "drum out tobacco."[3]

One C.O.S.T. group made a banner of handprints of people whose lives have been touched by the effects of smoking. Another group made kites bearing antismoking messages and flew them in a kite-flying contest at the Smithsonian Institution.

C.O.S.T. was started by a group of forty-three middle-school students in Runnemede, New Jersey, to help keep tobacco out of schools. When they heard how many teens start smoking every day and how unhealthy it is, they decided to do something about it. They began by researching why young people smoke and how tobacco companies target kids. They began a letter-writing campaign to eliminate vending machines in their town. They attended council meetings, talked to store owners, and got residents to sign a petition. Then they got their assemblywoman to draft a bill to ban area vending machines.[4]

Young people already have the personal power to report anyone who sells cigarettes to a minor. It is against the law to sell cigarettes to anyone under eighteen, and stores found doing so will be fined.

Some teens have worked as undercover agents in the fight against tobacco sales to minors. "They used to call me the Undercover Girl," said Alexa, an eleventh grader at Adlai E. Stevenson High School in the Bronx, New York.[5]

Alexa worked as a paid undercover agent to help the New York State Health Department gather information for an antismoking law. As one of thirty teens who spent six months asking to buy cigarettes at newsstands, candy stores, delicatessens, supermarkets, and drugstores, she was shocked at how easy it was. Alexa does not smoke and says she never will.

"I think it's baaaad! You get cancer from smoking. My health is first," said Alexa.[6]

As part of a Kick Butts Day protest, Molly, a student in Petaluma, California, decided she and her classmates would write an open letter to hometown actress Winona Ryder and ask the star, who has lit up cigarettes in several movies, to stop smoking on screen.

The story made the papers, and Ryder phoned Molly at school to say that she does not smoke or support smoking.[7]

Sometimes, the hardest thing to deal with when it comes to smoking is the damage it has done to people we love. To come to terms with this hurt, kids can make something positive out of their pain by contributing to the STAT and C.O.S.T. Web sites. These Web sites provide a place to share a photo, a poem, or some memories about loved ones who became sick or died from the harmful effects of smoking. These Web sites also make it easier to see that smoking does harm real people.

The best way to avoid nicotine addiction is never to start smoking. For those who do smoke, quitting is not always easy—but being healthier is well worth any short-term difficulties.

questions for discussion

1. At what age should people have the right to buy cigarettes and decide for themselves if they want to smoke?
2. Do you think cigarettes and other tobacco products should be made illegal in the same way that alcohol was during Prohibition (1920–1933 in the United States and 1917–1919 in Canada)? What do you think would happen if cigarettes and other tobacco products were suddenly illegal?
3. Should cigarette makers be held responsible for the diseases and deaths of people who smoke?
4. Do you think a woman who smokes while pregnant or around her children is committing child abuse?
5. If parents are aware of the fact that their children smoke, do you think it is acceptable for them to allow their children to smoke at home?
6. Should a person who smokes have to pay more for life insurance?
7. Should the tax on cigarettes be raised? If so, what should that extra money be used for?
8. What do you think is the most effective method for convincing young people not to smoke?
9. Should celebrities be allowed to smoke in movies and on television?
10. When people smoke, do you think that means those people do not like themselves?

chapter notes

Chapter 1. Hooked

1. Author interview with "Julia" December 1998.

2. U.S. Department of Health and Human Services, *Preventing Tobacco Use Among Young People: A Report of the Surgeon General* (Washington, D.C.: U.S. Dept. of Health and Human Services, 1994), p. 28.

3. Gladys Folkers and Jeanne Engelmann, *Taking Charge of My Mind & Body* (Minneapolis, Minn.: Free Spirit Publishing, 1997), p. 74.

4. Environmental Protection Agency Web site, "Facts About Smoking," © 1999, <http://www.usdoj.gov>, (January 2, 2000).

5. SmokeFree Educational Services, *The Truth About Secondhand Smoke* (New York: SmokeFree Educational Services, Inc., April 1995), p. 2.

6. Centers for Disease Control and Prevention, *Morbidity and Mortality Weekly Report* (Atlanta, Ga.: Centers for Disease Control and Prevention, November 1996), pp. 971–974.

7. American Cancer Society, *The Decision Is Yours* (Atlanta, Ga.: American Cancer Society, Inc., 1996), p. 4.

8. American Cancer Society, *Questions About Smoking, Tobacco, and Health* (Atlanta, Ga.: American Cancer Society, 1982), pp. 2–4.

9. Ibid.

Chapter 2. Social Issues

1. American Cancer Society, *Facts About Children and Tobacco Use* (Atlanta, Ga.: American Cancer Society, 1997), p. 2.

2. Ibid.

3. *The Surgeon General's Report 4 Kids* magazine, 1998, <http://www.cdc.gov/tobacco> (September 5, 1998).

4. *Facts About Children and Tobacco Use*, p. 2.

5. Centers for Disease Control, *Tips 4 Youth—Facts You Should Know, Teen Opinions on Smoking* (Washington, D.C.: Centers for Disease Control, 1998), p. 1.

6. Ibid.

7. Sandra Gallop, as told to Stephanie Dolgoff, "I Had A Killer Habit," *YM*, July 1997, pp. 82–87.

8. SmokeFree Educational Services, Inc., *The Truth About Secondhand Smoke* (New York: SmokeFree Educational Services, Inc., April 1995), p. 4.

9. Gallop, pp. 82–87.

10. Gladys Folkers and Jeanne Engelmann, *Taking Charge of My Mind & Body* (Minneapolis, Minn.: Free Spirit Publishing, 1997), p. 71.

11. American Cancer Society, *Facts About Children and Tobacco Use* (Atlanta, Ga.: American Cancer Society, 1997), p. 2.

12. *Tips 4 Youth*, p. 1.

Chapter 3. A Dangerous Experiment

1. Author telephone interview with "Michael," November 1998.

2. Arlene Hirschfelder, *Kick Butts! A Kid's Action Guide to a Tobacco-Free America* (Parsippany, N.J.: Julian Messner, 1998), p. 104.

3. The BADvertising Institute, © 1998, <http://world.std.com/~batteryb/> (September 27, 1998).

4. Andrew Tobias, *Kids Say Don't Smoke* (New York: Workman Publishing, 1991), p. 12.

5. *INFACT*, (New York: INFACT, The Apex Press, 1998), p. 4.

6. Gladys Folkers and Jeanne Engelmann, *Taking Charge of My Mind & Body* (Minneapolis, Minn.: Free Spirit Publishing, 1997), p. 65.

7. C.O.S.T. Kids Web site, © 1998, <http://www.costkids.org> (October 18, 1998).

8. Tobias, p. 78.

9. *INFACT*. pp. 51, 56, 86, 91.

10. Hirschfelder, p. 84.

11. National Cancer Society Anti-Smoking Campaign pamphlet, 1996.

12. U.S. Department of Health and Human Services, *Preventing Tobacco Use Among Young People: A Report of the Surgeon General* (Washington, D.C.: U.S. Department of Health and Human Services, 1994), p. 81.

13. Ibid.

14. Ibid., p. 28.

15. *Grolier Wellness Encyclopedia*, "Tobacco and Health," (Danbury, Conn.: Grolier Educational Corporation, 1992), vol. 14, p. 118.

16. Tobias, p. 64.

17. "Projected Smoking Related Deaths Among Youths—United States," *Morbidity and Mortality Weekly Report*, (Atlanta, Ga.: Centers for Disease Control and Prevention, 1996), vol. 45, pp. 971–974.

18. C.O.S.T. Kids Web site, 1998, <http://www.costkids.org> (October 18, 1998).

19. Ibid.

20. Ibid.

21. Jane Brody, "A Fatal Shift in Gender Gap," *The New York Times*, May 12, 1998, p. F7.

22. The American Cancer Society, *Cancer Facts and Figures—1998*, (Atlanta, Ga.: American Cancer Society, Inc., 1998), p. 3.

23. Ibid.

Chapter 4. The History of Nicotine Use

1. Arlene Hirschfelder, *Kick Butts! A Kid's Action Guide to a Tobacco-Free America* (Parsippany, N.J.: Julian Messner, 1998), p. 38.

2. Ibid., p. 39.

3. Patricia Allison and Jack Yost, *Hooked But Not Hopeless: Kicking Nicotine Addiction* (Portland, Oreg.: BridgeCity Books, 1996), p. 21.

4. Curtis W. Casewit, *The Stop Smoking Book for Teens* (New York: Simon & Schuster, 1980), p. 42.

5. Hirschfelder, p. 40.

6. *Grolier Wellness Encyclopedia*, "Tobacco and Health," (Danbury, Conn.: Grolier Educational Corporation, 1992), vol. 14, pp. 25–26.

7. SmokeFree Educational Services, *SmokeFree Air* (New York: SmokeFree Educational Services, 1998), p. 7.

8. Milwaukee Public Museum, *Tobacco, Pipes and Smoking Customs Bulletin* (Milwaukee, Wis.: Milwaukee Public Museum, 1934), pp. 48–49.

9. F.W. Fairhold, *Tobacco: Its History and Associations* (London: Chapman and Hall, 1959), p. 13.

10. Hirshfelder, p. 25.

11. *The World Book Encyclopedia*, Volume T, "Tobacco," (Chicago: World Book, Inc., 1986), p 243.

12. Ibid.

13. *Grolier Wellness Encyclopedia*, "Tobacco and Health," (Danbury, Conn.: Grolier Educational Corporation, 1992), vol. 14, pp. 25–26.

14. *The World Book Encyclopedia*, Volume T, "Tobacco," p. 243.

15. Ibid.

16. Ibid.

17. Julia Van Tine, "Stogie-Smoking Teens?" *Prevention*, December 1997, p. 51.

18. American Lung Association, *Facts About . . . Is There a Safe Tobacco?* (New York: American Lung Association, 1997) p. 2.

19. Ibid.

20. SmokeFree Educational Services, *SmokeFree Air* (New York: SmokeFree Educational Services, Inc., Fall/Winter 1998), p. 7.

21. Andrew Tobias, *Kids Say Don't Smoke* (New York: Workman Publishing, 1991), p. 24.

22. C.O.S.T Kids Web site, 1998, <http://www.costkids.org> (October 18, 1998).

23. Melissa Klein, "Tougher Penalties Urged on Tobacco Firms," Gannett Suburban Newspapers, *The Citizen Register*, (White Plains, N.Y.) April 3, 1998, p. 1A.

24. Ibid.

Chapter 5. Smoke No More

1. Curtis W. Casewit, *The Stop Smoking Book for Teens* (New York: Simon & Schuster, 1980), pp. 106–107.

2. Ibid., pp. 55–56.

3. American Cancer Society, *Smart Move! A Stop Smoking Guide* (Atlanta, Ga.: American Cancer Society, Inc., 1997), p. 2.

4. Centers for Disease Control and Prevention, *I Quit: What To Do When You're Sick of Smoking, Chewing or Dipping* (Washington, D.C.: Centers for Disease Control and Prevention, 1998), p. 1.

5. American Lung Association, *Is There a Safe Tobacco?* (New York: American Lung Association, 1992), p. 6.

6. Casewit, p. 70.

7. Gladys Folkers and Jeanne Engelmann, *Taking Charge of My Mind & Body* (Minneapolis, Minn.: Free Spirit Publishing, 1997), pp. 81–82.

8. American Cancer Society, p. 2.

9. Andrew Weil, *8 Weeks to Optimum Health* (New York: Alfred A. Knopf, 1997), p. 8.

Chapter 6. What You Can Do

1. Department of Health and Human Services, *Preventing Tobacco Use Among Young People: A Report of the Surgeon General* (Washington, D.C.: U.S. Department of Health and Human Services, 1994), p. 139.

2. C.O.S.T. Kids Web site, © 1998, <http://www.costkids.org> (October 18, 1998).

3. STAT Web site, © 1998, <http://www.stat.org> (October 18, 1998).

4. C.O.S.T. Kids Web site.

5. Robert D. McFadden, "Teen-Agers Turn Agents to Fight Illegal Sale of Cigarettes to Minors," *The New York Times*, November 13, 1998, pp. B1, B11.

6. "Some Smoke, Much Ire," *Time*, April 21, 1997, p. 125.

7. Ibid.

where to write for help

American Cancer Society
1599 Clifton Road N.E.
Atlanta, GA 30329
(800) ACS-2345
<http://www.cancer.org>

American Heart Association
7320 Greenville Ave.
Dallas, TX 75231
(800) 242-8721
<http://www.amhrt.org>

American Lung Association of New York
432 Park Avenue South
New York, NY 10016
(800) LUNG-USA
<http://www.lungusa.org>

Americans for Nonsmokers' Rights
2530 San Pablo Ave.
Berkeley, CA 94702
(510) 841-3032
<http://www.no-smoke.org>

Campaign for Tobacco-Free Kids
1707 L Street NW, Suite 800
Washington, DC 20036
(800) 284-KIDS
(202) 296-1662

Children Opposed to Smoking Tobacco (C.O.S.T.)
Mary Volz School
509 W. 3rd Avenue
Runnemede, NJ 08078
<http://www.costkids.org>

Office on Smoking and Health
Centers for Disease Control and Prevention
U.S. Department of Health and Human Services
Washington, DC 20201
(202) 401-0721

SmokeFree Educational Services, Inc.
375 South End Ave., #32F
New York, NY 10280-1085
(212) 912-0960
<http://www.smokescreen.org/ses>

Stop Teenage Addiction to Tobacco (STAT)
Northeastern University
Cushing Hall
360 Huntington Avenue
Boston, MA 02115
(617) 373-7828
<http://www.stat.org>

Internet Addresses

The Advocacy Institute
(provides information on tobacco control news)
<http://www.scarcnet.org/>

The BADvertising Institute
<http://world.std.com/~batteryb/>

Florida Kids Campaign Against Tobacco
<http://team.state.fl.us>

INFACT Tobacco Industry Campaign
<http://www.infact.org>
e-mail: <infact@igc.apc.org>

Kickbutt
<http://www.kickbutt.org>

National Center for Tobacco-Free Kids
<http://www.tobacco-freekids.org>

National Clearinghouse on Tobacco and Health
(a program of the Canadian Council for Tobacco Control)
<http://www.cctc.ca>

NicNet Nicotine and Tobacco Network
<http://tobacco.arizona.edu>

The Quit Net
<http://www.quitnet.org>

Smoke Free Kids
<http://www.smokefreekids.com/smoke.htm>

Smoke Free Maryland
<http://www.SmokeFreeMD.org>

The Surgeon General's Report 4 Kids Magazine
<http://www.cdc.gov/tobacco>

Teen Files: Truth or Dare
<http://www.paramountstations.com/common/teenfiles/smoking>

Tobacco Products Liability Project
(reports on tobacco cases going to trial and lies told by the tobacco industry)
<http://www.tobacco.neu.edu>

glossary

acupuncture—Chinese practice of gently inserting fine gold or silver needles in different pressure points on the body in order to cure diseases, relieve pain, or alleviate cravings.

addictive—Causing a person's body to depend on a chemical.

asthma—A condition in which breathing is often difficult and accompanied by wheezing, coughing, and gasping.

bronchitis—Inflammation of the bronchial tubes, the airways to the lungs.

cancer—A disease in which certain tissues of the body grow uncontrollably for no apparent reason and rob healthy tissues of the nutrients they need to survive.

carbon monoxide—A poisonous gas found in car exhaust and cigarettes.

cilia—Tiny hairs in the bronchi that clear mucus.

cocaine—An addictive and narcotic drug taken from coca leaves.

crack—A very addictive form of cocaine.

craving—An urgent need.

curing—A process of heating or smoking by which a product is preserved and made ready for use.

emphysema—A severe lung disease.

esophagus—The tube leading from the throat to the stomach.

flue—A passageway for carrying a current of air or smoke from one place to another.

heroin—An addictive narcotic made from morphine.

homicide—Murder.

hypnosis—A state resembling sleep that is induced by suggestions and during which a person may get cues to change his or her behavior.

mucus—A slippery secretion of the membranes in the nose.

nicotine—An addictive substance found in tobacco leaves.

paralysis—A condition of the nerves in which the body or parts of the body are no longer able to move.

peer pressure—Social pressure from people who are the same age or from the same background as oneself.

pneumonia—A disease in which the lungs become inflamed.

psychological—Relating to the mind.

pulse—The measurable beat resulting from the movement of blood through the body's arteries.

secondhand smoke—Smoke that is inhaled by a nonsmoker, simply because that person lives, works, or happens to be near a smoker.

self-esteem—Self-worth; feeling good about oneself.

stress—Strain or tension.

stroke—A sudden loss of consciousness or sensation caused when a blood vessel bursts or gets clogged. As a result, nerve cells in part of the brain cannot get oxygen and die, which can lead to paralysis and speech problems or death.

sudden infant death syndrome (SIDS)—Death due to unknown causes in an infant under one year who has previously been in good health.

suicide—The act of taking your own life.

tar—A sticky black substance found in tobacco.

toxic—Poisonous or lethal.

withdrawal—Physical and emotional changes that occur when a person stops using a drug.

further reading

Allison, Patricia, and Jack Yost. *Hooked But Not Helpless: Kicking Nicotine Addiction*. Portland, Oreg.: BridgeCity Books, 1996.

Folkers, Gladys and Jeanne Engelmann. *Taking Charge of My Mind & Body: A Girl's Guide to Outsmarting Alcohol, Drug, Smoking and Eating Problems*. Minneapolis, Minn.: Free Spirit Publishing, 1997.

Henningfield, Jack E. *Nicotine: An Old-Fashioned Addiction*. New York: Chelsea House Publishers, 1992.

Hirschfelder, Arlene. *Kick Butts! A Kid's Action Guide to a Tobacco-free America*. Parsippany, N.J.: Julian Messner, 1998.

Monroe, Judy. *Nicotine*. Springfield, N.J.: Enslow Publishers, Inc., 1995.

Tobias, Andrew. *Kids Say Don't Smoke*. New York: Workman Publishing, 1991.

index

A Portrait Of Me

Meet

CHRISTINE

Birthday: April 12

Best friends:

Joanne Spinoza
Diane Delaney
Aristotle "Ari" Kontos
("My brother from Mars!")

Hobbies:

Ballet, ballet, ballet
Checkers with Grandfather

Sports:

Volleyball
Aerobics

Favorite food (Yum!):

Hamburgers
French fries
Oranges and grapefruits
("Good for needle practice")

Favorite subjects:

Art
Music and Dance
Reading

Yuck!:

Arguing with Ari
Greek leftovers
A messy fridge
("Who moved my insulin *now*?")

Christine Kontos

THE KIDS ON THE BLOCK BOOK SERIES

A Portrait Of Me

Featuring Christine Kontos

Barbara Aiello and Jeffrey Shulman
Illustrated by Loel Barr

TWENTY-FIRST CENTURY BOOKS
FREDERICK, MARYLAND

Twenty-First Century Books
38 South Market Street
Frederick, Maryland 21701

Printed in the United States of America

9 8 7 6 5 4 3 2 1

Special Sales:

The Kids on the Block Book Series is available at quantity discounts with bulk purchase for educational, charitable, business, or sales promotional use. For information, please write to: Marketing Director, Twenty-First Century Books, 38 South Market Street, Frederick, Maryland, 21701.

Library of Congress Cataloging-in-Publication Data

Aiello, Barbara

A portrait of me: featuring Christine Kontos / by Barbara Aiello and Jeffrey Shulman; illustrated by Loel Barr.

(The Kids on the Block book series)

Summary: Eleven-year-old Christine copes successfully with her diabetes but finds it much more difficult to come to terms with the demands of her Greek-American heritage. Includes a section of questions and answers about diabetes and its treatment.

ISBN 0-941477-05-3

[1. Greek Americans — Fiction. 2. Diabetes — Fiction.] I. Shulman, Jeffrey, 1951— . II. Barr, Loel, ill. III. Title. IV. Series: Aiello, Barbara. Kids on the Block book series.

PZ7.A26924Po 1989 89-32318 CIP AP

[Fic]—dc20

To the children who teach us about differences—
and similarities

Dear Reader:

Who are The Kids on the Block? They are kids like you. They like to do the same things you do. They share your hopes and fears. And like you, they have differences. You'll meet kids who are blind or have cerebral palsy. You'll meet kids who are deaf or have asthma. And you'll meet kids whose lives have been changed by divorce or drugs.

In The Kids on the Block Book Series, you'll find their stories. You'll read stories about friendship and growing up, stories about changes and challenges. But you won't read about kids who are dependent, and you won't read about superheroes, either. The Kids on the Block are regular kids leading regular lives.

"I'm not an epileptic," one kid says. "I'm a person with epilepsy." And that is the point. These kids are people: different in the same ways that we are all different, alike in the same ways that we are all alike.

We hope you enjoy their stories.

Barbara Aiello
Jeffrey Shulman

CHAPTER 1

"We came on a boat that had been a coal ship. The conditions were very, very bad. And the weather was so terrible. The food was worse. But we managed to get here. We were allowed to go to Ellis Island. We were herded like sheep there to be examined, all very fearful that we might not be found healthy enough, that we might be sent back. My father referred to Ellis Island as the Palace of Tears because everyone was so fearful.

It was crowded. Ours was not the only immigrant ship. People were coming to the United States in droves from everywhere. Because this was the promised land.

This was the place for us."

"Did you find anything interesting?" Grandfather whispered in my ear.

His voice seemed to come out of the pages I was reading: from the long, fearful lines at Ellis Island, the place where so many people took their first step on American soil; from the ships crowded with hundreds of poor immigrants; from the little Greek villages where others waited their turn to make the hard and painful trip. Of course, it couldn't be. I knew that.

His voice sounded funny and different to me. I thought for a moment that I was hearing it for the very first time. But that couldn't be, I said to myself. It couldn't be.

Why was it, then, that when I looked up into the wrinkled eyes of my Grandfather, even his face was not the same? It, too, seemed to come out of the past, out of the many frightened and yet hopeful faces I had been looking at. Faces of Greeks, Italians,

Poles, Russians. Faces worn by weeks of the terrible journey. Faces lifted up to the promise of a new life.

"Oh, yes," I said, "I found so much."

Ellis Island. It was like some sort of magical place where the past still lives today. You know, like a time machine, where you can go back, back, back, and see what your grandparents were like when they were children. You can see their faces and read their stories. And you can see beyond that. You can see their homes and families, their parents and grandparents. You can see a long way back.

Okay, Christine, I wondered, what's going on here? What's all this looking back stuff? You're the one who's always looking ahead. You're the one who's going to be building the America of tomorrow. What about that little sign on your bedroom door: "Christine Kontos, Architect of the American Dream"? What's going on here? Christine, I thought, are you feeling all right?

Ellis Island. Its name was like some sort of magical spell. An island hidden in the misty past.

And I *had* found a lot, too. I guess you could say I found a portrait of me. Oh, I know, that doesn't make any sense. Well, it's complicated. Why don't I just start at the beginning?

CHAPTER 2

But where is the beginning?

Maybe when Ms. Shaw announced the theme for the winter dance recital. Or maybe when Ari and I had the big fight. Or—oh, I can't figure out beginnings anymore. I'll just start with me.

I'm Christine Kontos. I'm eleven years old and in the fifth grade at Woodburn School. I like art, music, and English, but what I really like the best is dance. Ballet. Especially, modern ballet. My best friend is Joanne Spinoza. She is fourteen, but what I like most about Joanne is that she never makes me *feel* eleven. She says I'm "a mature eleven-year-old." Isn't that great?

I have a family, of course. (Boy, do I ever have a family!) There's my Mom and Dad, my two sisters (Mary and Iantha), my three brothers (Ari, Peter, and Marc), my Grandfather and my Grandmother, one dog (Zeus), two cats (Mercury and Hera), and—oh, that's it. Well, that's enough, isn't it?

Most people know my Dad as Woodburn's "Coach" Kontos. But when he's not in his sweat suit, he really is an architect. "That's Greek," he likes to point out to me. "It means 'a master builder.' " A master builder: I love the sound of that. I remember when I told Dad I wanted to be an architect, too.

"Must be your Greek roots popping out at last," he laughed.

"What do you mean?" I asked. He was always making me sound like some sort of plant or something.

"The Greeks," he said, his index finger pointed in the air, "were master builders." He always speaks with that finger in the air. As a matter of fact, everybody in my family seems to speak with their hands. I tease my friend Mandy (she's deaf) that my family has its own sign language. Old World Greek, I call it. "Master builders," Dad was saying. "Look at the Parthenon."

"The Parthenon?" I asked. "Dad, you have to be kidding. I mean, I'm sure the Parthenon was okay in its day. But that day was a long, long time ago. The Parthenon must be a thousand years old."

"Actually," Dad said, "it's more like 2,500 years old."

"Just my point," I said, with *my* index finger high in the air. (So sometimes I speak Old World Greek, too. In this family you just can't help it. You have to be heard, don't you?) "Look at the World Trade Center, look at the Sears Tower," I said. "Now, that's master building."

"Maybe," Dad replied. "And, maybe, we'll have to wait 2,500 years to know for sure."

You never actually *win* an argument with a Kontos.

My Mom owns a restaurant—it's a Greek restaurant, of course—with my grandparents. The Olive Branch, it's called. It used to be called Kontos's Athenian Palace. That was before Mom and my grandparents remodeled it last year and gave it a brand new look, and a brand new name to match. Still, it's the same old Greek restaurant to me. I work there sometimes on the weekends. That's what the fight with Ari was all about. But hold on, I'll get to that.

Mom loves to cook Greek foods, like spanakopita, moussaka, souvlakia, dolmades—and lots of other strange dishes with strange names. "It's not the foods so much," she explained to me, "it's the traditions behind them. It's the spirit of the old country. It's a way of life I love and want to remember."

"Sure, Mom," I said in halfhearted agreement. But what it meant to me was lots of Greek leftovers. Lamb and pilaf and feta cheese, then more lamb and pilaf and feta cheese. "Why couldn't we be Italian?" I asked one night at dinner. "At least, then, we could be eating leftover pizza." The only Greek food I really like is baklava. It's like a pastry, with nuts wrapped in a special Greek dough, and it's topped with a delicious honey syrup. But I'm not supposed to eat it because of my diabetes. Leftovers and diabetes: that's what the Greek way of life used to mean to me.

Of course, you'll want to hear about my fight with Ari. But that's a long story. And what has all this got to do with Ellis Island? Just hold on. I'm getting there.

CHAPTER 3

It all started in dance class about a month ago.

"But let me make this clear," Ms. Shaw warned, trying to speak above all the excitement. "If you want to be in this year's dance recital, be prepared to work. W O R K. Work." Ms. Shaw liked to spell things out for us. It was kind of a pain. P A I N. Pain. But she was a wonderful teacher. I had been taking ballet lessons with her for nearly a year, a year of practicing all of the basic exercises: plié, and battement, rond de jambe à terre, and adagio—oh, I had practiced and practiced till I dreamed ballet. Sometimes I just wanted to scream, "Enough of exercises! I want to fly! I want to soar!"

"You may develop your own routine," Ms. Shaw was saying, "but remember our theme for this year's recital: 'A Portrait of You.' Here is your chance, boys and girls, to express yourself in dance. A chance to create a living portrait of you. Y O U. You."

Ms. Shaw suggested that we keep a dance notebook, a place to write down all our thoughts about our special portrait.

M E. Me. A portrait of me. What would it be? Whatever it was, I wanted it to be fresh and exciting and alive. I wanted it to tell the world who I was. I wanted it to say, "Look out! Here's something new, something unexpected. Here's Christine Kontos!" I wanted to take the world by surprise. I wanted to soar!

"Great news, everybody," I announced, as I soared into the kitchen of The Olive Branch. I worked there on weekends and sometimes after school, doing odd jobs in the kitchen, maybe helping clear the tables, and just generally trying to stay out of the way. It was a pretty busy place. I tried to convince Mom that working in a Greek restaurant would be bad for my diabetes—you know, I have to be real careful about what I eat and when I eat it.

"But, Christine," Mom observed, "you don't even like Greek food. Help me grate some more cheese, will you?"

I told you, you *never* win an argument with a Kontos.

"Great news, everybody," I exclaimed, "I'm going to be in Ms. Shaw's Christmas dance recital."

"That really is good news," my Grandma said. "I'll bet you're very pleased, Christina." Always Christina, I thought. When will I be plain old Christine to my grandparents?

"And I'll bet you will be the best one there." That was my Grandfather. He always thought I would be the best one, no matter what the occasion. "But I just have to tell you, Christina," he went on, "you've got those socks with no feet on again." He meant my leg warmers, of course. He was always kidding me about my exercise outfits. "Stella," he would say to my mother, "you'd think such a smart girl would know how to wear socks."

"Poppa," Mom would laugh, "she's a regular modern girl."

I told them all about the "Portrait of You" theme for the show. I told them how Ms. Shaw said it would be a chance to express myself in dance. I didn't have to tell them how excited I was. "But it'll be a lot of work," I explained. "We'll have to practice on Saturdays to get ready."

And that's what started the fight.

"But you're supposed to work here on Saturdays, Chris," Ari complained. Ari was my older brother, fifteen big years old. He loved the restaurant. He loved its spicy smell, the smell of basil and thyme, of marjoram and oregano. I was pretty much a hamburger and french fries girl myself. And so we'd fight over that. Ari couldn't understand why I didn't want to spend my afternoons peeling potatoes and washing spinach.

But it went deeper than that. Ari loved the old Greek ways. He was so much like my Grandfather, everyone said. And it was true. Sometimes, when I looked at Ari, I thought, "There goes my little grandfather." And I used to tell my friends that Ari was "fifteen and going on fifty." I thought he was old when he should be young. He was working when he should be free. Who knows what he thought of me?

"Well, I just won't be able to, Ari," I said back.

"That's typical."

"Typical of what?"

"Typical of you, that's what. Typical of your attitude. You're too busy to help. You've got too many important things to do."

"Children, please," interrupted Mom, "enough of this."

"Ari," Grandfather said in a comforting way, "it's all right. If Christina has other things to do, be happy for her. Let her do them. The restaurant is not for everybody."

"Nothing is," Grandmother added in a grandmotherly way.

"I guess," Ari grumbled. But you could tell he didn't mean it. He was simmering away like Mom's lentil soup. "I guess," he said again, "but it isn't fair. It's . . . it's . . . disloyal."

Disloyal? That was too much. I wasn't going to stand for it. "What is this?" I asked. "It's not disloyal to want to live my own life. I have my own dreams. And working here is just not part of them. I'm not interested in Greek foods and Greek this and Greek that. And I don't want to be stuck in some stupid Greek restaurant for the rest of my life!"

That quieted things in a hurry. I felt terrible the minute I said it. I meant to hurt Ari, but I knew I had hurt Mom and my grandparents, too. Now, I *felt* disloyal. I wanted to say, "I didn't really mean it that way," but it wouldn't have done any good. The quiet was too deep for that.

CHAPTER 4

Let me tell you about Aristotle Kontos. When I was little and scared to give myself insulin shots, Ari used to stand by my side and tell me funny stories to make me laugh. I learned to give myself shots by practicing on grapefruits and oranges, and it was Ari's idea to draw weird faces on them and pretend they were "fruit from Mars." He was the only one who could really make me accept my diabetes.

Ari made me feel like a regular member of the family. It wasn't easy, not being able to eat ice cream, sugary doughnuts—those kinds of things. But it was Ari who said, "If Chris can't have sweets, then neither will the rest of us." Well, it was also Ari who didn't last too long ("What?" he used to scream, "fruit again for dessert?"), but it was nice of him to try anyway. Sometimes, I'd reach into the fridge for a piece of fruit, and *all* the apples and oranges or whatever would have weird faces on them. My brother from Mars!

He used to say I was born stubborn. I remember when Ari would try to "tickle some sense" into me. Until the time I told him I was too old for that and quite sensible enough, thank you.

It was Ari who brought a scruffy looking puppy home from the pound. And it was Ari who taught me, and my brothers and sisters, how to take care of our new little ball of fur. It was Ari who named him Zeus.

I thought the world of Ari.

Now, I fight with him all the time. Why was he always angry with me? Why was I always angry with him? Only, it wasn't just with Ari, and that's what bothered me. It was with Mom, and

Grandma, and Grandfather, and The Olive Branch and—well, it seemed like I was fighting everyone and everything I knew.

But that was just the beginning. Believe me.

"Are you mad at me, Grandfather?" I asked quietly. We were in the kitchen, where I was helping him make a cucumber salad. Grandfather was old, and the creases and folds in his wrinkled skin made me think of getting old. But his hands were still swift and sure.

"Cut the cucumbers in cubes," he said. "No, of course not. I wish you and your brother wouldn't fight like cats and dogs."

"That's not what I mean," I replied.

"Well, what do you mean?" he asked. "Put the cubes in those big bowls while I get the yogurt."

"I mean, what I said about the restaurant. I didn't really mean it that way."

"Oh, I know you didn't. Now, don't worry yourself about that. Listen to your grandfather. It's like your mother said: you're a regular modern girl. Let's chop the garlic. But is that so different from my own parents? They left the old country to find a new life in America. They wanted that life for their children and grandchildren and"—Grandfather stopped his chopping for a moment and studied my face—"and their great-grandchildren." He placed his hand on my cheek. "I wish my mother could see this beautiful face. Because she would know that all the suffering, all the hardship, was worth it. I wish my father could hear you talk about being an architect. 'Imagine that,' I can hear him saying, 'Nico Kontos's great-granddaughter is an architect. An architect in America.' He would be so proud. We'll need the mint and the lemon juice. Don't forget the olive oil."

Grandfather was thinking about old, old times. I imagined him sitting in the square of his little hillside village, a little boy wondering what America was like. And if he would ever see it. "When my parents brought me to America," he went on, "they had dreams, too. But do you think they left Greece behind? No. They left family there. They left friends there. They left a life there. You can't just leave that behind. So you hold onto the old ways, the way you hold onto your memories. You can't just let them go."

"That's just it, Grandfather," I insisted, "they're memories. They're the past. I want more than memories. I have dreams for the future, Grandfather. Is there anything wrong with that?"

Grandfather was studying my face again. "Of course not," he replied. "Every family needs a dreamer. You be our dreamer, Christina." But I couldn't tell if he really meant it, or if he was just saying that for me. "But not our *day*dreamer," he finished. "Add the garlic, mint, and lemon juice to the yogurt. Just the right amount of oil, salt, and pepper. Pour the sauce over the cucumber. And there you have it: the best cucumber salad outside of Athens." It probably was, too. "Now, there's something to dream about," he said with pride and pleasure.

There was a funny sound in Grandfather's voice. I couldn't put my finger on it, but, trust me, it was there.

And, for a long time, I could still feel Grandfather's hand on my cheek.

CHAPTER 5

Practice, practice, and more practice. I tell you: when Ms. Shaw spelled out work, she was not kidding around. I knew getting ready for the recital was going to be hard, but I didn't think it was going to be *this* hard.

When I wasn't practicing dance, I was talking dance with Joanne or my other friends, and when I wasn't practicing or talking dance, I was thinking dance. I kept my notebook with me all the time. I even got in the habit of sort of singing softly to myself, "A Portrait of Me: What Could It Be?" It was really the only thing on my mind. Ari thought it was pretty weird, but, of course, he would. Come to think of it, it *was* pretty weird.

Well, what could my portrait be? One thing I did was to ask Mom and Dad and everyone what *they* thought. I put their ideas in my dance notebook.

From my father: "I see a dance vision of Christine Kontos, the world's greatest architect. I see a lone figure on the stage slowly rising to tower magnificently above the landscape. Say, that's pretty good, isn't it?" Right, Dad. I mean, let's not get too carried away or anything.

From my mother: "What about a modern routine? Combining ballet with some jazz steps and, maybe, aerobics. It would be perfect for you." Now, that *was* pretty good.

From Ari: "How about 'The Dance of a Pig-Headed Mule'?" Thank you, Ari. That was very helpful.

From my Grandmother: "Well, Christina, I think the most important thing is for you just to be yourself." It's Christine, Grandma, Christine.

From my Grandfather: "The goat dance of Greece. I'll bet it's the first time these people will see real Greek folk dancing. And who better to show it to them than a Kontos? Can you do that?" Maybe another time, Grandfather.

Now, where should I start? It seemed that everyone had a different idea of me. I guess the important thing was, what did *I* think of me, but I was more puzzled about that than ever. I used my notebook to help me sort out my thoughts. I wrote down all my favorite things to do. All my favorite foods. Favorite songs. Favorite people. One time I even tried to write down all the words I would use to describe myself. I had just about worn myself out with adjectives when I heard Mom calling.

"Christine." I was staring from my bedroom window at the last rays of the red-gold December sunset. "Almost dinner time."

"Okay," I hollered back. Time to give myself a shot of insulin. I have to do that twice a day, you know, but it only takes me a minute now. (Hey, maybe I could do "The Dance of the Human Pincushion." Well, maybe not.) I was thinking of the first time I gave myself a shot, how scary it was. Not anymore, I thought. I was about to go downstairs, but, first, I wrote one more word in my notebook: "fearless."

Thanks, Ari.

CHAPTER 6

Where do fights start? I'm no expert in fights, but I think they're like icebergs. You know how you only see the tip of an iceberg, but underneath it's super big and dangerous. Fights are like that. You only see the tip of the fight, and what you're fighting about may seem small and silly. But, underneath, where it really matters, there's a monster iceberg just waiting, waiting, waiting for you.

"Great, great news, everybody," I said, as we sat down to a Kontos Friday night dinner. I was soaring again. I was so excited I thought I might never get my feet back on the ground. I felt like a helium balloon. "I'm going to the ballet. I'm going to the Joffrey Ballet!"

Let me tell you about a Kontos Friday night. It was, without doubt, the best night of the week. We had Friday night dinner with Grandma and Grandfather. There was lamb and pilaf and feta cheese, of course ("Not again," I'd complain), and there was laughter and friendship and . . . and family. Old World Greek sign language flashed everywhere. And there were funny stories about the restaurant. There were even funnier stories about the old country. The old country. The way my grandparents talked about it, they made it sound like a dream—the kind you try to remember all day long, but it's always just a little out of reach. Sometimes, there was even a song or two.

"Slow down, Chris," Mom said. "Tell us all about it."

"The Joffrey Ballet will be here in January, and"—

"What's the Jeffrey Ballet?" Ari asked.

"Joffrey. The Joffrey Ballet, you knucklehead," I said.

"Hey, who are you calling"—

"All right, all right, you two," Mom stepped in, "let's not get started. Christine, we can do without the names, please."

"The Joffrey Ballet is my favorite. And Ms. Shaw wants to take the whole class. Can I go, Mom? Can I? Oh, please say yes."

"Well, I don't see why not," she replied. That was as good as a yes, wasn't it? They were going to have to tie me to the ground with a rope.

Ari wasn't too happy, you could tell. Just what is it with big brothers, anyway? They're like pins, always ready to burst your bubble. "I still think it's a funny name," he said.

"You would, *Aristotle* Kontos," I said.

He was getting angry. "What's that supposed to mean?"

"You figure it out!" Well, I had a right to get angry, too.

"Can we *please* get through one dinner without a fight," Dad said impatiently. "Why don't we try it tonight and see how we like it? Just this once. Okay?"

Okay, Dad. But what about that nice iceberg there? Don't you see it? You know, the one with the Kontos name on it. *The one we're about to hit.* Ladies and gentlemen, to the lifeboats, please. Hurry, now.

Grandfather tried to steer our dinner into calmer waters. He would always ask how we spent our week. "The Weekly Update," he called it. "Ari," he began, "what's the good news with you?"

"I'm still working on my history report about immigration, Grandfather." Oh, that stupid report. That's the only thing Ari has talked about for weeks. "It's not just numbers and dates and stuff like that, though. I want to understand what it was *really* like. I want to write down the stories you and Grandma tell, and show people how it felt to leave everything behind for a strange, new country, what it felt like to . . . to . . . well, to see the Statue of Liberty for the first time."

It figures, doesn't it? When we were little, we went to see the Statue of Liberty. It was a wet and foggy day. I remember how miserable the cold drizzle made me feel. That's about all I want to remember.

"And, you, Christina," Grandfather turned his attention to me, "you had big news today, didn't you?"

Just thinking about the ballet got me excited again. I told Grandfather all about the Joffrey. "It's like a dream come true," I said.

"And when is the ballet, Christina?" Grandmother asked. It was a simple question. Or so I thought at the time.

"January 6th," I said. It was a simple answer. At least, I thought so at the time.

Have you ever heard the sound of complete silence? It's the sound you hear just before your lovely ship of dreams hits the biggest iceberg in the ocean.

"January 6th?" Mom asked.

"Why, yes," I said, "January 6th."

"But, Chris," she said with surprise, "you know January 6th is the Feast of the Epiphany. I'm afraid you"—

I didn't hear the rest of it, but I didn't have to hear it to know that I was shipwrecked. I had forgotten that January 6th was the Epiphany. How I forgot that I don't know. You see, my family's religion is Greek Orthodox, and for us January 6th is a very special holiday. One of our Christmas holidays. I guess I was just so busy with the dance recital that . . . well, that I forgot. I just forgot.

"I'm sorry, Christine," Mom finally said.

I didn't know what to say. But I had to say something, didn't I? "But nobody celebrates January 6th. Why can't we just have a normal holiday, like everyone else? Why do we always have to be different?"

"We *do* have a normal Christmas," Ari insisted.

"You stay out of this, Ari," I shouted. The last thing I needed now was for him to butt in. "Can't I miss it just this once?"

"I'm afraid not," Dad said. "You know how important"—

"I know how important the ballet is, too. It's not like this is a *real* religious holiday. I can see my gifts when I get home. Nobody else"—

"She's embarrassed to be Greek," Ari said. "That's what this is all about."

"Ari," Mom tried to say, "this is not"—

"I am not," I said back to Ari. "I am not."

"There they go again," my sister Mary complained. "Like a broken record."

"I wish it *were* broken," sighed Mom. "You two fight worse than Zeus and Hera." When Zeus heard his name, he barked in agreement.

"Isn't anybody on my side?" I cried out.

"It's not a question of sides, Christina," Grandma said. "It's a holy day for us, the day the three kings brought their gifts to the child Jesus."

I felt like screaming, "I know, Grandma, I know. I've heard it a thousand times." But I didn't dare.

Grandma continued. "They traveled for days and days to show their love. I think we can give up one day to show ours. That's what the Epiphany is all about, Christina. It's more than getting gifts. It's about the gift of giving. I'm surprised at you."

"Your grandmother is right, Christine Kontos," Mom said firmly. "This is not a question of sides. It's a question of family. Like it or not, you're still a part of this family, and you will be for quite some time. I'm sorry. I wish you could go to the ballet. I know what it means to you. But you can't. And that's final."

"It's not fair!" I said, as I stormed off to my room. "And it's not final!"

CHAPTER 7

It was a rainy Saturday, and I was stuck inside. What I usually do on a rainy-Saturday-stuck-inside day is talk on the phone. Just to a few friends. You know, just for a few hours. About everything. And nothing. It drives everyone crazy.

But not today. Today, I stayed in my room. I was angry at the whole world. And it seemed like the whole world was angry at me.

I heard a knock on the door. It was Grandfather. "Excuse me," he said, "but has anyone seen my old checkers partner?" That was me. I loved to play checkers with Grandfather. We would sit by the window, with the checkerboard between us, and Zeus (ever since he was a puppy) would curl up by our feet. Grandfather would tell stories about growing up in Greece. Once in a while, we would even play checkers. And once in a while, he let me win.

"You know, Christina," Grandfather said between moves, "I have to go to New York soon for business. I don't see why you couldn't come along. We could do a little sightseeing. Maybe even take in a ballet."

"Really, Grandfather?"

"Really," he said. "If your mother and father don't mind."

"Oh, that would be great!" I exclaimed. "The ballet in New York! Things are going to work out, after all."

"Of course, they are," Grandfather replied, softly patting my cheek. "They always do, don't they?" But there was that funny sound in his voice again. He sounded, somehow, worried.

“Thanks to you, Grandfather,” I answered.

He was quiet for a moment. “Not thanks to me,” he finally said with a sigh. “I can take you to the ballet, but I can’t bring peace to this family. I can’t”—

“But I don’t understand,” I interrupted. “Why can’t everyone leave me alone? Why is it always the past? Why is it always the family? Why can’t I just be myself?”

“Yourself?” asked Grandfather. “Well, who are you if not part of a family? Where do you come from if not from your family?”

“I want to know where I’m going, not where I come from. Is that so horrible?”

“No, I suppose not,” he said.

“Why can’t Ari understand that?”

“He understands,” Grandfather replied. “He’s proud of you.”

“Well, he has a strange way of showing it,” I said.

Grandfather laughed a little. “I guess that’s true.”

“It’s because he lives in the past, Grandfather. That’s why he hates me.”

“Ari doesn’t hate you, Christina. He loves you, even if he does have a strange way of showing it. I think he’s just a little afraid, that’s all.”

“Afraid of what?” I asked.

“Maybe he’s afraid that if he lets go of the past, he’ll lose something he wants to hold onto. Maybe something he wants to hold onto too much.”

“Maybe,” I muttered. It didn’t make sense to me. I was tired of the whole business. Why couldn’t Grandfather get Ari off my back? He knew it was Ari’s problem, after all. But before I was able to ask Grandfather to talk to Ari, he spoke first.

“And what are *you* afraid of, Christina?” Grandfather asked.

CHAPTER 8

Monday was the worst day of my life. It's funny. The one day I'd like so much to forget is the day I remember so clearly.

I had to explain to Ms. Shaw why I couldn't see the ballet. "There will be other times, Christine," she said.

"I guess so" was my sullen response.

"Maybe you could become Jewish, like me," my friend Leslie suggested. "Then, your parents would have to let you go."

I didn't think they'd go for that one.

I was on my way home from school, just a block from our house. I was walking with Joanne. Joanne and I were on the safety patrol at Woodburn. She was on the senior patrol; I was a junior aide. We were still wearing our bright orange belts. It hadn't been a great day. I got so tired and dizzy on the safety patrol, I had to sit down and eat some emergency candy. The "candy cure," Joanne calls it. I guess (I mean, I *know*) I should have eaten all my lunch. I was just so busy.

I felt better on the way home, though. Joanne was talking nonstop about some new boy she met, but I wasn't paying much attention. I was thinking about the recital ("What could it be?"), I was thinking about New York, I was thinking about me.

Oh, Christine, why weren't you paying attention?

It all happened so quickly. I saw Zeus bounding up the block to meet me. He always does. He was so happy to see me, and I was just as happy to see him. He waits on our side of the street. He always does. Together, we run the rest of the way home.

But somehow today was different. Today, Zeus didn't wait. (But he always does!) I saw him leap into the street. (Why didn't he wait?) I heard the terrible screech of brakes. There was nothing I could do. I heard the terrible sound of Zeus's yelp.

"Oh, God, please don't let him die." Over and over I prayed to myself, leaning over Zeus, "Oh, God, please don't let him die." He was hurt really bad.

Joanne raced to my house to get help. I saw Ari running. "Oh, Ari," I was crying, "please don't let him die."

"Let me take you to the vet," the man who drove the car said. Ari picked Zeus up and held him so gently. And Joanne sat beside me.

We waited and waited while the vet tried to help Zeus. But when he came out at last, "I'm sorry" was all he said.

I cried like a baby. I didn't want to. I didn't want to act like a little kid, but I couldn't help myself. Joanne tried to put her arm around me, but it wasn't Joanne I needed then. That day, I cried like a baby in my brother's arms.

Later that night, Ari came to my room. "Mind if I come in?" he asked.

Of course, I didn't mind. We might fight like cats and dogs, but, somehow, I always knew that when I really needed him, Ari would be there.

Ari and I sat together in my room for a long time that night. The quiet seemed to grow around us, the way stars come out one by one till the sky is filled with them.

I was thinking about Zeus when he was a puppy. How he used to hide when it was time for his bath. How he tried to make friends with our cats, Mercury and Hera. How he nuzzled me awake in the morning with his cold nose. How he grew and grew. "That dog is eating us out of house and home," Dad used to say. But Dad loved him, too.

"It's hard to believe," I said, "that Zeus is gone. Just like that. Just this morning I was playing with him. And, now, it's all memories. That's all that's left. Memories."

The moon rose white in the dark night sky.

"That's a lot," Ari said quietly.

"What do you mean?" I asked.

"I wish I could explain, Chris. But I really don't know how. Grandfather says that growing up means changes—some good, some not so good. You know, Chris, he's seen so many changes in his life. More than I can imagine. More than I ever want to see. Maybe I'm afraid of so many changes."

Ari stopped and took my hand. "Nothing lasts forever, Chris. Except our memories. Maybe that's why I feel so strongly about our family and roots. Maybe that's why I get so angry with you. I mean, I know I'm old-fashioned." Ari paused again, while we both felt the quiet of the bright winter night. "Maybe that's why I wrote my report on Ellis Island."

Ari and I sat together in my room for a long time that night. When he left, I thought about a lot of things. I thought about Zeus and how gently Ari held him. I thought about Grandfather, the way he put his hand on my cheek, the funny, worried sound in his voice.

I knocked quietly on Ari's door.

"Come in," I heard him say. I opened the door halfway and stuck my head inside.

"What's up, Chris?" he said.

"Can I read it?" I asked. "Can I read your report?"

CHAPTER 9

I told you I couldn't figure out beginnings anymore. You might say reading Ari's report was a new beginning for me.

Voices from Ellis Island
by Aristotle Kontos

Nothing shows the spirit of America better than the Statue of Liberty. For millions of immigrant Americans it meant a dream come true. It meant that they had, at last, reached the land of promise, the land of their hopes and dreams.

Ellis Island is a small spot of land in the shadow of the Statue of Liberty. For 15 million new Americans, it was their entrance way to a new world and a new life.

Many years later, hundreds of these newcomers to America remembered the most important trip of their lives. They spoke of their old homes and their journey to a new home. This is the true voice of Ellis Island.

What was so neat about Ari's report was that he used the real words, and real pictures, of the people who came to America, people whose first steps in their new land were through the great halls of Ellis Island. I noticed right away all the different names: Tartarini, Blau, Devlin, Vasily, Nagy, Chletsos, Berger, and on and on. Names of Poles, Russians, Slavs, Irish, Greeks, Italians. Names that told a hundred different stories. Names that all told the same story.

And they were so young when they came over. Just my age, many of them. They had to leave their families and their friends. *"I remember how many nights I used to cry,"* one woman said, *"but it had to be done."* It had to be done? Could I ever do that? I tried to imagine myself making that long and lonely voyage. Where would I find the courage?

They remembered the awful trip on the ships. They lived for weeks in steerage, in the bottom of the boat, where it was dirty and crowded. There was always bad food and sometimes bad weather. But they tried to make the best of it. One woman (she was Greek) remembered one "bright night on the deck":

> *"I was born with the music in my body. When they have this big doings in the villages, they would dress me in the little Grecian outfits, and I danced. That night, there was such a bright night on the deck. So they say, 'How about you, little girl? You know how to dance?' I say, 'You bet I know how to dance.' I never forget that. I was the life of the party."*

They remembered when they first saw the Statue of Liberty:

> *"It was a most beautiful thing. The torch was burning. I still remember the light. I keep on looking and looking. And a man came to me and says, 'What is it, girl?' I says, 'Do you know this Statue of Liberty? Do you know what it means?' He says, 'It's just a statue.' I says, 'No. That's the freedom of the world. This lady opens her arms for people. We come from all over the world. The torch up there: it says, Welcome.' I stayed there for over two hours just staring at her. I thought it was the prettiest thing I ever seen in my life."*

They remembered being herded into long lines to be questioned and examined. Some remembered being separated from their families, perhaps forever.

They told about their new lives. Learning a new language, learning new ways. But they didn't forget the old ways. It was like Grandfather said: they were dreamers like me, but they held onto their memories, too. Dad says that the taller a building you want to make, the deeper a foundation you have to dig. It was that way with them. Their memories gave them the strength to dream new dreams for the future:

> *"If you drop everything of your own kind, it's like cutting off part of you. You may be able to do without your arm, but is it the best thing for you to do? You need both arms, both legs. My son Michael brings up his Greek background all the time.*
>
> *I'm an American in America, in the United States. When something is Greek, the Greek comes out in me. I speak Greek with those who speak Greek with me. In the church it's Greek. We have certain customs we celebrate, and I feel Greek then. So I'm really part of both lives.*
>
> *Should I throw away the Greek? It's part of our lives. It's part of our roots. Otherwise, I couldn't be a whole person. My son feels the Greek in him. It is a big dimension in his life. And it should be that way. How about his children? Even they have a little feeling and knowledge. I have tried to give them a background because I feel it's a strength to know your roots. It gives you a sense of security."*

The past really is part of you. We *are* born with what has come before.

"Did you find anything interesting?" Grandfather whispered in my ear.

"Grandfather, I didn't hear you come in," I said.

"That's what happens when you get so involved in your reading," he said. "Ari tells me you asked to read his report. Did you find anything interesting?"

"Oh, yes," I said. "I found so much." I told you, I found a portrait of me. I don't know if I can put it into the right words, words that will make sense, but I understood . . . no, I felt, for the first time, how much a part of my own life the past really was. It's like this: I want to be an architect or a ballet star or whatever, and maybe I will be it and maybe I won't be, but I have that chance because my parents and my grandparents and my great-grandparents gave me that chance. And I will give that chance to my children, too, when I teach them how to dream—and when I teach them how to remember.

CHAPTER 10

"Ladies and gentlemen," Ari announced, "it is my very great pleasure to present the newest wonder in the world of dance. Here to entertain you, here to enthrall you: direct from her bedroom—Christine Kontos."

"For goodness sake, Ari," I whispered from the hallway, "it's only a rehearsal."

It was time to show my family "A Portrait of Me." I knew it was only a rehearsal, but I was nervous anyway. I mean, if *they* didn't like it, who would?

A portrait of me: so what could it be?

"I call my performance 'Christine Kontos: Past, Present, and Future,' " I said to my family audience. "It's 'A Portrait of Me.' I hope you like it. Thank you."

I had been working on my dance for days. It really was a portrait of me. I thought about what Grandfather had asked. You know, what was I afraid of. I didn't know the answer yet, but I did know that ever since I was little, ever since I found out I had diabetes, I didn't want to be babied by anyone. I didn't want to depend on other people for help. I wanted to be independent. Well, maybe I was too independent. Maybe I was afraid to need other people. I didn't know the whole answer yet, but I did know that my family was more important than a ballet (even if it was the Joffrey). I knew that my family wanted me to be a part of it. And I knew that I wanted to be a part of it, too.

My dance had three parts. (Ms. Shaw helped me find the right music, and Grandma made me a very special costume.) It began with the movements and rhythms of Greek folk dances that Grandfather showed me. I wore the traditional dress of the Greek countryside. Then, lo and behold, I was transformed (more of Grandma's magic costume) into a ballerina and danced to the music of *The Nutcracker Suite.* But I didn't stop there. With a flourish of my hand, I left my ballerina costume on the floor, and there was the modern Christine in tights and leotard dancing to "Bad" by Michael Jackson.

All that in fifteen minutes. I was exhausted. “Well, what did you think?” I asked when I finished, breathless with excitement.

“Wonderful,” said Grandma.

“You’ll be the best one there,” Grandfather said. Well, what did you expect him to say?

“It was just about the weirdest thing I ever saw in my life,” Ari said. I gave him a dirty look. “But I liked it! I liked it!”

“It was very good, Christine,” Mom said. I thought she was going to cry.

“Bravo! Bravo!” Dad exclaimed. “A virtuoso performance. This calls for a celebration. How about dinner out tonight?”

There were cheers all around at Dad’s suggestion.

“Greek?” I asked. What else? I thought.

“I was thinking Chinese,” he said with a big smile.

“Chinese it is,” I said happily.

Didn’t I tell you? Never argue with a Kontos.

Questions for Christine

There are lots of kids with diabetes. Many people don't know what diabetes is all about. Maybe you have a question, too.

Q. What is diabetes?

A. The best way to tell you about diabetes is to describe how your body uses food to do all the things a body likes to do. When you have diabetes, it means your body cannot use food in the regular way. Let me explain.

Just like your family's car, your own body needs fuel to run properly. Of course, you can't just fill up at the pump. Your body gets its fuel from the food you eat. Your body turns the food you eat into fuel for energy: energy for growing, thinking, playing, dreaming; energy for everything you do. That's why it's really important to eat right. If your body doesn't get food, it runs out of steam, and if it doesn't get the right food, it won't run properly. "Remember," my doctor tells me, "you are what you eat."

The way the body turns food into fuel for energy is called "metabolism." There are different kinds of fuels, but one of the most important is called "glucose" or "sugar."

Have you ever heard of the pancreas? Probably not, but you would have if you had diabetes. The pancreas, an organ near the stomach and intestines, makes something called "insulin." Insulin helps the body make use of the sugar it needs for fuel. It helps turn the sugar in your blood into the energy your body (and everybody!) needs. This way, insulin helps to keep just the right amount of sugar in the blood.

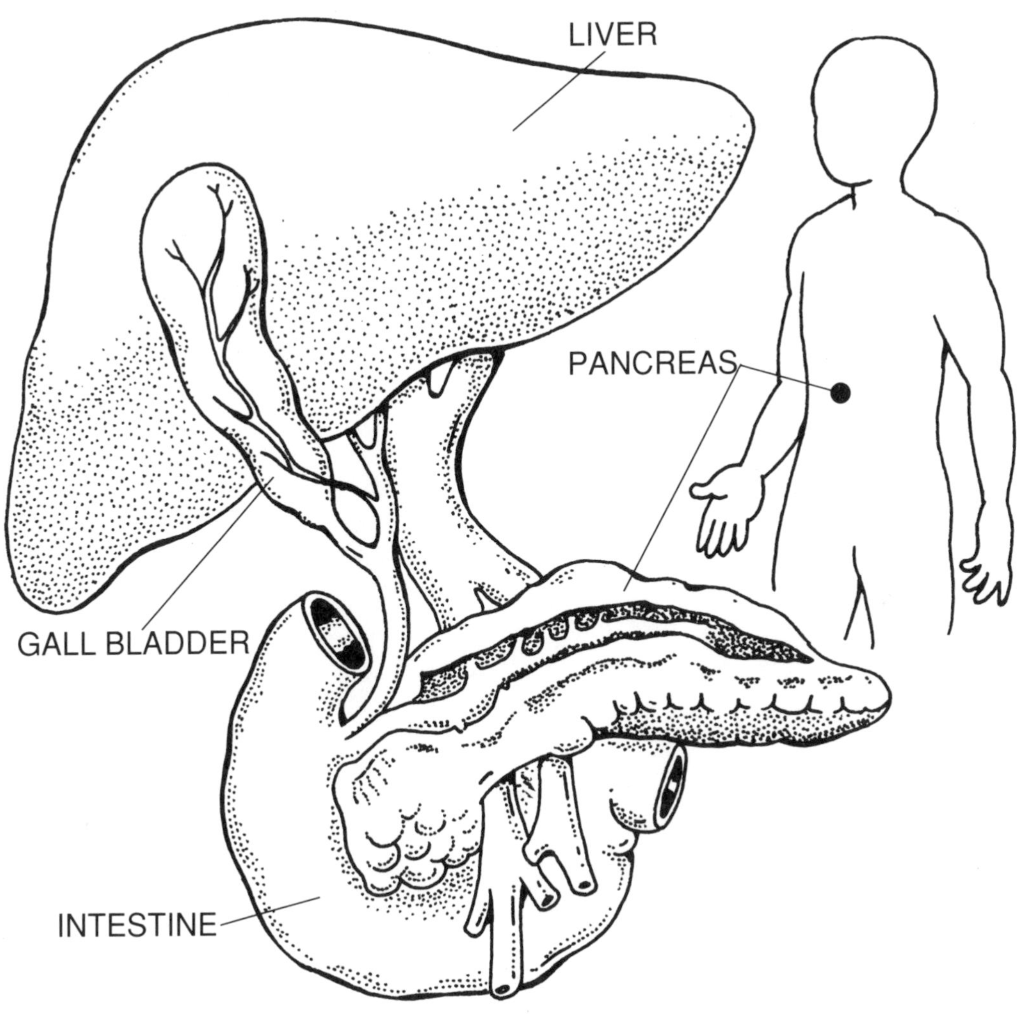

See, the amount of sugar in your body is not always the same. There's more sugar in your blood after a meal, when your body has loaded up its fuel supply. There's less sugar in your blood after exercise, when your body is using up its fuel supply. The pancreas makes just the right amount of insulin for your body: more if your blood sugar level is high and less if it is low. It helps you keep the levels of insulin and sugar in balance.

But when you have the kind of diabetes I do, the pancreas doesn't make any insulin or just doesn't make enough. The body can't turn sugar into energy. The level of sugar in the blood gets too high—and you get sick. Several years ago, I began to lose weight. It seemed like I was thirsty, really thirsty, and hungry all the time. And I had to urinate a lot. (I mean, I really *had* to go.) When the doctor tested the sugar level in my blood, he found out I had diabetes.

Q. Is there a cure?

A. There is no cure, but there are ways to treat diabetes. My doctor tells me that the main idea in treating diabetes is to keep my metabolism in balance. That means that I must get the right amount of food, exercise, and insulin to keep my sugar at just the right level. If I eat too many sweets, or get too little exercise, or don't take enough insulin, the sugar in my blood will get too high, and I'll get sick. But I'll also get sick if the sugar in my blood gets too low. If I miss a meal, there won't be enough sugar in my blood for my regular dose of insulin.

It may seem like I can't win. But I can be a winner if I do three things: give myself shots of insulin, eat a balanced diet, and get regular exercise. If I do that, I'll be able to do just about everything I want to do, even with diabetes. Lots of people do. Famous people like Catfish Hunter, the baseball player. Or Mary Tyler Moore, a television star. And lots and lots of people who aren't famous, too. Like me. (I'm not famous—yet!)

Q. Why is exercise so important?

A. When I exercise, my body uses more sugar for energy. That helps the insulin do its job, and I am able to keep my daily dose of insulin low. Besides, exercise is good for everyone.

Q. Why do you give yourself shots of insulin?

A. Because my pancreas doesn't make enough insulin, I have to add insulin to my body myself. I give myself a shot or injection of insulin two times a day, once before breakfast and once before dinner. This insulin helps my body use the sugar in my blood and keeps it at a healthy level, just like the insulin made by your pancreas.

But it doesn't work exactly the same way. If you don't have diabetes, your pancreas makes just the right amount of insulin depending on what your body needs. But I have to be careful that my insulin dose and sugar level are right for one another. That's why watching my diet and getting regular exercise are so important to me.

Q. How can you give yourself shots? Isn't it disgusting?

A. At first it was, and scary, too. But now it doesn't bother me at all. When I was very little, my Mom and Dad gave me the shots. Then, I went to a special camp for kids who have diabetes, where I learned how to do it myself. I remember when I first showed Ari how I give myself a shot. I thought he was going to faint. But it's not so bad. This is what I do:

- I get all the stuff I need: a syringe, my insulin, and cotton balls with alcohol on them. I use a real syringe and a real needle, just like doctors and nurses do.
- I wash my hands, and clean the insulin bottle with a cotton ball. It's important to keep everything I need super clean, including me.
- I put the needle into the bottle and fill the syringe with the proper dose of insulin.
- I pick a spot on my skin where I'm going to give myself the shot. It might be my arm, or leg, or stomach. I pick different spots for different days. If I picked the same spot all the time, it would get very sore.
- I wipe the spot with a cotton ball and some alcohol. The alcohol kills germs that can cause an infection.
- I pinch the skin to make a little bulge or fold.
- I put the needle into the fold of skin, then I let go of the pinch of skin, and I push down on the syringe. The insulin goes into my body.
- I take the needle out carefully and wipe the spot of skin with alcohol again.
- I throw the syringe away in a trash can I keep locked.
- That's all! Now, I'm ready to go. See: that wasn't so bad, was it?

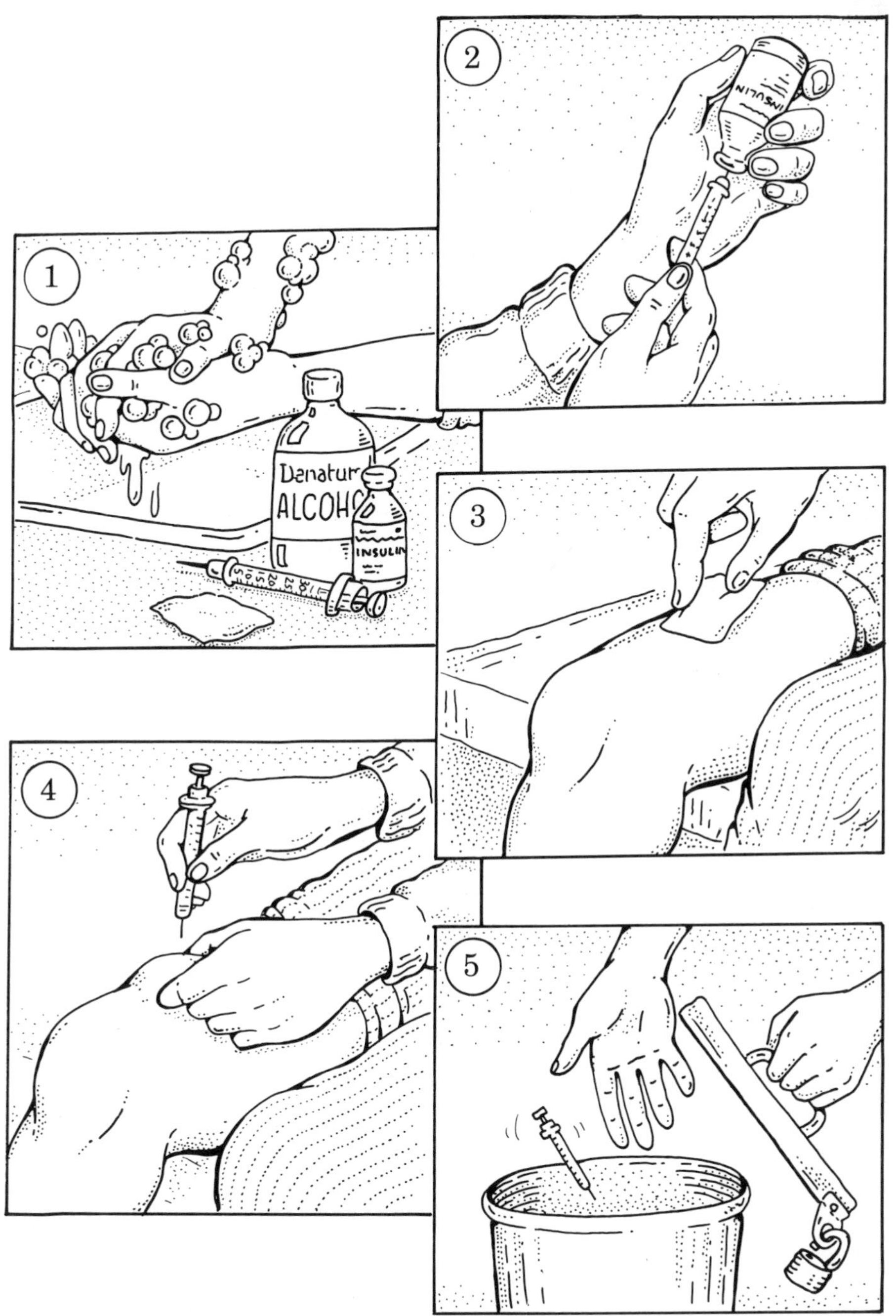
1
Denatur
ALCOH
INSULIN
2
INSULIN
3
4
5

Q. Doesn't it hurt?

A. Not if you do it right. It just feels like a little pinch. But it's very important to remember that giving yourself a shot is not a game. You should never play with a real needle, and never, never handle a used or dirty needle.

Q. Can you get AIDS from using a needle?

A. Not from one of my needles. You can get the AIDS virus or other diseases by using a needle that someone else has already used. And that is why you should never use or play with a dirty needle. When I'm done with my shot, I throw it away in a safe place. The life of that needle is over!

Q. How did you get diabetes?

A. That's a good question. A lot of people think you can get diabetes by eating too much candy or drinking too much soda. Well, you can't get diabetes that way, but you sure can get a ton of cavities!

There are two kinds of diabetes. I have the kind of diabetes children mostly get, where the pancreas doesn't make insulin. No one knows for sure how you get diabetes. Doctors think the kind of diabetes I have may be caused by two things. One is heredity. That means the chance of getting diabetes is passed along in a family from one generation (like my grandparents) to another (like my parents) to another (like me). It doesn't mean that everyone in a family will get diabetes, but you're more likely to get it if it "runs" in your family.

But there is more to getting it than just heredity. My kind of diabetes may be caused by a virus infection, a virus that hurts the body's immune system. (The immune system is the way your body fights infections.) Perhaps one day we'll know for sure. But what *is* important to know is that you won't catch diabetes by being near someone who has it. So you don't have to be afraid of getting close. I can't give you diabetes.

Q. Why can't you eat candy and other sweet things?

A. I wish I could. But sweets like candy, cake, cookies, soda, and ice cream will raise the level of sugar in my blood too high. When *you* eat a lot of sweets, your pancreas starts pumping out the insulin to turn all that sugar into energy. But *I* have to keep my blood sugar level at the right amount for my dose of insulin, not too high and not too low. That means I have to pay careful attention to my diet. I eat a nutritious, well-balanced diet. That would be good for you, too!

If I eat too many sweets, I get sick. It's kind of a pain. I mean, how would you like to go to a party and worry about the cake and ice cream? But I got used to it, and so did my friends. With a little planning, I don't have to miss out at all. I remember at Diane's birthday party, her mother made an angel food cake, which is low in sugar. That was a nice surprise. And these days, everybody's drinking sugar-free soft drinks.

Sometimes, I bring my own food with me. Have you ever tried carrot sticks at the movies instead of candy? I know what you're thinking, but give it a try: they really taste good, even to a sweet tooth like me.

Q. But once you needed emergency candy. Why?

A. I know it may sound strange, but sometimes I need to eat something sugary real fast. I give myself a shot of insulin twice a day to help turn my blood sugar into body fuel. But what if I forget to eat or if I exercise more than usual? Then, there's *too little* sugar in my body and *too much* insulin. This is called an "insulin reaction." I get dizzy and sweaty, and if I don't eat something sweet right away, I could get real sick. So I keep candy with me just in case. That's what Joanne calls the "candy cure."

Q. But how do you know if your sugar level is right?

A. You can tell if you have a high sugar level by testing your blood. I test my blood two or three times a day by pricking my finger to get a tiny bit of blood. I wipe the blood on a special test strip and use a special meter to test for the result. It might look like this:

This way, I can tell if I am getting just the right amount of insulin and exercise, and eating the right kinds of food, to keep the sugar in my blood at a safe level. And I keep a record of my blood test results to show the doctor. If there is a problem, my doctor may want to adjust my insulin dose.

Q. Is it hard to have diabetes?

A. Sure, sometimes it's hard. Most kids don't have to worry about eating just the right food at the right time. That can be real hard. Shots are no great thrill, either. Believe me, if I had the choice, I would choose *not* to give myself two shots every day. There are some things I may not be able to do when I grow up, like fly airplanes.

And I don't like being teased at all.

But after a while, you get used to treating your diabetes. It just becomes a part of your life that you don't think about that much. Oh, every now and then I get a craving for a hot fudge sundae, but I don't really feel like I'm missing out on anything important. I don't really want to fly airplanes anyway.

And what about the people who tease me? I figure they just don't understand. Sure, diabetes is different. But I try to explain that "different" isn't better or worse. There's something different about everyone. Being different is what makes me, *me*: it's what makes you, *you*. I just want to be the best *me* I can. And what do you want to be?

About The Kids on the Block

Founded in 1977 by Barbara Aiello, The Kids on the Block puppet program was formed to introduce young audiences to the topic of children with disabilities. Since then the goals and programs of The Kids on the Block have evolved and broadened to encompass a wide spectrum of individual differences and social concerns.

Barbara Aiello is nationally recognized for her work in special education. The former editor of *Teaching Exceptional Children*, Ms. Aiello has won numerous awards for her work with The Kids on the Block, including the President's Committee on Employment of the Handicapped Distinguished Service Award, the Easter Seal Communications Award for Outstanding Public Service, and the Epilepsy Foundation of America's Outstanding Achievement Award. Her puppets have appeared in all 50 states and throughout the world. In addition, over 1,000 groups in the United States and abroad make The Kids on the Block puppets an effective part of their community programs.

For More Information

The Kids on the Block
9385-C Gerwig Lane
Columbia, Maryland 21046
800-368-KIDS

American Diabetes Association
National Service Center
1660 Duke St.
Alexandria, VA 22314
1-800-ADA-DISC
Check the white pages of your telephone directory for local Affiliate of the American Diabetes Association.

Joslin Diabetes Center
1 Joslin Place
Boston, MA 02215
617-732-2514

Juvenile Diabetes Foundation, The International Research Foundation
432 Park Ave., South
New York, NY 10016
1-800-JDF-CURE
Check telephone directory for local JDF Chapter.

National Diabetes Information Clearinghouse
Box NDIC
Bethesda, MD 20892
301-468-2162